ABSOLUTE BEGINNER'S GUIDE

TO

Upgrading and Fixing Your PC

Michael Miller

800 East 96th Street
Indianapolis, Indiana 46240

Absolute Beginner's Guide to Upgrading and Fixing Your PC

International Standard Book Number: 0-7897-3045-6

Library of Congress Catalog Card Number: 2003108676

Printed in the United States of America

First Printing: September 2003

04   03   02   01   4   3   2   1

Bulk Sales

Que offers excellent discounts on this book when ordered in quantity for bulk purchases or special sales. For more information, please contact:

U.S. Corporate and Government Sales
1-800-382-3419
corpsales@pearsontechgroup.com

For sales outside of the U.S., please contact:

International Sales
+1-317-581-3793
international@pearsontechgroup.com

Trademarks

All terms mentioned in this book that are known to be trademarks or service marks have been appropriately capitalized. Que cannot attest to the accuracy of this information. Use of a term in this book should not be regarded as affecting the validity of any trademark or service mark.

Warning and Disclaimer

Every effort has been made to make this book as complete and as accurate as possible, but no warranty or fitness is implied. The information provided is on an "as is" basis. The author and the publisher shall have neither liability nor responsibility to any person or entity with respect to any loss or damages arising from the information contained in this book.

Associate Publisher
Greg Wiegand

Executive Editor
Rick Kughen

Development Editor
Rick Kughen

Technical Editor
David Eytchison

Project Editor
Sheila Schroeder

Managing Editor
Charlotte Clapp

Copy Editor
Kate Givens

Indexer
Mandie Frank

Proofreader
Suzanne Thomas

Team Coordinator
Sharry Lee Gregory

Interior Designer
Anne Jones

Cover Designer
Dan Armstrong

Page Layout
Julie Parks

Contents at a Glance

Table of Contents

About the Author

Michael Miller is a successful and prolific author with a reputation for practical advice and technical accuracy and an unerring empathy for the needs of his readers.

Mr. Miller has written more than four dozen how-to and reference books since 1989, for Que and other major publishers. His most recent books include *Absolute Beginner's Guide to Computer Basics*, *Absolute Beginner's Guide to eBay*, and *TechTV's Microsoft Windows XP for Home Users, 2nd Edition*. He is known for his casual, easy-to-read writing style and his practical, real-world advice[md]as well as his ability to explain a wide variety of complex topics to an everyday audience.

Mr. Miller is also president of The Molehill Group, a strategic consulting and authoring firm based in Carmel, Indiana. As a consultant, he specializes in providing strategic advice to and writing business plans for Internet- and technology-based businesses.

You can email Mr. Miller directly at upgrade@molehillgroup.com. His Web site is located at www.molehillgroup.com.

Dedication

To my brother Mark, who's never seen a computer upgrade that worked right out of the box.

Acknowledgments

Thanks to the usual suspects at Que, including but not limited to Greg Wiegand, Rick Kughen, David Eytchison, Sheila Schroeder, Mandie Frank, and Suzanne Thomas.

Tell Us What You Think!

As the reader of this book, *you* are our most important critic and commentator. We value your opinion and want to know what we're doing right, what we could do better, what areas you'd like to see us publish in, and any other words of wisdom you're willing to pass our way.

As an Associate Publisher for Que, I welcome your comments. You can fax, email, or write me directly to let me know what you did or didn't like about this book—as well as what we can do to make our books stronger.

Please note that I cannot help you with technical problems related to the topic of this book, and that due to the high volume of mail I receive, I might not be able to reply to every message.

When you write, please be sure to include this book's title and author as well as your name and phone or fax number. I will carefully review your comments and share them with the author and editors who worked on the book.

Email: feedback@quepublishing.com

Mail: Greg Wiegand

Que
800 East 96th Street
Indianapolis, IN 46240 USA

Introduction

I've been working with computers for more than 20 years now. The first machines I used were big and slow and very finicky, and as far removed from "user friendly" as you can imagine. It took a lot of trial and error (and blood, sweat, and tears) to get those early PCs to do anything, so users got used to opening up the case and replacing this or the other part just to keep things up and running.

Computers then were kind of like the technological equivalent of an old Model T—in a world where everyone had to be their own mechanic.

Fortunately for all of us, computers got smaller and faster and easier to use. They also got more reliable, although they're still far from perfect. Not a week goes by that I don't get a call from some friend or family member telling me that their PC won't do this or that, and pleading for just a little bit of help.

Well, that's what this book offers—a bit of help.

Absolute Beginner's Guide to Upgrading and Fixing Your PC will help you in lots of ways. This book will help you better understand how your PC works, so that you can more easily get it to do what you want it to do. This book will also help you upgrade some or all of the components of your computer system, so that it will run faster or more reliably or just be able to do more things better. And, finally, this book will help you when things go wrong—you'll learn how to track down and fix all sorts of pesky PC problems.

This book will help you do all those things, even (and especially) if you're an absolute beginner where computers are concerned. You don't have to be a techie to keep your computer up and running. The advice I give you is simple and practical and easy to do—for anyone.

That means, of course, that there are some more advanced upgrades and repairs that I don't go into. That's okay; my motto is if you need anything more than a screwdriver, let a professional do it. The good news is that there's a lot of cool and useful stuff you can do with just a screwdriver—or even your bare hands!

(By the way, if you're interested in more technically advanced hardware issues than what I cover in this book, I heartily recommend what is now a classic in the computer book publishing industry: Que's *Upgrading and Repairing PCs*, a 1000+ page tome by the extremely knowledgeable Scott Mueller. It picks up where this book leaves off—and then some!)

How This Book Is Organized

Absolute Beginner's Guide to Upgrading and Fixing Your PC is organized into six main parts, as follows:

- **Part 1, Before You Upgrade**, gives you a quick refresher course on computer hardware basics and shows you how to prepare your system for an upgrade.

- **Part 2, Essential Hardware Upgrades**, provides step-by-step instructions on how to upgrade your PC's key pieces of hardware: system inputs, hard disk, CD/DVD drives, memory, mice, keyboards, printers, video cards and monitors, and sound cards and speakers.

- **Part 3, Upgrading for Specific Applications**, helps you decide what components of your system to upgrade for different uses—downloading and listening to music, storing and editing digital pictures, watching and editing movies and home videos, and playing the latest PC games.

- **Part 4, Upgrading Your Entire System**, is all about the really big upgrades; you'll learn how to connect and configure a small wired or wireless network, speed up your Internet connection, install Windows XP, and upgrade to a brand new computer.

- **Part 5, Preventing PC Problems**, discusses essential system maintenance, and what you can do to avoid computer viruses and Internet attacks.

- **Part 6, Troubleshooting Common Problems**, presents a huge number of common PC problems—along with probable causes and likely solutions.

Taken together, the 30 chapters in this book will help anyone—even absolute beginners—get the most out of their computer systems, and keep their PCs up and running. Just read what you need, and before long you'll have one of the best-performing computer systems on the block!

Conventions Used in This Book

I hope that this book is easy enough to figure out on its own, without requiring its own instruction manual. As you read through the pages, however, it helps to know precisely how I've presented specific types of information.

Menu Commands

Most computer programs operate via a series of pull-down menus. You use your mouse to pull down a menu and then select an option from that menu. This sort of operation is indicated like this throughout the book:

Select File, Save

or

Click the Start button and select All Programs, Accessories, Notepad.

All you have to do is follow the instructions in order, using your mouse to click each item in turn. When there are submenus tacked onto the main menu (as in the All Programs, Accessories, Notepad example), just keep clicking the selections until you come to the last one—which should open the program or activate the command you want!

Shortcut Key Combinations

When you're using your computer keyboard, sometimes you have to press two keys at the same time. These "two-key" combinations are called *shortcut keys* and are shown as the key names joined with a plus sign (+). For example, Ctrl+W indicates that you should press the W key while holding down the Ctrl key. It's no more complex than that.

Other Commands

Some of the operations in this book involve entering a command at the Windows command prompt. (This is virtually identical to entering MS-DOS commands, if you've been around computers long enough to remember a world before Windows.) When there's a command to enter, it will be noted like this:

chkdsk

You should enter the command, as written, at the command prompt, and then press the Enter key on your keyboard to execute the command.

Web Page Addresses

There are a lot of Web page addresses in this book. (That's because you'll probably be spending a lot of time on the Internet.) They're noted as such:

www.molehillgroup.com

Technically, a Web page address is supposed to start with http:// (as in http://www.molehillgroup.com). Because Internet Explorer and other Web browsers automatically insert this piece of the address, however, you don't have to type it—and I haven't included it in any of the addresses in this book.

Special Elements

This book includes a few special elements that provide additional information not included in the basic text. These elements are designed to supplement the text to make your learning faster, easier, and more efficient.

A *note* is designed to provide information that is generally useful but not specifically necessary for what you're doing at the moment. Some are like extended tips—interesting, but not essential.

A *tip* is a piece of advice— a little trick, actually—that helps you use your computer more effectively or maneuver around problems or limitations.

Mike Sez

This element is my personal opinion or recommendation regarding the topic at hand. Remember—I might not always be right, but I'll always have an opinion!

caution

A *caution* will tell you to beware of a potentially dangerous operation. In some cases, ignoring a caution could cause you significant problem— so pay attention to them!

Let Me Know What You Think

I always love to hear from readers. If you want to contact me, feel free to email me at upgrade@molehillgroup.com. I can't promise that I'll answer every message, but I will promise that I'll read each one!

If you want to learn more about me and any new books I have cooking, check out my Molehill Group Web site at www.molehillgroup.com. Who knows—you might find some other books there that you'd like to read.

PART i

Before You Upgrade

1

HARDWARE BASICS FOR THE ABSOLUTE BEGINNER

Before you pop open your system unit and start plugging and unplugging cables, it might be a good idea to take a quick refresher course in computer basics. We'll start by looking at each of the parts of your computer system, from the system unit (and everything inside) to monitors, speakers, and keyboards. Then we'll examine what exactly happens when you turn on your PC—what we call the startup process.

Remember, this chapter is just an overview; we'll go into more detail about upgrading and troubleshooting all these components later in the book. So if you already know all there is to know about the various types of computer hardware in your system, feel free to skip this chapter. But if you're an absolute beginner when it comes to how your computer works, this is the chapter for you!

Getting to Know Your Personal Computer System

We'll start by looking at the physical components of your system—the stuff we call computer *hardware*. As you can see in Figure 1.1, there are a lot of different pieces and parts that make up a typical computer system. You should note, however, that no two computer systems are identical because you can always add new components to your system or disconnect other pieces you don't need.

FIGURE 1.1

A typical personal computer system.

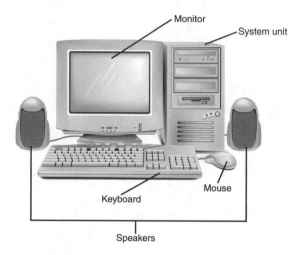

These items are the basic elements you'll find in almost all computer systems. Of course, you can add lots of other items to your personal system, including *printers* (to make printouts of documents and pictures), *scanners* (to change a hardcopy document or picture to electronic format), *PC cameras* (to send live video of yourself to friends and family), *digital cameras* (to transfer your snapshots to electronic format), and *joysticks* (to play the most challenging PC games). You can even add the appropriate items to connect multiple PCs together in a *network*.

Your PC's System Unit—The Mother Ship

The most important piece of hardware in your computer system is the *system unit*. This is the big ugly box that houses your disk drives and many other components.

You should keep your system unit in a well-ventilated location free of excess dust and smoke. (The moving parts in your computer don't like dust and dirt or any other such contaminants that can muck up the way they work.) Because your computer generates heat when it operates, you must leave enough room around the system unit for the heat to dissipate. *Never* place your computer in a confined, poorly ventilated space; your PC might overheat and shut down (or even damage critical internal components) if it isn't sufficiently ventilated.

For extra protection for your computer, connect the power cable on your system unit to a *surge suppressor* rather than directly into an electrical outlet. A surge suppressor—which looks like a power strip with multiple outlets—protects your PC from power line surges that could damage its delicate internal parts. When a power surge temporarily *spikes* your line voltage (causes the voltage to momentarily increase above normal levels), a surge suppressor shuts down power to your system, acting like a circuit breaker or fuse.

The back of the system unit typically is covered with all types of connectors. This is because all the other parts of your computer system connect to your system unit, and they all have to have a place to plug in. And, because each component has its own unique type of connector, you end up with the assortment of jacks (called *ports* in the computer world) that you see in Figure 1.2. The back of your PC might look somewhat different

note

Desktop computer systems have separate system units, monitors, keyboards, and mice; portable PCs have all their components crammed into a single, lightweight case—which makes them much harder to upgrade!

tip

Although a surge suppressor will protect your system from electrical spikes, you'll still lose any data you were working on if your power goes out. If you use your PC for applications in which you can't afford even a momentary shutdown, you should invest in a battery-operated backup power supply (also called an *uninterruptible power supply*, or *UPS*). These devices send auxiliary power to your PC during power outages—and provide "clean" power in areas where power line spikes and brownouts are common.

than the one pictured here, depending on the manufacturer, but this should help you identify the major connectors.

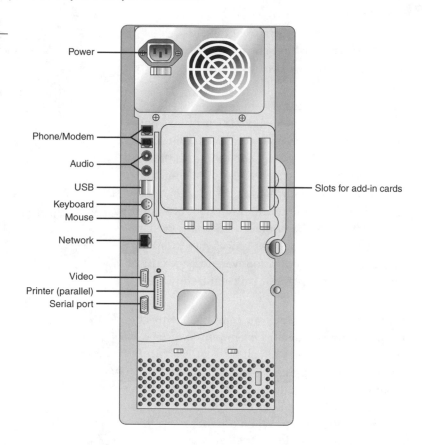

FIGURE 1.2
The back of a typical system unit—just look at all those different connectors!

Power

Phone/Modem

Audio

USB

Keyboard

Mouse

Network

Video

Printer (parallel)

Serial port

Slots for add-in cards

The cables that connect your peripherals to your system unit can be a source of trouble if they're not connected correctly. Make sure that you plug all cables securely into their sockets; in fact, screw them into place if you can. Make certain, too, that the cables don't have abrupt bends or kinks in them. If your cables aren't as straight as possible, the wires inside them might break or become damaged.

Inside the Case

All the good stuff in your system unit is inside the case. With most system units, you can remove the case to peek and poke around inside.

To remove your system unit's case, look for some big screws or thumbscrews on either the side or back of the case. (Even better—read your PC's instruction manual for instructions specific to your unit.) With the screws loosened or removed, you should then be able to either slide off the entire case, or pop open the top or back.

When you open the case on your system unit, you see all sorts of computer chips and circuit boards. The really big board located at the base of the computer (into which everything else is plugged) is called the *motherboard*, because it's the "mother" for your microprocessor and memory chips, as well as for the other internal components that enable your system to function. This motherboard (like the one shown in Figure 1.3) contains several slots, into which you can plug additional *boards* (also called *expansion cards*, or just *cards*) that perform specific functions. Different computers use different types of motherboards, so the layout will differ from PC to PC.

caution

Always turn off and unplug your computer before attempting to remove the system unit's case—and be careful about touching anything inside! Not only can you shock yourself, but if you have any built-up static electricity, you can seriously damage the sensitive chips and electronic components with an innocent touch.

FIGURE 1.3

The inside of a typical system unit—a big motherboard with lots of add-on boards attached.

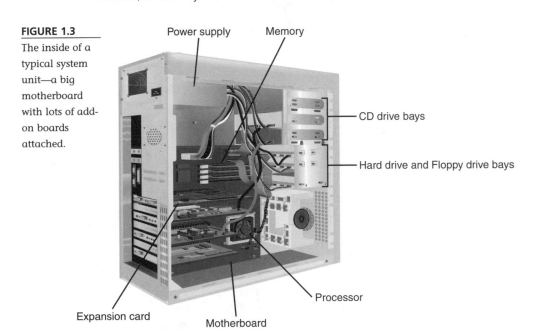

Power supply   Memory

CD drive bays

Hard drive and Floppy drive bays

Processor

Expansion card

Motherboard

If add-on cards aren't inserted correctly, your entire system could fail to function. In addition, if the switches or jumpers on a card are set in the wrong positions, that card—or your entire system—might seriously malfunction. (Don't worry, I cover setting switches and jumpers in Chapter 2, "Preparing Your System for an Upgrade.")

Some cards also require you to run software-based setup programs to configure parts of your system. Whatever the case, always be sure to consult the instructions that come with each card to make certain everything is set correctly before you button up the case and turn on the power again.

You might even find it necessary to make adjustments to your operating system or to specific software programs so that you can use your new cards. Check each program to determine whether it must be adjusted or set up individually to operate with your new card.

Microprocessors: The Main Engine

We're not done looking at the system unit just yet. Buried somewhere on that big motherboard is a specific chip that controls your entire computer system. This chip is called a *microprocessor* or a *central processing unit (CPU)*.

The microprocessor is the brain inside your system. It processes all the instructions necessary for your computer to perform its duties. The more powerful the microprocessor chip, the faster and more efficiently your system runs.

Microprocessors carry out the various instructions that let your computer compute. Every input and output device hooked up to a computer—the keyboard, printer, monitor, and so on—either issues or receives instructions that the microprocessor then processes. Your software programs also issue instructions that must be implemented by the microprocessor. This chip truly is the workhorse of your system; it affects just about everything your computer does.

Different computers have different types of microprocessor chips. Many IBM-compatible computers use chips manufactured by Intel. Some use Intel-compatible chips manufactured by AMD and other firms. But all IBM-compatible computers that run the Windows operating system use Intel-compatible chips.

note

The Apple Macintosh uses chips made by Motorola that are totally different from the Intel-compatible chips. Because of the different processor configurations, software written for the Macintosh won't run on IBM-compatible computers and vice versa.

In addition to having different chip manufacturers (and different chip families from the same manufacturer), you'll also run into microprocessor chips that run at different speeds. CPU speed is measured in megahertz (MHz); a CPU with a speed of 1MHz can run at one million clock ticks per second! The higher the megahertz, the faster the chip runs. If you're still shopping for a new PC, look for one with the combination of a powerful microprocessor and a high clock speed for best performance.

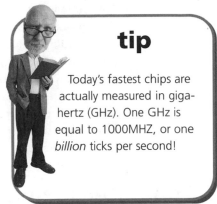

tip

Today's fastest chips are actually measured in gigahertz (GHz). One GHz is equal to 1000MHZ, or one *billion* ticks per second!

To see which microprocessor is installed in your system, use the Windows System Properties utility. If your computer is running Windows XP, all you have to do is follow these steps:

1. Click the Start button to display the Start menu.
2. Select Control Panel to open the Control Panel folder.
3. Select the System icon to open the System Properties dialog box, shown in Figure 1.4.
4. Select the General tab.

FIGURE 1.4

Use the System Properties dialog box to find out what processor your computer is running.

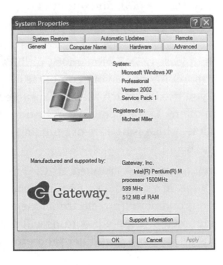

The System section of this dialog box tells you which version of Windows you're running; the Registered To section tells you who you are (or, rather, how your version of Windows is registered); and the Manufactured and Supported By section tells which processor you have and how much memory (RAM) you have installed.

Fortunately, not much can go wrong with a microprocessor, short of it completely failing—and microprocessor failure is fairly rare, especially if you keep your PC in a well-ventilated place. You might, however, notice that some software programs run very slowly (if at all) on underpowered machines—that is, machines with older or slower chips. If in doubt, check the software's packaging or documentation, or ask the software publisher (or your dealer) if a particular program is designed to run on your PC. You might just have to avoid purchasing certain programs—or else upgrade to a newer, more powerful computer that can run all the programs you want it to run.

Computer Memory: Temporary Storage

Before your CPU can process any instructions you give it, those instructions must be stored somewhere, in preparation for access by the microprocessor. These instructions—along with other data processed by your system—are temporarily held in the computer's *random access memory (RAM)*. All computers have some amount of memory, which is created by a number of memory chips. The more memory that is available in a machine, the more instructions and data that can be stored at one time.

Memory is measured in terms of *bytes*. One byte is equal to approximately one character in a word processing document. A unit equaling approximately one thousand bytes (1,024, to be exact) is called a *kilobyte (KB)*, and a unit of approximately one thousand (1,024) kilobytes is called a *megabyte (MB)*. A thousand megabytes is a *gigabyte (GB)*.

Most computers today come with at least 128MB of memory, and it's not uncommon to find machines with 512MB or more. To enable your computer to run as many programs as quickly as possible, you need as much memory installed in your system as it can accept—or that you can afford. Extra memory can be added to a computer by installing a new memory module, which is as easy as plugging a "stick" directly into a slot on your system's motherboard.

If your computer doesn't have enough memory installed, its CPU must constantly retrieve data from permanent storage on its hard disk. This method of data retrieval is slower than retrieving instructions and data from electronic memory. In fact, if your machine doesn't have enough memory, some programs will run very slowly (or you might experience random system crashes), and other programs won't run at all!

Hard Disk Drives: Long-Term Storage

Another important physical component inside your system unit is the *hard disk drive*. The hard disk permanently stores all your important data. Some hard disks can store more than 100 gigabytes of data. (Contrast this to your system's random access memory, which stores only a few hundred megabytes of data—temporarily.)

A hard disk consists of numerous metallic platters. These platters store data *magnetically*. Special read/write *heads* realign magnetic particles on the platters, much like a recording head records data onto magnetic recording tape.

Before data can be stored on any disk, including your system's hard disk, that disk must first be *formatted*. A disk that has not been formatted cannot accept any data. When you format a hard disk, your computer prepares the surface of the disk to accept and store data magnetically.

caution

If you try to reformat your hard disk, you'll erase all the programs and data that have been installed—so don't do it unless you know what you're doing and are prepared to lose your stuff!

Of course, when you buy a new PC, your hard disk is already formatted for you. (And, in most cases, your operating system and key programs also are preinstalled.)

Your hard disk can cause you a great deal of trouble if you don't treat it right. Because a hard disk is a physical device that spins at a high rate of speed, it can actually wear out over time. The disk might start spinning at the wrong speed, or the platters that make up the disk might themselves become damaged. If your system is located in an area with too much dust or smoke, the disk platters can become contaminated; a contaminated disk might not read or write data correctly. In addition, a rough jolt to your system unit (and thus to the hard disk) can cause the disk's read/write heads to collide with the platters and result in damaged hardware and data—which is a good reason to turn off your PC before moving it.

Eventually, too, the platters and the read/write head might become misaligned, due to nothing more than age and use. When this happens, consult a technician. Your disk might be salvageable, or it might have to be replaced.

The data on your hard disk also can be subject to various problems, many of which are caused by human error. If you accidentally format a hard disk that has data on it, for example, you lose all that data. You can accidentally erase varying amounts of data on your hard disk, too, if you're careless in deleting files. What's more, if computer viruses manage to infect your system, they can scramble your valuable data, making your hard disk function abnormally, if at all. So always take extra care when working with your hard disk; if you don't, all its gigabytes of data can very suddenly—and quite painfully—become inaccessible.

Diskette Drives: Portable Storage

Along with a hard disk drive, most computers have a *removable disk drive*. Removable disks—often called *floppy disks* or *diskettes*—work much like hard disks except that they consist of thin sheets of a magnetic-tape–like material instead of hard metallic platters.

Because removable diskettes are more portable than hard disks, they're typically used to store data that's transported physically from PC to PC. And disks are useful, too, for storing backup copies of the data on your PC's hard disk.

The head in a diskette drive works just like the read/write head of a hard disk drive. The only difference is that the diskette drives aren't sealed from the elements, as are hard disk drives. Diskette drives,

therefore, are even more susceptible to dirt, dust, and smoke than are their "hardier" cousins. If you seem to encounter more than a few read/write errors when you use different diskettes, the diskette drive itself might require realignment or even replacement.

Diskettes are susceptible to every ailment that can possibly befall a hard disk—and then some. Because diskettes are portable, they can become damaged during transit. And because data is stored on diskettes magnetically, placing a diskette too close to a magnetic source (such as a stereo speaker, a ringing telephone, or your computer monitor) can erase its data.

CD Drives: Storage on a Disc

There's a third type of disk that is now standard on personal computer systems. This disc is called a *CD-ROM*. (The initials stand for *compact disc—read-only memory*.)

CD-ROMs look just like the compact discs you play on your audio system. They're also very similar in the way they store data (audio data in the case of regular CDs; computer data in the case of CD-ROMs).

Information on a CD-ROM is encoded in the form of microscopic pits (representing the 1s and 0s of computer binary language) below the disc's surface. The information is arranged in a series of tracks and sectors, and read via a drive that uses a consumer-grade laser. The laser beam follows the tracks of the disc and reads the pits, translating the data into a form your system can understand.

By the way, the *ROM* part of CD-ROM means that you can only read data from the disk; unlike normal hard disks and diskettes, you can't write new data to a standard CD-ROM. However, recordable (CD-R) and rewritable (CD-RW) drives are available that *do* let you write data to CD discs—although they're a bit more expensive than standard read-only CD-ROM drives.

note

A drive that handles both recordable and rewritable discs is referred to as CD-R/RW.

Most CD-ROM (and DVD) problems have to do with dirty or scratched discs, or with dirty laser assemblies. Cleaning a disc is easy—just use a soft cloth. If you have a scratch on a disc, you can try one of the so-called "CD scratch repair" kits sold at some stores, although I've found they really don't work that well; once a disc is scratched, the damage is generally permanent. (Which argues in favor of handling your discs as carefully as you do your audio CDs—and only by the edges, never touching the surface of the disc itself.)

You should also avoid writing on the shiny side of disc, which is the side the laser reads. If you want to write on a disc, use a Sharpie on the label side. And don't use anything other than a Sharpie-like marker, as it could make the disc unusable.

tip

Many new drives combine normal CD-ROM, CD-R/RW, and DVD capabilities into a single unit.

If the lens that focuses the laser in your CD-ROM or DVD drive gets dirty, the laser can become unfocused and have difficulty reading the information from the disc. The solution to this problem is to use a commercial laser lens cleaner that you insert just like you do a CD-ROM disc.

DVD Drives: Even More Storage on a Disc

Beyond the CD-ROM is the new *DVD* medium. DVDs can contain 4.7GB or more data (compared to 650MB–700MB for a typical CD-ROM), and therefore are ideally suited for large applications or games that otherwise would require multiple CDs. Similar to standard CD-ROMs, most DVDs are read-only—although all DVD drives can also read CD-ROM discs. In addition, most DVD drives play full-length DVD movies, which turns your PC into a mini movie machine.

And, just as there are recordable CD-ROM drives, you can also find recordable DVD drives. These DVD-R drives are a little pricey, but costs are coming down—and they let you record an entire movie on a single disc.

Keyboards: Fingertip Input

Computers receive data by reading it from disk, accepting it electronically over a modem, or receiving input directly from you, the user. You provide your input by way of an *input device*; the most common input device is the keyboard.

A computer keyboard looks and functions just like a typewriter keyboard, but with a few more keys. When you press a key on your keyboard, it sends an electronic signal to your system unit; if for any reason the system unit doesn't receive this signal, your keystrokes do absolutely nothing. The most common keyboard problems can usually be traced to some sort of obstacle that's preventing the signals from reaching your system unit. The culprit might be a loose connection, excess dirt or dust—or maybe even a crumb from that Twinkie you ate while working with your files the other night.

To avoid loose connections that could interrupt signals from your keyboard, always make certain the keyboard is securely connected to your system unit. Try also to keep your keyboard free of dust, dirt, and other foreign matter that could block signals to the system unit. And always take care when handling or transporting your keyboard so as not to damage it.

Mice: Point-and-Click Input Devices

It's a funny name, but a necessary device.

A computer *mouse* is a small handheld device. Most mice consist of an oblong case with a roller underneath and two or three buttons on top or along the sides. When you move the mouse along a desktop, an onscreen pointer (called a *cursor*) moves in response. When you click (press and release) a mouse button, this motion initiates an action in your program.

Mice come in all shapes and sizes. Some have wires, and some are wireless. Some are relatively oval in shape, and others are all curvy to better fit in the palm of your hand. Some have the typical roller ball underneath, and others use an optical sensor to determine where and how much you're rolling. Some even have extra buttons that can be programmed for specific functions or a scroll wheel you can use to scroll through long documents or Web pages.

Of course, a mouse is just *one* type of input device you can hook up to your PC. Trackballs, joysticks, game controllers, and pen pads all count as input devices, whether they work in conjunction with a mouse or replace it. You can use one of these alternative devices to replace your original mouse or (in some cases) to supplement it.

If you have a portable PC, you don't have a separate mouse, but rather a built-in pointing device of some sort—a touchpad, rollerball, or track stick (the thing that looks like a little rubber eraser). Fortunately, you don't have to use the built-in pointing device on a portable PC; most portables let you attach an external mouse, which then overrides the internal device.

Just as with the keyboard, the most common mouse problems result from loose connections. These usually occur when the mouse somehow becomes unplugged from the computer (such as when you tug too hard on it or accidentally roll it off the desk). Because the mouse is a mechanical device, its roller ball can eventually wear out with use, making cursor movement difficult. The constant movement of the mouse across a desk surface can often damage the mouse cable, too. If your mouse's behavior becomes too erratic, it might be time to either clean or replace the little rodent.

If you have more than one input device connected to your computer—a mouse and a joystick, for example—these two devices can sometimes interfere with one another. I've seen instances where changing the settings on a joystick affected the behavior of a mouse. Always look for unwanted interaction when you have two similar devices connected to one PC.

Video Cards and Monitors: Getting the Picture

Operating a computer would be difficult if you didn't constantly receive visual feedback showing you what your machine is doing. This vital function is provided by your computer's monitor.

The traditional computer monitor is a lot like a little television set. Your microprocessor electronically transmits words and pictures (*text* and *graphics*, in PC lingo) to your monitor, in some approximation of how these visuals would appear on paper. You view the monitor and respond according to what you see onscreen.

Although the traditional monitor uses a picture tube (similar to the one in a normal television set) to display its picture, another type of monitor does away with the tube. A so-called *flat-screen* monitor uses an LCD display instead—which is not only flat, but also very thin. (These are the same types of displays used in portable PCs.)

You measure the size of a monitor by measuring from corner to corner, diagonally. This measurement is different for tube-type monitors than it is for flat-screen monitors, however. That's because a flat-screen monitor displays its images all the way to the edge of the screen, and traditional tube-type monitors don't. For that reason, a 15" flat-screen monitor has the same viewable picture area as a 17" tube-type monitor.

Note, however, that the monitor itself does not generate the images it displays. These images are electronically crafted by a *video card* installed inside your system unit. To work correctly, both video card and monitor must be matched to display images of the same resolution.

Resolution refers to the size of the images that can be displayed onscreen and is measured in pixels. A *pixel* is a single dot on your screen; a full picture is composed of thousands of pixels. The higher the resolution, the sharper the resolution—which lets you display more (smaller) elements onscreen. Resolution is expressed in numbers of pixels, in both the horizontal and vertical directions. Most newer video cards and monitors can display a resolution of at least 1024×768.

Your system's video setup can be the source of numerous problems. If your card and monitor are mismatched, for example, you might receive distorted images on your monitor—if, in fact, you see anything at all. (You might have to reset the switches on the video card itself to establish the correct setup for your system.) Configuring Windows for the wrong video card can result in display problems, too. And, as with most peripheral-based problems, a loose connection between the monitor and the system unit is Public Enemy Number One. So, to ensure great reception on your monitor, just as you would with your television, make sure that everything is plugged in, set up, and adjusted correctly.

Sound Cards and Speakers: Making Noise

Most PCs come with some sort of speaker system. That might be an internal speaker (although those are becoming increasingly rare) or two or more external speakers. In fact, some systems come with multiple-speaker audio systems, complete with sub-woofers and so-called 3D or surround sound.

All speaker systems are driven by a sound card or motherboard-driven audio circuit inside your system unit. If you upgrade your speaker system, you also might need to upgrade your sound card accordingly.

Because speakers have no moving parts, they seldom go bad. If your PC goes silent, the problem probably lies in the configuration of a specific software program, in the workings of your sound card, or in the connection of the speakers to your system unit—but *not* in the speakers themselves.

Modems: Getting Connected

Almost all PC systems today include a *modem*. A modem enables your computer to connect to a telephone or cable line and transmit data to and from the Internet.

Modems come in either internal (card-based) or external models that hook up to an open port on the back of your system. If you connect to the Internet via a broadband connection, you probably have an external cable or DSL modem. These devices work just like traditional phone line modems, but are specifically designed to work with the data transmitted over digital cable and DSL lines.

When you connect a modem to your system, take care that all its settings are configured correctly for your computer—and that you have the correct device drivers installed. You also must create a dial-up connection in Windows to connect to an Internet service provider; you need to input the right information to establish your connection and account—which can sometimes be a chore.

note

The word *modem* stands for "modulate-demodulate," which is how digital data is sent over traditional analog phone lines. The data is "modulated" for transmittal, and "demodulated" upon receipt.

Network Devices: Sharing Files and Peripherals

When you need to share files, printers, or an Internet connection between two or more PCs, you need to hook all your computers together into a *network*. Connecting multiple computers is actually fairly simple, and many new PCs come preconfigured with all the network hardware to do the job.

The most common type of network is a wired network using Ethernet cables and hardware. For this type of network, you need to install and configure a *network interface card (NIC)* in each of your PCs. If you're connecting more than two computers in your network, each network card then has to be connected to a *hub*, which is a simple device that functions like the hub of a wheel and serves as the central point in your network.

Also popular—and more convenient, in many cases—is the *wireless* network. Wireless networks use radio frequency (RF) signals to transmit data from one PC to another. To make your network wireless, you need to add a wireless *router* or *base station*, and then add wireless adapters to each of your PCs.

The main problems you run into with home and small business networks is setting them up. Although it's easier to set up a network on a Windows XP system than it is on most older systems, there is still a fair amount of technical configuration that you have to work through. After you have the network set up, however, the only problems you're likely to encounter involve the typical connection issues—or, in the case of wireless networks, interference with other wireless devices in the vicinity.

Printers: Making Hard Copies

Your monitor displays images in real time, but they're fleeting. For permanent records of your work, you must add a printer to your system. Printers create hard copy output from your software programs.

You can choose from various types of printers for your system, depending on your exact printing needs. *Laser* printers work much like copying machines, applying toner (powdered ink) to paper by using a small laser. *Inkjet* printers, on the other hand, shoot jets of ink to the paper's surface to create the printed image.

You also can choose from either black-and-white or color printers. Black-and-white printers are faster than color printers and better if you're printing memos, letters, and other single-color documents. Color printers, however, are great if you have kids, and they're essential if you want to print pictures taken with a digital camera.

You can run into problems with any type of printer. Not only are the usual problems with hookup and setup to be expected, but printers also require constant maintenance to stay in top operating condition. For example, laser printers require regular replacement of their toner cartridges as well as frequent paper-path cleaning; inkjet printers require new ink cartridges and maintenance to keep the ink jets from getting clogged.

The Operating System: Windows to the World of Computing

Before you can use all the pieces and parts of your computer to do anything, you need to know how to operate Microsoft Windows. This is because Windows pretty much runs your computer for you; if you don't know your way around Windows, you won't be able to do much of anything on your new PC.

Windows is a piece of software called an *operating system*. An operating system does what its name implies—it *operates* your computer *system*, working in the background every time you turn on your PC.

Equally important, Windows is what you see when you first turn on your computer, after everything powers on and boots up. The "desktop" that fills your screen is part of Windows, as is the taskbar at the bottom of the screen and the big menu that pops up when you click the Start button.

The version of Windows installed on most new PCs is Windows XP. There are actually two different flavors of Windows XP: Windows XP Home Edition is designed for home and small-business users; Windows XP Professional Edition is designed for larger businesses and corporate users. They both share the same basic functionality; XP Professional just has a few more features specially for large corporate networks.

note

This book is written for PCs running Windows XP, Windows Me, or Windows 98. If your PC is running a different version of Windows, most of the advice here is still good, although not all the step-by-step instructions will apply.

If you have an older PC, it might be running an older version of Windows, such as Windows 95, Windows 98, or Windows Me (Millennium Edition)—and if you're computing in a large corporation, you might be using Windows NT or Windows 2000. All of these Windows operate in the same general fashion, even if some of the specific details are different.

Understanding the Startup Process

So what happens when you first turn on your computer? What complex chain of events is initiated when you flip your power switch to the "on" position?

The first thing that happens is that power is sent through the PC's power supply to the boards in the system unit. This initial power surge (called a *power-on reset*) resets your system's memory, microprocessor, and other electronics. Then your system, using instructions stored in its *basic input/output system* (*BIOS*), does a *power-on self test* (*POST*). During this test, you see some messages scroll down your screen, letting you know how much RAM is available and that the system checks out as expected.

After the self-test, your computer tries to access drive A, looking for a bootable diskette. A bootable diskette contains important system files necessary for your system to operate—files that are normally "hidden," and not displayed in a normal directory listing.

If a bootable diskette is in drive A, your system proceeds based on the startup files on this diskette; if not, your system proceeds to the next bootable drive, which is probably your CD-ROM drive. (This is certainly the case in all newer systems, from about Windows 98 on; older systems typically can't boot from the CD-ROM drive.) If there's no bootable disc in your CD-ROM drive, your system (finally!) proceeds to drive C to look for the system files.

When your computer accesses drive C, it reads into memory the contents of the disk's *boot sector*, which tells the system how to load the operating system.

If you're running Windows XP, NT, or 2000, your system now loads the Windows operating system. If you're running an older version of Windows, however, your system doesn't load Windows just yet; instead, it loads a copy of the older DOS operating system. This is because all versions of Windows up to and including Windows 98 were based on DOS, and actually sat on top of the older operating system. In any case, this all happens in the background—you don't actually see DOS on your screen.

Your system then begins to load Windows and reads important settings from the Windows Registry, a database that contains all of your system configuration settings. As Windows loads, it also loads a variety of device drivers, as specified by the Windows Registry. Device drivers are small files that enable various pieces of hardware to operate; they're loaded into your system's memory, where they're immediately available for use.

Finally, after all the settings have been checked and all the drivers loaded, Windows itself is launched. You see a "loading" screen (which replaces the text-based screen you've seen up till now), hear "The Microsoft Sound," and then the Windows interface begins to build, element by element, until you can see the entire desktop and can use your system.

All this activity is accompanied by beeps and whirrs and clicks and flashing lights, which just indicate that your system is doing its job. If you don't hear all the beeps and whirrs and clicks and see the flashing lights, and if your system doesn't load the boot program, the system files, and Windows, you have a problem.

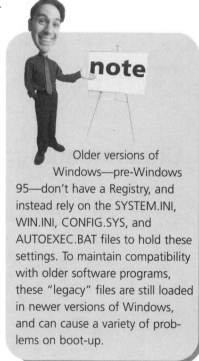

note

Older versions of Windows—pre-Windows 95—don't have a Registry, and instead rely on the SYSTEM.INI, WIN.INI, CONFIG.SYS, and AUTOEXEC.BAT files to hold these settings. To maintain compatibility with older software programs, these "legacy" files are still loaded in newer versions of Windows, and can cause a variety of problems on boot-up.

THE ABSOLUTE MINIMUM

Here are the key points to remember from this chapter:

- Your computer system is composed of various pieces of hardware, almost all of which plug into that big beige (or gray or black) box called the system unit.

- The system unit is the brains and engine of your computer system; it contains the microprocessor, memory, disk drives, and all the connections for your other system components.

- Data is temporarily stored in your system's memory; you store data permanently on some type of disk drive—either a hard disk, floppy disk, or CD-ROM.

- You interface with your computer hardware via a piece of software called an operating system. The operating system on your new computer is probably some version of Microsoft Windows.

- When you turn on your computer, it goes through a series of self-tests, loads basic system settings, and then starts the Windows operating system.

2

PREPARING YOUR SYSTEM FOR AN UPGRADE

If your PC is more than a year old, you can probably improve its performance and capabilities by upgrading one or more components. Whether you're adding more memory, moving to a larger hard disk, adding a faster modem, or changing audio or video cards, you can keep your system up-to-date without buying a completely new system.

To Upgrade or Not to Upgrade—That Is the Question

Paradoxically, it's easier to upgrade a newer PC than it is an older one; of course, if you have a newer PC, you have less need to upgrade. In fact, if your computer is *too* old, you'll find upgrading both problematic and overly expensive; when you add up the costs of the new components you want to add, you'll probably find that it's cheaper to buy a new PC.

How old is too old? Some techies use the "three years and out" rule and say that if your PC is more than three years old, don't bother upgrading. There's a good reason for this, as really old PCs often don't have the oomph necessary to accept newer, higher-performing components. It's also possible that some components of your old PC might be obsolete; this is a particular problem when upgrading memory on a system that uses SIMM or early SDRAM-NIMM modules.

Cost is also a factor. As low-priced as new PCs are these days, you don't want to put too much money into an old machine when a few bucks more will buy you a brand-new system.

Here is a good example of how buying a new PC is often more cost-effective than punching up an old one. I recently contemplated upgrading a five year-old Pentium II to serve as a digital audio workstation for my home recording projects. To bring the old unit up to spec, I would have had to add 128MB of memory ($50), a 40GB hard disk ($150), a USB expander hub ($30), a new sound card ($120), and a full copy of Windows XP ($200). When I added it all up, I would have spent $550 to have a souped-up Pentium II running at a relatively pokey 300MHz. Instead, I opted to buy a new low-end computer (sans monitor and speakers, which I already had) for just $499. For $50 *less* than what I would have spent on the upgrade, I got my 256MB total memory, 40GB hard disk, fancy sound card, six USB 2.0 ports, and Windows XP—all pre-installed and running on a speedy 1.67GHz AMD Athlon XP microprocessor. Less money, less work—not a hard decision!

Of course, some minor upgrades are both feasible and affordable, even if your PC is more than three years old. Memory, for example, is a cheap and easy upgrade that can boost the performance of just about any PC. Adding a second hard drive—especially if your PC has a USB connector, so you can add an external model—

note

Don't let all these acronyms tax your (human) memory; learn more about different types of computer memory in Chapter 6, "You Must Remember This: Upgrading System Memory."

is also relatively cheap and easy, and a real godsend if you're running short on storage space for all your graphics and music files.

If your computer is a Pentium III or later and has at least one free USB port, you don't need to worry. Upgrading a newer system is comparatively easy, if not always cheap!

What to Upgrade

When it comes to adding stuff to your PC, what are the most popular upgrades? Memory is always good (you can never have too much memory!), but other upgrades are driven more by the particular applications for which you use your computer. For example, if you play a lot of PC games you should consider upgrading your system's video card and monitor; if you listen to a lot of MP3 files, consider better speakers and a fast CD burner.

Table 2.1 shows the most popular hardware you can add to your system—along with why you'd want to make that upgrade, and the approximate cost of the new hardware.

Table 2.1   Popular Hardware Upgrades

Hardware	Approximate Cost	Reason to Upgrade
Memory	$40–$60 (128MB module)	To increase the speed at which your applications run, the number of programs that can run at the same time, and the size of individual files you can work with
Ports	$20–$100	To let you add more or different devices to your system; this is a good option if you've run out of USB ports, for example, or need to connect multiple printers and only have a single parallel port (another option—adding an external USB hub to increase the number of USB connections in your system)
Video card	$20–$400	To display higher-resolution pictures and graphics, provide smoother playback for visually demanding PC games, or add a second monitor for some high-end programming or development activities
Monitor (traditional)	$100–$500	For a larger viewing area—especially if you're playing graphics-intensive games or watching DVD movies

Table 2.1 (continued)

Hardware	Approximate Cost	Reason to Upgrade
Monitor (LCD)	$300–$2000	For a flatter display and to free up some desk space (plus, they look really cool!)
Sound card	$20–$250	To improve the audio capabilities of your PC system; this is particularly important if you're listening to high-quality MP3 files, watching surround-sound DVD movies, playing PC games with so-called 3D sound, or mixing and recording your own digital audio
Speakers	$15–$200	To upgrade the quality of your computer's sound system; speaker systems with sub-woofers are particularly popular
Keyboard	$15–$100	To upgrade to a more ergonomic or wireless model
Mouse	$5–$60	To upgrade to a different type of controller (such as a trackball), a more fully featured unit, a more reliable optical model, or a wireless model
Joystick or other game controller	$10–$300	To get better action with your favorite games
Modem	$15–$150	In case your PC doesn't have a state-of-the-art 56.6Kbps model, or if you're upgrading to broadband DSL or cable service
CD-ROM drive	$20–$150	In case your computer doesn't have one, or to upgrade to a faster unit
CD-R/RW drive (burner)	$30–$200	To add recordable/rewritable capabilities to your system
DVD-ROM	$50–$200	To add DVD capability to your system
DVD-R/RW (burner)	$250–$450	To let you burn your own DVD movies
Hard drive	$70–$400	To increase the storage capacity of your system (can be either external or internal)
Removable drive	$20–$200	To add removable storage capacity to your system—typically in the form of a Zip drive (or a floppy, if your system didn't come with a 3 1/2" drive)
Media card reader	$15–$50	So you can read data from devices that use various types of flash memory cards
Network interface card (NIC)	$10–$30	To connect your computer to a local area network

Table 2.1   (continued)

Hardware	Approximate Cost	Reason to Upgrade
Wireless network adapter	$30–$80	To connect your computer to a wireless network
Scanner	$50–$300	So you can scan photographs and documents into a digital format to store on your computer's hard drive
Printer	$50–$1000	To improve the quality of your printouts, to add color to your printouts, to add photo-quality printing to your system
PC camera	$20–$200	To send live video of yourself to friends and family, to participate in live video chat, or to set up your own Webcam on the Internet
Digital media hub	$150–$500	Connects your PC to your home audio system, so you can listen to digital audio files and Internet radio on your big system

There are also parts of your system that you *can* upgrade or replace, but probably don't want to because the process is too difficult. These components include your PC's microprocessor chip and power supply. If you have lots of hands-on experience under the hood of your computer, you might be comfortable performing this type of major upgrade. If you're technically timid or an absolute beginner, leave these types of upgrades to a professional.

Before You Upgrade

Before you dive headfirst into the upgrading waters, it helps to know what you're getting yourself into. If nothing else, you need to know whether your system can accept the upgrade you want to make; not all PCs are compatible with all the new peripherals on the market today.

Then there is the unsettling fact that even the simplest upgrades—the ones where you plug a new peripheral into an open port—don't always go smoothly. On the off chance that your upgrade either doesn't take or somehow messes up something else in your

note

All the prices here and elsewhere in this book are approximate, and subject to change. In general, the cost of PC equipment decreases over time, and if you shop around a little you'll get a better deal than if you buy from the first store you walk into. So don't take these prices as gospel—do your homework to find the best bang for your buck when you're ready to upgrade!

system, you want to be able to undo the damage and return your system to its pre-upgrade (or *working*) state.

That said, here is a checklist of what you need to prepare *before* you attempt a PC upgrade:

Pre-Upgrade Checklist

- ☐ Assemble your upgrade toolkit.
- ☐ Print out a system hardware report, so you'll know exactly what hardware is installed on your system.
- ☐ Determine whether the peripheral you want to add will work on your system.
- ☐ Make a note of your system's key configuration settings.
- ☐ Gather your original Windows installation CD or disks—including an emergency startup disk or CD, just in case your system won't restart normally.
- ☐ Make a backup of your important data files.
- ☐ If you're running Windows XP or Windows Me, set a System Restore point.
- ☐ Read the instructions of the item you want to install.

Assembling an Upgrade Toolkit

As the first point on the Upgrade Checklist indicated, you should assemble an upgrade toolkit. Figure 2.1 shows all the tools you'll need to perform the various types of upgrades you can make to your personal computer system.

FIGURE 2.1
Your complete
PC upgrade
toolkit—two
screwdrivers.

Phillips

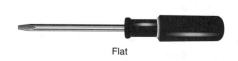

Flat

That's right. All you need are two screwdrivers—flat-head and Phillips-head.

In fact, if you're adding an external peripheral to you system, you won't even need a screwdriver; all you have to do is plug the new peripheral into one of the connectors on the back of the system. You'll use your screwdriver only if you need to open the case of your system unit and install a new card.

Creating a System Hardware Report with Device Manager

Now that we have the tool gathering out of the way, let's look at the rest of the pre-upgrade preparation. It's good practice to know what hardware is installed on your PC before you install any new equipment. Fortunately, Windows provides a utility, called the Device Manager, that provides various reports that detail the devices installed on your system and which resources they're using.

To use Device Manager to create a system hardware report, follow these steps (in Windows XP):

1. Click the Start button and select the Control Panel option to open the Control Panel.

2. Select Performance and Maintenance, System, to open the System Properties dialog box.

3. Select the Hardware tab and click the Device Manager button to open the Device Manager utility, shown in Figure 2.2.

Mike Sez

Before any hard-core techies start jumping up and down and waving their arms and shouting about "chip pullers" and other fancy tools, it's time to make an important point. Yes, there are some advanced hardware upgrades (such as changing microprocessor chips) that do require different tools. But, as an absolute beginner, you shouldn't be attempting those types of upgrades. The general rule is this: If it takes more than a screwdriver, let a professional do it.

FIGURE 2.2

Use the Device Manager to print details about your installed hardware.

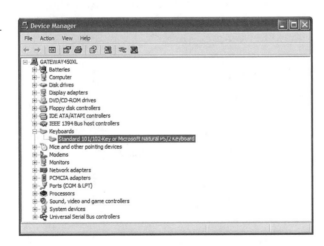

4. Select View, Devices by Type to list all devices by class.

5. To print a report for a specific class or device, select the name in the devices list and then click the Print button. When the Print dialog box appears, select the type of report to print, as described in Table 2.2. Click OK in the Print dialog box to print the report on the selected output device.

Table 2.2 System Hardware Reports

Report	Description
System Summary	Lists the resources on your system, as well as which hardware is using each resource.
Selected Class or Device	Lists the resources and device drivers used by the device selected in the device list.
All Devices and System Summary	Lists all the hardware on your system, including a list of all resources used by the hardware.

Use the All Devices and System Summary report to determine whether you have a potential conflict with new hardware that you are preparing to install in your computer. Print the report, highlight all IRQ, I/O, and MEM settings, and then compare these to the settings that the new device(s) can be set to.

Print a More Detailed Report with Microsoft System Information

You can also use the Microsoft System Information utility (shown in Figure 2.3) to print out more detailed reports on your system status. Because Microsoft System Information gives you a snapshot of your entire system configuration, this is a great resource for anyone—including technical support staff—trying to troubleshoot Windows problems; this kind of specific information is necessary to figure out what might be conflicting with what.

FIGURE 2.3

The Microsoft System Information utility is a great way to learn about your system components.

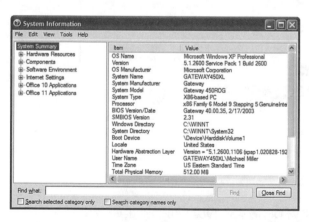

To use the Microsoft System Information utility, follow these steps:

1. Click the Start button and select All Programs, Accessories, System Tools, System Information.

2. When the Microsoft System Information utility launches, click the item in the left-hand pane you want to examine; the contents of that view will appear in the right-hand pane.

tip

To see changes made to your system components over time, select View, System History.

Microsoft System Information organizes your system data into several major categories, displayed in a kind of resource "tree" in the left-hand pane. The most important of these categories are

- **Hardware Resources**—This view displays hardware-specific settings—DMA, IRQs, I/O addresses, memory addresses, and so on. Select **Conflicts/Sharing** to identify devices that are sharing resources or are in conflict.

- **Components**—This view displays information about your Windows configuration. Look here to determine the status of your device drivers and network resources.

- **Software Environment**—This view displays a snapshot of the software loaded in your system's memory.

To print out a complete listing of all system parameters, click the Print button. (Depending on your particular system, the printout can run up to 100 pages!) If you'd prefer to save your system information in a text file for future viewing, select File, Export, and then select a filename and location for the text file.

Backing Up Your Data

The next thing you need to do before you upgrade is prepare for the worst-case scenario, in which your upgrade completely fries your system and you lose access to all the data stored on your hard disk. While this is a highly unlikely scenario, it can happen—and you don't want to be caught short if it does!

The only way to protect against a catastrophic loss of data is to create a backup copy of that data. Then, if you have to start rebuilding your system from scratch, you can restore the lost data from the backup copy.

You can back up your data to any number of media. In the old days it was common to use floppy disks for backup; given the size of today's data files (especially graphics and sound files), the meager 1.44MB capacity of a floppy disk just isn't big enough. Better to back up to a Zip disk, a tape cassette, or a CD-R/RW disc.

If you have all your data files in a single folder and are backing up to a large-enough medium (such as a CD-R/RW), the easiest way to back up the data is just to copy the folder. If your files are scattered all over your hard drive or (especially) if you'll need to use multiple media (more than one disk or tape, that is), you'll want to use a backup software program.

Fortunately, you don't have to go out and purchase a separate backup program because Windows has its own built-in backup utility, called (surprisingly enough) Microsoft Backup. To learn how to use Microsoft Backup to back up your data files, turn to Chapter 19, "Simple Steps to Keep Your System in Tip-Top Shape."

Setting a System Restore Point

If you're running Windows XP or Windows Me, another good preventative measure to take is to set a System Restore point. System Restore is a new utility that takes a snapshot of your key system settings. If some of your system settings get messed up during an upgrade, you can use System Restore to return your system to its pre-upgrade configuration.

To learn how to set a System Restore point, see Chapter 21, "How to Deal with a Finicky PC."

An Upgrade Roadmap

Now that your preparation is complete, it's time to perform the upgrade itself. What you do next depends on whether you're adding an internal or an external peripheral.

Figure 2.4 provides a roadmap you can use for implementing your upgrade.

Upgrading from the Outside

The easiest way to add new devices to your system is to add them via an external connector; this way, you don't have to open your PC's case to make the upgrade.

Of course, the easiest way isn't always the *best* way. That's because some types of peripherals run faster if they're installed internally rather than externally. For example, an internal hard disk will probably run faster than an external one. Still, for most users, an external connection—preferably via USB—is the way to go.

> **tip**
>
> Most peripherals you add to your system come with their own sets of instructions and their own installation disks or CDs. You should *always* read and follow the manufacturer's instructions—even if they contradict the general upgrade instructions presented in this book. In all instances, specific instructions outrank general advice!

FIGURE 2.4

To add a peripheral to your computer system, follow this upgrade roadmap.

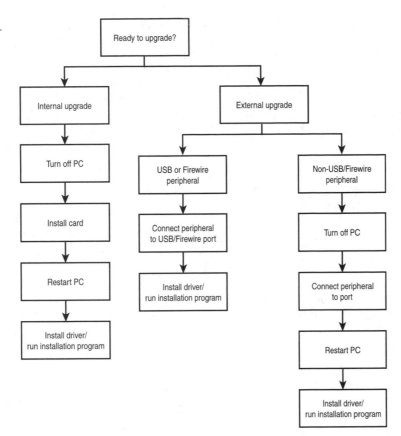

That said, there are many different types of external connectors available—each optimized to send and receive specific types of data. And, because different types of hardware connect via different types of connectors, it's important to know the different types of ports and connectors with which you might be working.

Table 2.3 shows the many types of external connectors available on a typical PC. These connectors are most likely located on the back of your system unit, although some computers have auxiliary ports (typically for USB and FireWire) on the front, as well. Note, however, that not all PCs will have all types of connectors.

Table 2.3   Common External Connectors

Connector	Type	Common Uses	Description
	Serial	Modems, printers, mice	A serial port (sometimes called an *RS-232* or COM port) is an interface that enables communication one bit at a time, in one direction at a time
	Parallel	Printers, scanners	A parallel port (often called a *printer port*) is an interface that can handle communications going in two directions at once
	USB	Any—printers, scanners, modems, external sound cards, mice, keyboards, joysticks, CD-ROM/DVD drives, external hard drives, cameras	A USB (*Universal Serial Bus*) port is a newer, faster, more intelligent type of serial port; USB devices can be added while the computer is still running, which you can't do with other types of connections; the newer USB 2.0 standard is much faster than the existing 1.1 variety
	FireWire	Digital video cameras, external hard drives, CD burners	FireWire (also called *IEEE 1394*) is an interface that enables hot-pluggable, high-speed data transmission

Table 2.3 (continued)

Connector	Type	Common Uses	Description
	SCSI	External hard drives, CD burners, CD-ROM/DVD drives, Zip drives, tape backups	The SCSI (*computer system interface*—pronounced "scuzzy") port is a high-speed parallel interface, typically used to connect mass storage media
	Gameport	Joysticks and other controllers; MIDI devices (with adapter)	Use the gameport to connect all your gaming controllers; this port also functions as a MIDI port when you use the proper MIDI-to-15 pin adapter
	Mouse	Mice, trackballs, other pointing devices	The mouse port (sometimes called a *PS/2 port*) is used to connect wired pointing devices, as well as the wireless receiver used by wireless mice
	Keyboard	Keyboard	The keyboard connector (also sometimes called a PS/2 port) is used to connect both wired keyboards and the wireless receiver used by wireless keyboards
	Audio Out	Powered speakers, audio amplifiers/receivers	The audio out jack feeds a line-level output that can be used by any audio amplifier or set of powered computer speakers

Table 2.3   (continued)

Connector	Type	Common Uses	Description
	Audio In	External audio devices (CD players, turntables, cassette decks)	Some advanced sound cards let you plug in typical audio components, so you can record their output to digital files on your hard disk
	S/PDIF	Digital audio	The S/PDIF (Sony/Philips Digital Interface) connector is used to transmit high-end digital audio (typically from a DVD player) to and from a sound-card
	Digital DIN	Speaker systems	A 9-pin digital interface used to connect high-end multiple-speaker systems
	Microphone	Microphone	Accepts input from consumer-grade microphones
	Headphone	Headphone	With the right plug adapter, any set of headphones can be plugged into this jack
	MIDI	Musical keyboards, audio mixers, other MIDI-compatible devices	This jack is used to connect musical instruments and other devices using the MIDI (Musical Instrument Digital Interface) standard
	VGA	Computer monitors	This is the 15-pin adapter used to connect almost all traditional CRT computer monitors

Table 2.3 (continued)

Connector	Type	Common Uses	Description
	DVI-I	LCD monitors	DVI (Digital Video Interface) is used to connect some newer LCD monitors, and provides a crisper picture than the older VGA connection
	Video Out	Television monitors	This composite video output that can feed your computer display signal to any television set with a similar video input.
	S-Video	Television monitors	This connector also feeds your computer display signal to a television monitor; S-Video provides a crisper picture than composite video, and should be used when available
	Ethernet	Wired networks	Ethernet enables connection to wired networks at speeds up to 100Mps
	Telephone	Telephone lines	The telephone connector is part of your system's modem; use this connector to plug into a telephone line to connect to the Internet (some PCs have both telephone in and telephone out connectors, thus enabling a through feed of the phone line signal when you're not online)

Table 2.3 (continued)

Connector	Type	Common Uses	Description
EtherLink II	PC Card	PC Card devices, from modems to hard drives	The Personal Computer Memory Card International Association (PCM-CIA) established the standard for the PC Card interface used on most of today's portable PCs; on a portable PC, the PC Card slot can be used to connect all manner of devices

On newer PCs, many of these connectors are color-coded, which makes it easier to figure out which cable plugs into where. Table 2.4 provides the color coding (specified by Microsoft in its PC 99 Connector Guidelines) for common types of connectors. To see these colors in living color, go to the Color Coding for Connectors page on the PC Design Guide Web site (www.pcdesguide.org/documents/pc99icons.htm).

Table 2.4 Connector Color Codes

Connector	Color
VGA (analog) monitor	Blue
Digital monitor	White
Video out	Yellow
Mouse	Green
Keyboard	Purple
Serial	Teal or turquoise
Parallel (printer)	Burgundy
USB	Black
FireWire (IEEE 1394)	Gray
Audio line out (left)	Red
Audio line out (right)	White

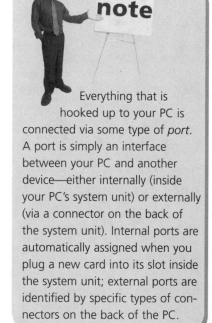

note

Everything that is hooked up to your PC is connected via some type of *port*. A port is simply an interface between your PC and another device—either internally (inside your PC's system unit) or externally (via a connector on the back of the system unit). Internal ports are automatically assigned when you plug a new card into its slot inside the system unit; external ports are identified by specific types of connectors on the back of the PC.

Table 2.4 (continued)

Connector	Color
Audio line out (headphones)	Lime
Speaker out/subwoofer	Orange
Right-to-left speaker	Brown
Audio line in	Light blue
Microphone	Pink
Gameport/MIDI	Gold

Upgrading via USB

The most common external connector today is the USB port. USB is a great concept (and truly "universal") in that virtually every type of new peripheral comes in a USB version. Want to add a second hard disk? Don't open the PC case; get the USB version. Want to add a new printer? Forget the parallel port; get the USB version. Want to add a wireless network adapter? Don't bother with Ethernet cards; get the USB version.

See a trend here? The easiest way to upgrade your system is via USB. If you have a choice, get the USB-compatible peripheral. It will make the job of upgrading *extremely* easy.

Another nice thing about USB, in addition to its universality, is that USB peripherals are *hot swappable*. That means you can just plug the new device into the USB port, and Windows will automatically recognize it in real time; you don't need to reboot your machine to finish the installation.

There are currently two flavors of USB available. The older USB standard, version 1.1, has been around for awhile and, if your PC is more than a year or so old, is probably the type of USB you have installed. The newer USB 2.0 protocol is much faster than USB 1.1, and is now standard on most new computers. See the icons in Figure 2.5 to make sure you're using the right version of USB for your system.

caution

Older PCs produced before the PC 99 Connector Guidelines might use different color coding. When in doubt, consult the instruction manual!

"Mike Sez"

USB is so popular today that it's possible to run out of USB connectors on your PC. If that happens to you, buy an add-on USB hub, which lets you plug multiple USB peripherals into a single USB port.

FIGURE 2.5
USB 1.1 and 2.0
icons.

Supports USB 1.1   Supports USB 2.0

Because USB 2.0 ports are fully backward-compatible with older USB 1.1 devices, you can't go wrong with the newer version. For this reason, installing a USB 2.0 port (via expansion card) is a very popular and inexpensive upgrade if you have an older PC.

I'll assume you're sold on USB, and proceed to the upgrade instructions. To add a USB peripheral to your system, follow these steps:

1. Connect the new peripheral to an open USB connector on your system unit, as shown in Figure 2.6.

2. Windows should automatically recognize the new peripheral and either install the proper driver automatically, or prompt you to provide a CD or disk containing the driver file. Follow the onscreen instructions to finish installing the driver.

FIGURE 2.6
Connecting a
peripheral via
the USB port.

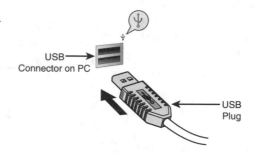

USB
Connector on PC

USB
Plug

note

That's it! The only variation on this procedure is if the peripheral's manufacturer recommends using its own installation program, typically provided on the installation CD. If this is the case, follow the manufacturer's instructions to perform the installation and setup.

By the way, FireWire peripherals are also hot swappable, and just as easy to install as USB devices. So if you're installing a FireWire-compatible device, follow the same procedure as you would for a USB device.

A *device driver* is a small software program that enables your PC to communicate with and control a specific device. Windows XP includes built-in device drivers for many popular peripherals. If Windows doesn't include a particular driver, you typically can find the driver on the peripheral's installation disk or on the peripheral manufacturer's Web site.

Upgrading via Serial, Parallel, and Other External Ports

When you're connecting to something other than a USB or FireWire port (such as a serial or parallel port), you need to follow a slightly different procedure. The big difference is that you need to turn off your PC before you connect the new device. Just follow these steps:

1. Close Windows and turn off your computer.

2. Find an open port on the back of your system unit, and connect the new peripheral.

3. If the peripheral needs to be plugged in, do that now; if the plug uses thumb screws, secure them after plugging it in.

4. Restart your system.

5. As Windows starts, it should recognize the new device and either install the proper drivers automatically or ask you to supply the device drivers (via CD or disk).

6. Windows installs the drivers and finishes the startup procedure. Your new device should now be operational.

note

As with USB devices, if your new peripheral comes with its own unique installation instructions, follow those steps instead of these general ones.

Upgrading from the Inside

Adding an internal device—usually through a plug-in card—is slightly more difficult than adding an external device, primarily because you have to use your screwdriver and get "under the hood" of your system unit. Other than the extra screwing and plugging, however, the process is pretty much the same as with external devices.

The one major difference is recognizing the type of card you're installing and the type of expansion slots you have available—and making sure they match. There are three major types of expansion slots used on today's PCs, as detailed in Table 2.5.

Table 2.5 Types of Internal Expansion Slots

Card/Slot	Type	Description
	ISA	ISA (*Industry Standard Architecture*) slots have been around since the dawn of the PC era; they're big, they're dumb, and they are for all practical purposes, outdated and unused on today's newer PCs—so don't be alarmed if your PC doesn't have any of these.
	PCI	PCI (*Peripheral Component Interconnect*) slots are about a decade old now, but still widely used on today's PCs; these slots accept relatively small cards and are good for everything except really fast video.
	AGP	AGP (*Accelerated Graphics Port*) slots are used primarily for speedy 3D graphics cards.

In general, you'll want to use PCI cards and slots for all your internal upgrades *except* video; if you're adding a new video card, get an AGP model. And, if at all possible, avoid the older ISA cards—unless you have a really old PC that doesn't have any open PCI slots.

After you have the cards and slots all figured out, follow these steps to add the new card to your system:

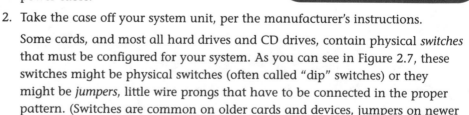

caution

Never open up the system unit with the power still on. Electricity is no fun to play with!

1. Turn off your computer and unplug the power cable.

2. Take the case off your system unit, per the manufacturer's instructions.

   Some cards, and most all hard drives and CD drives, contain physical *switches* that must be configured for your system. As you can see in Figure 2.7, these switches might be physical switches (often called "dip" switches) or they might be *jumpers*, little wire prongs that have to be connected in the proper pattern. (Switches are common on older cards and devices, jumpers on newer ones.) You don't need any special tools to set dip switches or jumpers, although a set of long-nosed pliers might be useful if the jumpers on a card are lodged too tightly. If your new card has switches or jumpers that need to be configured, do this before inserting the card into your system unit.

caution

Because electrical discharges can damage critical electronic components, you should avoid creating static electricity when working inside your system unit. That means working on a clean wooden or tile surface—*not* a carpet—and wearing cotton or other natural-fiber clothing. You might also want to consider using an anti-static work mat or an anti-static grounding strap, both available at Radio Shack and most computer retailers.

FIGURE 2.7

The dip switches and jumpers you'll find on a typical expansion card.

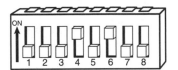

4. Find an open card slot inside the system unit. If you need to remove the slot's cover (on the back of the system unit), do so now, as shown in Figure 2.8. (And if things are too tight inside the case to insert the card, consider using another slot—you don't have to use slots sequentially, you can leave some empty slots between cards.)

FIGURE 2.8

Removing the slot's cover.

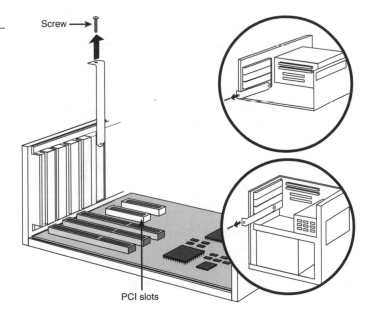

Screw

PCI slots

5. Insert the new card according to the manufacturer's instructions, as shown in Figure 2.9. (Make sure the card is firmly plugged in; if you can wiggle it, you haven't made a good connection.)

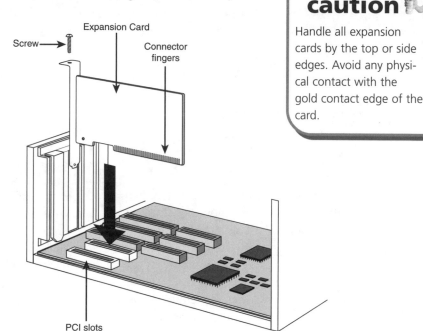

FIGURE 2.9

When inserting a card into a slot, press firmly!

caution

Handle all expansion cards by the top or side edges. Avoid any physical contact with the gold contact edge of the card.

6. After the card is appropriately seated and screwed in, put the case back on the system unit, plug in the unit, and restart your system.

7. After Windows starts, it should recognize the new device and automatically install the appropriate driver.

Using the Windows Add Hardware Wizard

Whether you're adding an internal or external component, both your system and Windows should recognize the new device without any manual prompting. If, however, Windows doesn't

tip

You probably want to see whether the new component configures properly and works fine before you close your system unit back up. For that reason, you might want to leave the case off until you're convinced everything is working okay and you don't need to do any more fiddling around inside your PC.

recognize your new device, you can install it manually via the Add Hardware Wizard. To use the Add Hardware Wizard in Windows XP, follow these steps:

1. Click the Start button and then select the Control Panel option to open the Control Panel folder.

2. Select Printers and Other Hardware, Add Hardware, to open the Add Hardware Wizard, shown in Figure 2.10.

FIGURE 2.10

Use the Add Hardware Wizard to add new hardware to your computer system.

3. Click the Next button.

4. If you're asked if you've already installed any new hardware, select Yes and click Next.

5. Windows now evaluates your system and displays a list of installed devices. To add a new device, select Add a New Hardware Device from the list, and click the Next button.

6. When the next screen appears, select Search For and Install the Hardware Automatically; then click Next.

7. Windows now looks for new plug-and-play hardware. If it can identify the new hardware, the wizard continues with the installation. If it can't find a new device, it tells you so. If this is your situation, click Next to begin a manual installation.

8. Select the type of device you want to install, and then click Next.

9. On the next screen, select the manufacturer and specific device. If you want to install the drivers that came with the device, click the Have Disk button and follow the onscreen instructions. To use a built-in Windows driver, click the Next button.

10. When the necessary files have been loaded, follow the onscreen instructions to complete the installation.

Note, however, that in most cases new hardware is detected automatically by Windows, thus eliminating the need for this somewhat more complicated procedure.

Configuring System Settings

Some devices you add to your PC—in particular, memory and disk drives—might need to be configured at the system level, before you ever get into Windows. As you learned back in Chapter 1, "Hardware Basics for the Absolute Beginner," these settings make up your system's BIOS, and are stored in a special battery-powered memory called CMOS (*Complimentary Metal-Oxide Semiconductor*) RAM.

To change the settings stored in your system's BIOS, you need to reboot your computer and then interrupt the startup process before Windows launches. Most systems, on startup, display an onscreen message that tells you what key to press to access your BIOS settings; it's typically one of the function keys, such as F2 or F8 or F10. (If you don't see this message, look in your computer's instruction manual for the setup key.) Table 2.6 shows the startup interrupt key for some common types of computer BIOS.

Table 2.6   Startup Interrupt Keys

Computer BIOS	Key(s)
AMI BIOS	Del
Award BIOS	Del *or* Ctrl+Alt+Esc
Compaq	F10
IBM Aptivas and Thinkpads	F1
Microid Research (MR BIOS)	Esc
Phoenix BIOS	F2
Toshiba notebooks/laptops	Esc, then F1 at prompt

When you enter the BIOS setup utility, you can change a number of basic system settings, such as which disk drives boot first, or what kind of hard disk you have, or how much memory is installed. There are typically several "pages" of settings in this utility, so make sure you page through until you find the settings you want to change.

After you make any changes to your system's BIOS, follow the onscreen instructions to save your settings and exit the setup utility. Your computer will then resume the startup process, using the new settings you just entered.

What to Do if the Upgrade Goes Wrong

In most cases, upgrading your computer system is every bit as easy as I've outlined in this chapter. Just plug in the new peripheral or insert the new card, and you're ready to go.

But what happens if—just *if*—the upgrade doesn't go right? What if the new peripheral isn't recognized? What if the new peripheral somehow causes an existing device not to work? Or, heaven forbid, what if you install the new peripheral but then your PC doesn't work at all?

caution

Be careful when changing system settings with the Setup utility; if you make the wrong choices, you can make your system unbootable!

Believe it or not, these things happen. If they happen to you, you want to keep a cool head and then begin a detailed course of troubleshooting. Fortunately, the entire last half of this book is dedicated to the troubleshooting process, so if you run into upgrade problems, turn to the appropriate chapter in Part VI, "Troubleshooting Common Problems," and work from there.

And, whatever else happens, don't panic!

THE ABSOLUTE MINIMUM

When you're ready to upgrade your computer system, here are the key points to remember:

- Before you buy any new peripherals, consider whether it's more cost-effective to upgrade your old PC or buy a new one—and remember, the decision gets harder if your PC is more than three years old.

- The most popular (and cost-effective) PC upgrades continue to be memory and storage.

- Before you upgrade, print out a report of your system's hardware and settings, back up your important data, and (if you're running Windows XP or Windows Me) set a System Restore point.

- Always, *always* read and follow the installation instructions that come with your new peripheral.

- If the upgrade requires anything more than a screwdriver, let a professional do it.

- If you have the choice, go with an external peripheral that uses a USB connection.

- In most cases, Windows should automatically recognize the new peripheral and install the proper device drivers; if not, run the Add Hardware Wizard to complete the installation and configuration.

- If you need to reconfigure your system's BIOS, you'll need to interrupt the startup procedure and enter the setup utility.

PART

Essential Hardware Upgrades

3

PORTS AHOY: UPGRADING SYSTEM INPUTS

Here is an indisputable reason to upgrade your computer system: you buy a new peripheral, and have no free ports to connect it to. It happens, and it happens a lot. Let's say you want to add a second printer to your system (like a color photo printer; they're quite popular these days). Most printers only come with a single parallel port, to which you probably have your existing printer connected. So when you go to plug in your new printer, you're out of luck.

The answer, of course, is to add a second parallel port to your system. (Another solution is to buy a USB printer and connect to a free USB port; let's not ignore easy fixes!)

Or maybe you've become enamored of USB devices, and completely filled all of your system's USB connections. Buy one more USB-compatible peripheral, and then what do you do? Here you have a choice; you can increase the number of connections available by adding an external USB hub, or you can add an extra USB card to your system.

Here's another one. You want to connect your new digital video camcorder to your PC to edit your home movies. But your camcorder connects via FireWire, and your PC doesn't have a FireWire connector. The solution? Add a FireWire port to your system unit.

This chapter shows you how to add extra ports to your computer system. Some of these upgrades are external (like the USB hub) and some require opening up your PC's case. Fortunately, they're all relatively easy procedures.

What Ports Can You Add?

Let's do a quick rundown on the types of ports you can add to your computer system:

- **Parallel** ports are used primarily for connecting printers to your system
- **Serial** ports are used to connect some types of mice, keyboards, and printers, as well as PDAs, PC cameras, and other assorted peripherals
- **USB** ports are used to connect just about any type of peripheral; peripherals conforming to the new USB 2.0 standard run much faster than the existing 1.1 devices
- **FireWire (IEEE 1394)** ports are used to connect fast digital devices, such as digital video recorders and digital still cameras
- **SCSI** ports are used to connect fast external hard drives

Most computers today come with a single parallel port, one or two serial ports, a FireWire port, and anywhere from a couple to a half-dozen USB ports. As you can see, if you add enough new devices to your system, you easily run out of available connectors.

> **caution**
>
> To install a USB 1.1 port on your system, your computer must be running Windows 98 or later. To install a USB 2.0 port, your computer must be running Windows XP with Service Pack 1 installed. To install a FireWire port, your computer must be running Windows 98 or later.

Buying a Port Expansion Card

Fortunately, adding a new port—of any kind—is as easy as installing a new card (like the one in Figure 3.1) in your system unit.

Not only is this particular upgrade relatively easy, it's also relatively inexpensive. You can find parallel, serial, and USB expansion cards for as little as $20 or so; FireWire and SCSI cards run a bit more.

In addition, many port expansion cards contain more than one type of port. So you can install one card to gain extra serial and parallel ports, or get a combination of USB and FireWire ports on a single card.

If you need a quick refresher course in the different types of ports and connectors, turn to Table 2.3, Common External Connectors, in Chapter 2, "Preparing Your System for an Upgrade."

FIGURE 3.1

A typical port expansion card—this one adds two USB ports.

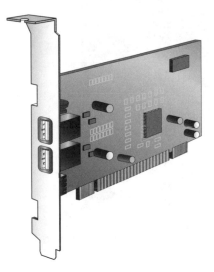

Mike Sez

If you have the choice, you're better off buying a peripheral that plugs into an existing USB port than one that requires a new parallel or serial connection. It's easier to connect a device to an open USB connector than it is to install a new parallel or serial card.

When you're shopping for a port expansion card, check out the product models from these manufacturers—most of these companies also make external port expansion devices:

- Adaptec (www.adaptec.com)
- Belkin (www.belkin.com)
- IOGEAR (www.iogear.com)
- SIIG (www.siig.com)
- StarTech (www.startech.com)

Upgrade #1: Adding a New Port Card

To install a port expansion card, grab your Phillips head screwdriver and follow these steps:

1. Close Windows and power off your PC.
2. Disconnect your PC from its power source.
3. Open the system unit case.
4. Locate an unused PCI card slot (see Figure 3.2).

FIGURE 3.2

Locate an empty PCI slot; if you have several empty slots, leave an empty slot between an old card and the new one you're installing.

5. Remove the cover to the selected slot (on the back of the system unit).
6. Insert the card into the open slot (see Figure 3.3).
7. Screw the card bracket into place, using the screw from the slot cover (see Figure 3.4).
8. Reinstall the system unit cover and reconnect the PC to its power source.
9. Restart your computer.
10. When prompted, install the drivers for your new card.

That's it. As soon as your computer is configured for the new ports, they're ready to use!

FIGURE 3.3
Use firm pressure to push the card into the slot—and make sure that the card is firmly seated.

FIGURE 3.4
Be careful when screwing the card into place; it's easy to slip and damage nearby components with the tip of your screwdriver.

Upgrade #2: Adding an External USB Hub

Here's an even easier upgrade. If your system already has one or more USB connectors, you can add extra ports by using an external device called a USB hub, shown in Figure 3.5. The hub connects to an open USB port on your PC; you can then connect multiple USB devices to the hub.

Add a USB hub to increase the number of USB ports on your system.

Follow these steps to connect a USB hub to your system; there's no need to turn off your computer before proceeding.

1. If you don't have a free USB port on your system, unplug one of your current USB peripherals.

2. Plug the USB hub into the open USB port on your system unit.

3. If you purchased a self-powered USB hub, connect it to its power source.

4. Connect any new or existing USB peripherals to the USB hub.

note

USB is a particularly expandable technology. The USB standard enables you to daisy chain up to 127 USB devices to your system!

Upgrade #3: Adding Ports to a Portable PC

Adding a new port to a portable PC is particularly problematic. (My apologies for the alliteration!) You can't add a new port via internal card, so you're limited to going the USB route, or adding an expansion port on a PC Card. Either of these options is equally viable.

If you go the PC Card route, you need to be aware of which type of PC Card slot you have on your portable. Older portable PCs used a 16-bit PC Card slot, which isn't very versatile; you can't use it for USB, FireWire, or fast SCSI adapters. Most newer portables have 32-bit PC Card slots, which can handle just about anything you throw at them. (Check the specifications page of your PC's instruction manual to determine what type of PC Card slots you have.)

caution

Some older PCs have trouble working with some external USB hubs; they might require constant rebooting to recognize the hub. If this happens to you, try plugging the hub into a different internal port, or try using a different brand of hub.

THE ABSOLUTE MINIMUM

When it comes time to expand the ports on your PC, remember these important points:

- You can add just about any type of port to your system by installing a port expansion card.
- To install a port expansion card, all you need is a free PCI expansion slot—and a screwdriver.
- An easier way to expand the number of USB ports in your system is to use an external USB hub.
- You can expand the ports on a portable PC via either USB or PC Card.

IN THIS CHAPTER

- Understanding hard disk drives
- Adding an external hard drive
- Adding a second internal hard drive
- Replacing your existing hard drive
- Adding an internal floppy or Zip drive
- Adding a memory card reader

BIGGER IS BETTER: UPGRADING SYSTEM STORAGE

Your computer stores its data on various types of disks. Permanent storage is typically on one or more hard disks installed in your PC's system unit; temporary storage is often on removable disks or CD-ROM discs.

The computer industry uses two different types of technology to read and write data to these various types of disks. *Magnetic disks*, such as hard disks and floppy disks, store data on thin metal or metal-coated disks, using magnetic fields. *Optical disks*, such as CDs and DVDs, store data in miniature pits that are read by a focused laser beam. In both cases, information is encoded in the 1s and 0s typical of digital data.

When you want to store more stuff on your computer system, it's time to talk about upgrading your system storage. That might mean replacing your existing hard drive with a bigger unit, or adding a second hard drive (either internally or externally). You can also upgrade your system storage by adding a new floppy or CD-ROM drive, or a reader for flash memory cards.

This chapter focuses on magnetic disk storage—specifically, hard drives and floppy drives. And, as a bonus, you'll learn how to add a memory card reader to your system. If you want to install a new optical drive, you'll have to skip ahead to Chapter 5, "Optical Tricks: Upgrading CD and DVD Drives."

Understanding Hard Disk Drives

Before we get into installing hard disk drives, let's take a minute to examine how a hard drive works. As you can see in Figure 4.1, a hard drive consists of multiple rigid-metal platters, stacked on a spindle inside a sealed enclosure. The spindle is attached to a motor that spins the platters at very high speeds.

FIGURE 4.1

The inside of a hard drive looks like this.

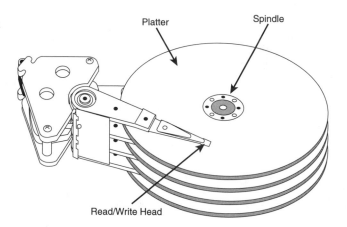

Hard disk platters are coated with a special material that enables the storage of information in magnetic patterns. Data is written to and read from the platter by means of an electromagnetic read/write head. Each platter is divided into *sectors*; each sector contains 512 bytes of data.

Understanding Hard Drive Specs

When you go shopping for a new hard drive, you need to understand the relevant specifications in order to make an informed buying decision—and get the right hard drive for your system. This information, typically available somewhere on the drive's packaging—tells you how much data the disk can hold, and how fast it can access that data. (Faster is better, of course—and also more expensive.)

Of these specs, you'll want to focus your attention on size, speed, and price. Given the low prices of hard drives today, you'll probably want to spend a few extra bucks to get a larger-capacity drive—if your system can handle it. If you're using disk-intensive applications (such as PC games or audio/video editing programs), you'll also want to spring for the faster 7,200 RPM models. And, of course, price is always a factor; make sure you make the price/performance compromise that works best for your specific needs.

Capacity

Disk drive size is typically measured in gigabytes (GB). The bigger the drive, the higher the price.

Access Time

Access time is the amount of time it takes for the heads to locate a specific piece of data on the hard drive. Manufacturers typically specify the "average access time," because the actual seek time varies depending on the location of the heads and where the next bit of data is stored.

Spin Rate

This spec measures the speed at which the platters spin, in revolutions per minute (RPM). Faster-spinning drives result in faster data transfer rates (discussed next); most drives today spin at either 5,400 RPM or 7,200 RPM. The slower speed is acceptable for traditional office use, but you'll want a faster drive if you're doing a lot of audio or video-related tasks.

caution

It's actually possible to buy too big a hard drive. If you're running Windows 95 or earlier, your operating system will only support drives up to 32GB in size. If you're running Windows 98, Windows Me, Windows XP, Windows NT, or Windows 2000, you can use drives that exceed the 32GB limit.

Data Transfer Rate

The data transfer rate is the speed at which the system copies data from the hard drive to your computer (and vice versa). This spec is typically measured in terms of a *programmed input/output* (*PIO*) or *Ultra Direct Memory Access* (*UDMA*) mode. For example, a drive with a peak transfer rate of 100MBps is labeled UDMA 100 (also known as UDMA mode 5). Make sure the PIO or UDMA mode of your new hard drive matches the specs of your system unit—although, in most cases, if you get a faster hard drive than your system can handle, it can be configured to run at a slower mode to ensure compatibility.

Drive Interface Type

There are several different interfaces available that control the communication between your hard drive and your PC. The two primary interfaces in use today are

- **IDE** (Integrated Drive Electronics). This is the most popular hard drive interface currently in use. (Some vendors use the terms *ATA*—for *AT attachment*—or IDE/ATA to describe drives of this type.) IDE drives use 40-pin connectors, and are quite easy to install and configure. Every PC made today can accept IDE drives; in addition, other types of storage devices, such as CD/DVD and Zip drives, also use the IDE interface.

- **SCSI** (Small Computer System Interface). This is a more expensive, difficult-to-configure interface primarily used in systems designed for high-end audio/video editing.

Most hard drives today use some variation of these two interfaces. The IDE/ATA standard, especially, has inspired a raft of progeny, all promising faster performance than the basic IDE interface. These subsets of IDE include UDMA, UIDE, AT-6, Fast ATA, and Ultra ATA. All of these interfaces utilize the basic IDE-type connector, so compatibility generally isn't a huge problem.

If you're working with an older PC, you might encounter some additional, now-obsolete interfaces, such as ST-506, ESDI, and MCA-IDE. If your system uses any of these interfaces, it's an antique; junk the thing and buy a new PC!

> **"Mike Sez"**
>
> Given the higher expense and more difficult installation associated with SCSI, I recommend you go with an IDE drive—which is what we'll focus on for the balance of this chapter.

Disk Drive Manufacturers

When you're looking for a new hard disk, it pays to stick to the major manufacturers. Here are some of the companies that specialize in magnetic storage media:

- LaCie (www.lacie.com)
- Maxtor (www.maxtor.com)
- Western Digital (www.westerndigital.com)

Upgrade #1: Adding an External Hard Drive

The easiest type of hard drive to install is the external variety. These drives typically install via either USB or FireWire.

Installation of an external hard drive is relatively simple. Just follow these steps:

1. Plug the new drive into a live electrical outlet.

2. Connect the drive to an open USB or FireWire port on your PC.

3. If your new drive came with an installation CD (and it probably did), insert the CD into your CD-ROM drive and run the installation program. Otherwise, Windows should recognize the new drive and automatically install the proper device drivers.

Once installed, an external drive assumes the next highest available drive letter on your system. So, for example, if your current hard drive is drive C:, the new external drive will be drive D:. (If your CD-ROM drive was formerly drive D:, it will now become drive E:; when it comes to letters, your system likes to group similar types of drives together.)

> **Mike Sez**
>
> If you're looking for ease of installation, an external hard drive is ideal—especially if you use a FireWire or fast USB 2.0 connection. If you want the fastest possible access speeds, however, you should go with an internal hard drive. In addition, you can't use an external hard drive as your sole or primary drive; you can't boot your system from an external drive.

Upgrade #2: Adding a Second Internal Hard Drive

If you're installing an additional internal hard drive, the process is more complicated—primarily because of all the physical issues involved. Frankly, it's a pain to root around inside the drive bays of your system unit, which is why I prefer installing external drives whenever possible.

The back of the drive unit is where you make all your connections. As you can see in Figure 4.2, most internal hard disk drives include power and data connectors, as well as a set of jumpers that determine how the drive will be used in your system. Familiarize yourself with these connectors before you perform the upgrade.

FIGURE 4.2

The back of an internal hard drive.

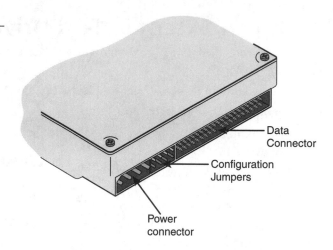

Data Connector

Configuration Jumpers

Power connector

If you insist on adding a second internal drive, make sure you have your screwdriver handy and that your system unit is in a comfortable workspace. You might even want to grab a small flashlight to help you see into all the nooks and crannies inside your PC.

Installing the Drive

Ready to begin the installation? Then follow these steps:

1. Close Windows and power off your PC.

2. Disconnect your PC from its power source.

3. Open the system unit case.

4. Set the drive selection jumper on the new hard drive (see Figure 4.3). You typically have three options: *master*, *slave*, and *cable select*. Because this will be your second hard drive, you'll probably select *slave*—unless, that is, your system is set up to automatically determine which drive is which, in which case you'll select the *cable select* setting. You'll have to consult the hard drive's instructions to determine where the drive selection jumper is located, and how to position it. (It's different with every manufacturer.) Often, the jumper settings are silk-screened on the drive itself, so be sure to check it first!

tip

Cable select is the preferred setting for most newer PCs, especially those capable of running UDMA 66 and faster modes. You can also check the jumper setting on your existing hard drive; if it's set for cable select, use this setting for your new drive, too. Otherwise, use the slave setting.

FIGURE 4.3

Use a pair of needle nose pliers or a pair of tweezers to move the jumper block into the correct position.

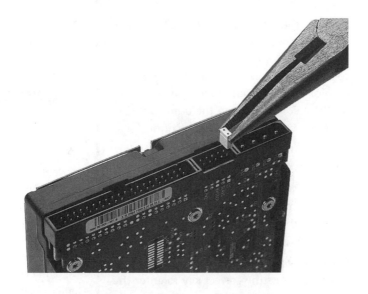

5. Locate an empty drive bay in your system unit and position the drive next to the bay. *Don't* slide the drive into the bay just yet.

6. Connect the internal power cable to your new hard drive, as shown in Figure 4.4.

FIGURE 4.4

Attaching the power and data cables to the hard drive.

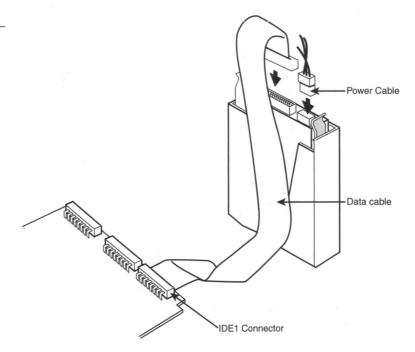

Power Cable

Data cable

IDE1 Connector

7. Connect the internal data cable to the hard drive. (You use the same cable to connect the slave drive and the master drive; the slave connector is typically color-coded gray, whereas the master connector is color-coded black.) Make sure you line up the colored stripe on the data cable with pin 1 on the drive's data connector.

8. Slide the new drive into the drive bay. If necessary, fasten the drive into the bay with the supplied screws; most newer drives should just snap into place.

9. Reinstall the system unit cover and reconnect the PC to its power source.

10. Power on your PC. When your system starts up, press the correct key to enter the BIOS setup utility.

11. Use the arrow keys to move to the section of the utility that holds the hard disk configuration information and select the Auto Detect or Auto Detect Drives option.

12. Save your configuration changes, exit the BIOS setup utility, and allow your computer to continue the startup process.

13. If your hard drive came with its own installation program, run it now to prepare your hard drive for use. If it didn't, you may need to partition and format the drive before you can use it. If this is the case, read on to the next section.

> **caution**
> If your drive bays are enclosed in a metal cage, you'll need to remove the cage before inserting the new drive. In addition, if you're trying to fit a 3.5-inch drive into a 5.25-inch bay, you'll need to use a frame adapter to make the thing fit. (If your new drive didn't come with a frame adapter—actually a set of rails—you can buy it separately.)

> **note**
> Make sure you read the drive's instructions to determine what you need to do to complete the installation and configuration process.

Partitioning and Formatting with Windows XP

Before you can use a new hard drive, you first must create one or more partitions on the disk, and then you must format it. Fortunately, many new hard drives come pre-partitioned and pre-formatted, making the installation process that much simpler.

If your computer is running Windows XP, all your partitioning and formatting can be done from a new utility (based on a similar Windows 2000 utility) called

Computer Management. This single utility lets you manage all manner of hardware processes from a single interface.

To use Computer Management to partition and format your new hard disk, follow these steps:

1. From within Windows XP, open the Control Panel and select Performance and Maintenance, Administrative Tools.

2. When the Administrative Tools folder opens, select Computer Management.

3. When the Computer Management utility launches (as shown in Figure 4.5), select Disk Management in the left-hand pane. This displays information about the various hard disks installed on your system.

4. Right-click the listing for your new hard drive, and then select New Partition. This launches the New Partition Wizard. Click the Next button.

5. Select Extended Partition, and then click Next.

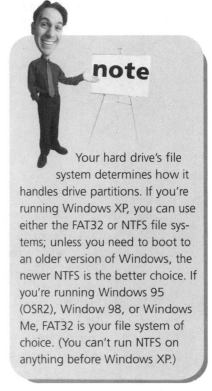

note

Your hard drive's file system determines how it handles drive partitions. If you're running Windows XP, you can use either the FAT32 or NTFS file systems; unless you need to boot to an older version of Windows, the newer NTFS is the better choice. If you're running Windows 95 (OSR2), Window 98, or Windows Me, FAT32 is your file system of choice. (You can't run NTFS on anything before Windows XP.)

FIGURE 4.5

Using Windows XP's Computer Management utility.

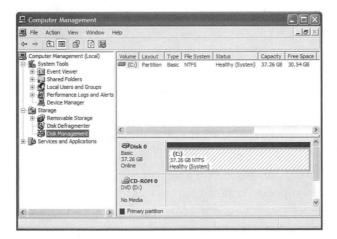

6. Accept the full capacity listed, and then click Next.

7. Click Finish to complete the partitioning.

8. Your new hard drive is now listed as free space in the Computer Management utility. Right-click the listing for the new drive again, and then select New Logical Drive. This restarts the New Partition Wizard.

9. To use the entire partition as a single drive, click Next.

10. To use the default drive letter, click Next.

11. Select the Format This Partition option, select a file system, and then click Next.

12. Click Finish to perform the formatting.

Using the Computer Management utility is actually easier than it looks, thanks to the New Partition Wizard. Just follow the onscreen instructions and keep clicking Next, and the job will be done in no time!

tip

You can also open Computer Management by right-clicking the My Computer icon.

caution

Do *not* partition or format an existing hard disk drive, unless you're really, really sure you want to return your hard drive to its original from-the-factory condition. Either of these two operations will delete all data on the drive!

Partitioning and Formatting Pre-Windows XP

If you're running an older version of Windows, you have to partition and format your hard drive manually. It isn't that hard really; we'll start with the portioning process, which uses a DOS-based utility called FDISK.

Follow these steps:

1. From within Windows, click the Start button and select Run. When the Run dialog box appears, enter **FDISK** into the Open box and click OK.

2. When FDISK starts (in a DOS window), you'll be asked if you want to enable large disk support. Answer Yes.

3. The FDISK menu is now displayed. Select the drive you want to partition, and then choose option 1 (Create DOS Partition or Logical DOS Drive).

4. When asked if you want to use the entire drive for your DOS partition, answer Yes. (If you're asked whether you want to enable FAT32 support, also answer Yes.)

5. After the partition is created, follow the onscreen prompts to exit FDISK and restart your computer.

After your new drive has been partitioned, you have to format it for use. To format a new hard drive manually, follow these steps:

1. From within Windows, open My Computer.

2. Right-click the drive you want to format, and select Format from the pop-up menu.

3. When the Format Local Disk dialog box appears (see Figure 4.6), select the File System you want to use (only select NTFS if you're running Windows XP; for older operating systems, choose FAT32), enter a label for the disk, select the Quick Format option, and then click Start.

caution

Do *not* run FDISK on an existing hard disk drive, unless you're really, really sure you want to return your hard drive to its original from-the-factory condition. Partitioning the drive will delete all data on the drive!

FIGURE 4.6

Formatting your new hard drive.

After your new drive has been partitioned and formatted, it's ready to store whatever data you need stored.

Upgrade #3: Replacing Your Existing Hard Drive

It's one thing to add a second hard drive to your system. It's quite another to replace your existing hard drive—you know, the one that holds all your existing data and software programs, as well as your operating system.

Physically, replacing the drive is as simple as taking the old one out of your system unit and plugging the new one into the same spot. The big challenge in replacing a hard drive is how to transfer your existing stuff from the old drive to the new one.

One approach is to back up all your data and programs from your old drive, and then restore them to your new drive after it has been installed. This is a big pain in the rear, but it works.

A better approach is to install the new hard drive in your system unit as your master drive, but keep the old drive installed as your second, or slave, drive. When you do this, you can then copy all the data and programs from the old (now slave) drive to your new (master) drive. Plus, you get the benefit of having two hard drives on your system—and every little bit of storage space helps!

If you take this approach, I recommend purchasing a software program to help you with the disk copying chores. The best of these programs are PowerQuest's DriveCopy (www.powerquest.com/drivecopy/) and Symantec's Norton Ghost (www.symantec.com/sabu/ghost/ghost_personal/). These programs pretty much automate the process of creating an exact mirror of your old drive on your new drive—including the operating system and all your data and applications.

Here's how you want to replace an existing hard drive:

1. Follow the instructions in the Upgrade #2 section to install and configure the new hard drive in your system unit. You should initially set the jumper settings to make the new drive your *slave* drive.

2. Run the drive copy software to copy the contents of your old drive to your new drive.

3. Get back inside your system unit and change the jumper settings on your old drive to the *slave* setting, and then change the jumper settings on your new drive to the *master* setting.

4. Assuming that your new hard drive is working fine as your main drive C:, reformat your old hard drive (which should now be drive D:) to wipe off all the old data, applications, and operating system.

Your new hard drive should now mirror the operation of your old drive—but with more free space, presumably. You can now use your old hard drive for additional data storage.

Upgrade #4: Adding an Internal Floppy or Zip Drive

Some new PCs come with no removable media, save for the now ever-present CD-ROM drive. If you want to use old-fashioned 3.5-inch floppy disks, you'll have to add your own floppy drive.

Naturally, the easiest way to add a floppy drive is with a USB-compatible external model. However, many of us are more comfortable inserting our floppies into the front of the system unit; if this is you, you'll want to do an internal installation.

To add a floppy drive to your machine (or to replace an existing floppy drive), just follow these steps:

1. Close Windows and power off your PC.

2. Disconnect your PC from its power source.

3. Open the system unit case.

4. Locate an empty 3.5-inch drive bay and pop out the corresponding plastic face on the front of the system unit. (Or, if you're replacing an existing drive, identify and remove the old one—taking care to unplug the power and data cables first.)

5. Locate a free power cable and data cable.

6. Slide the new drive into the bay and align it with the hole in the front of the system unit.

7. Attach the power and data cables to the drive. (Some data cables might have connectors for both 3.5-inch and the older 5.25-inch drives; use the 3.5-inch connector.)

8. Fasten the drive to the bay.

9. Reconnect your PC to an AC power supply, power it up, and test the drive. (Formatting a new disk is a good test.)

10. Assuming everything works okay, reinstall the system unit cover.

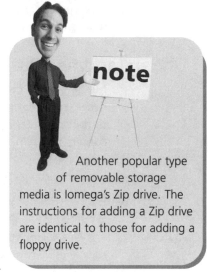

note

Another popular type of removable storage media is Iomega's Zip drive. The instructions for adding a Zip drive are identical to those for adding a floppy drive.

caution

Most floppy connectors aren't keyed to prevent improper connection. If your drive light stays on all the time, the connector is reversed; fix the problem by reconnecting the cable the other way.

Upgrade #5: Adding a Memory Card Reader

If you have a digital still camera, PDA, portable MP3 player, or other device that uses memory card storage, you need to somehow get data from that memory card into your PC. Although you can connect your camera or other device directly, it may be more convenient to use a memory card reader. All you have to do is insert your memory card into the reader, and then your computer will recognize the card as it would any removable storage device.

Understanding Flash Memory Storage

Memory cards don't have any moving parts; instead, they use *flash memory* (some-times called *flash RAM*) to store data on tiny, nonvolatile memory chips. Unlike tradi-tional computer RAM, which is wiped clean when the power is turned off, the contents of a flash memory device don't evaporate when the host unit powers down. Flash memory data is always there, ready to be addressed when the power is turned back on—or when you insert the card into a new device, like a card reader.

Because different devices have different storage needs, there are several different types of memory cards available—all non-interchangeable. These include

- **CompactFlash** (CF), a small, thin, squarish memory card used in a variety of electronics devices, including PDAs, digital cameras, digital voice recorders, set-top television boxes, and so on.

- **SmartMedia** (SM), a smaller, lighter-weight card than CF, specifically designed for portable digital devices such as digital cameras, portable MP3 players, PDAs, and the like.

- **MultiMedia Card** (MMC), a postage stamp-sized card with low power con-sumption, originally targeted at the mobile phone and pager markets, but now used in a variety of other devices, including digital video cameras, global positioning systems, portable MP3 players, and PDAs.

- **Secure Digital** (SD), another small card that builds on the MMC format with additional capacity and a digital copyright security scheme, popular in many new PDAs.

- **Memory Stick**, a storage device about the size and shape of a pack of chew-ing gum, used almost exclusively by Sony in its many different portable digi-tal devices (digital cameras, portable MP3 players, PDAs, and so on).

Most memory card readers will accept all five of these media types, so you don't have to buy different readers if you have devices that use different types of cards.

Installing a Memory Card Reader

There are two types of memory card readers available. An external reader connects to your PC via a USB port, no fuss no muss. An internal reader installs inside your system unit, typically in one of the empty drive bays in the front of the case. As you might expect, I recommend you use the external type; they're much easier to install and configure.

To install an external reader, just plug it into a free USB port. To install an internal reader, follow the instructions for adding a new removable disk drive earlier in this chapter.

Windows should automatically recognize the media card reader as a new drive, and assign it a drive letter. You can now start transferring data to and from your memory cards, as if they were normal disk drives.

An Alternate Type of Flash Memory: USB Drives

Another popular form of flash storage, although not technically a card, is the *USB drive*. This type of removable "drive" is actually a flash memory device designed to function like removable disk storage.

As you can see in Figure 4.7, these devices are small enough to be carried in your pocket or hung on your keychain. They plug directly into an open USB port on your computer, and are instantly recognized as a new disk drives by Windows. No special installation is necessary.

FIGURE 4.7
Easy flash storage with a USB drive.

THE ABSOLUTE MINIMUM

That's a lot of material to cover for one chapter! Just remember the following points if you plan on upgrading your system's storage:

- The easiest upgrade for any type of drive is the external one, via either USB or FireWire.

- When you're shopping for a new hard drive, look at capacity, speed, price, and interface type.

- The most common hard drive interface today is IDE. (You can also choose a SCSI interface, but it will cost you more—and be more difficult to configure.)

- When you install a new internal hard drive, you'll probably have to reset your computer's BIOS settings—as well as partition and format the new drive.

- Installing an internal floppy drive is much like installing a hard drive, but without all the BIOS, partitioning, and formatting stuff.

- You can also add a memory card reader to your system—and, again, the external type is preferable to the internal one.

5

OPTICAL TRICKS: UPGRADING CD AND DVD DRIVES

If your PC doesn't yet have a CD-ROM drive, if you need faster CD access and playback, or if you want to add CD burning capabilities to your system, you need to add some sort of new CD drive to your PC. In addition, you might want to think about upgrading to a combination CD/DVD drive, so you can play back DVD movies on your computer system. And, while you're assembling a wish list, how about a DVD burner, so you can burn your own home movies on DVD discs?

For all these reasons, adding a CD or DVD drive is one of the most popular upgrades today. Read on to learn how to add one of these drives to your computer system.

Understanding Optical Storage

CDs and DVDs are both optical storage media. That means they store data optically instead of magnetically, like hard drives do. In an optical system, data is etched into the tracks of a disc in the form of tiny pits. A laser beam is used to "read" the pits; this information, in the form of digital 1s and 0s, is then translated into digital files (for computer use), audio files (for music), or audio/video files (for movies).

Figure 5.1 shows how an optical storage system works.

FIGURE 5.1

How a laser reads data from a CD or DVD.

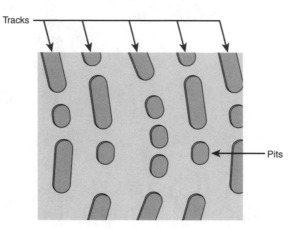

Tracks

Pits

A big difference between a CD and a DVD is storage capacity. Because DVDs place their pits and tracks closer together, they can store much larger amounts of data than the older CD format. CDs can store from 650MB to 700MB of data, whereas DVDs can store 4.7GB or more, depending on the specific DVD format. (It's that extra storage capacity that enables an entire movie to be stored on a single DVD.)

> **note**
>
> CD storage capacity depends on the blank media you use. The original 74-minute CD-R discs hold 650MB, whereas the newer 80-minute discs hold 700MB.

CD Formats

The term CD stands for *compact disc*. Read-only CDs come in two flavors; straight audio CDs contain audio data and can be read by any audio CD player or computer CD drive, whereas CD-ROMs (*compact disc read-only memory*) contain digital computer data and can only be read by the types of CD-ROM drives you find in your friendly PC. Any CD drive you buy for your computer is capable of reading both data CD-ROMs and audio CDs.

When it comes to burning your own CDs, you have two formats with which to familiarize yourself. The CD-R (*compact disc recordable*) format lets you record *once* to a CD. You can record either computer data or audio files to a CD-R disc; CD-R discs can be played in any computer CD-ROM drive, and some (but not all) recent audio CD players (home and auto CD players included)—assuming, of course, you recorded audio files to the disc.

The second burnable format is CD-RW (*compact disc rewritable*). CD-RW discs let you rewrite data multiple times to the same disc. There are two big drawbacks to the CD-RW format: the discs themselves are more expensive than blank CD-R discs, and the discs you burn on your system aren't always playable on other drives.

Most drives available today are classified as CD-R/RW, meaning they can handle both recording and rewriting.

DVD Formats

DVD formats are a lot more confusing than CD formats. That's because major DVD manufacturers are still fighting among themselves to create the "standard" recording format.

Regular playback-only DVDs are like playback-only CDs. There are two types—video DVDs, which hold movies, and data DVD-ROMs, which hold computer data. Like the CD world, the DVD drive in a computer system can read both types of DVDs; the DVD player in a home theater system can only play video DVDs.

The confusing part comes when you want to burn your own DVDs. Not only are DVD burning drives quite expensive, there's also no single format established for DVD burning. Pay careful attention here, because all of the competing formats are similar to each other—especially in their naming. Don't believe me? Then check out the different formats in Table 5.1.

note

The process of storing data on a CD or DVD is called *burning* a disc.

Mike Sez

Given the extremely low price of CD-R discs—and their near-universal playback capabilities—I recommend using the CD-R format for all your disc burning operations.

note

DVD really isn't an acronym for anything in particular. Some manufacturers claim that it stands for *digital versatile disc* or *digital video disc*, but it's really just a bunch of initials with no literal meaning.

Table 5.1 DVD Recording Formats

Format	Description
DVD-R	DVD-*recordable*, for one-time writing to disc; used primarily to record video for playback on standard DVD players. This format is compatible with about 89% of existing DVD players.
DVD+R	Similar to DVD-R, but with a few extra technical bells and whistles. This format is compatible with about 83% of existing DVD players.
DVD-RAM	DVD-*random access memory*, with random read/write access.
DVD-RW	DVD-*rewritable*, similar to DVD-RAM but with sequential read/write access. This format is compatible with about 72% of existing DVD players.
DVD+RW	Similar to DVD-RW, but with a few extra technical bells and whistles. This format is compatible with about 72% of existing DVD players.
DVD-R/W	Similar to DVD-RW, but capable of recording on double-sided discs.
DVD+R/W	Similar to DVD+RW, but capable of recording on double-sided discs.

Notice the (slight) differences? Still confused? Me too!

Fortunately, we're seeing more and more DVD recorders that conform to more than one of these formats. So if you insist on buying a DVD burner today, look for a model that reads and writes multiple formats—especially including the main "minus" and "plus" formats.

Of course, you can always wait for this format war to play itself out and then purchase the winning format. Unless you have desperate need for DVD burning *today*, this might be the best course to take.

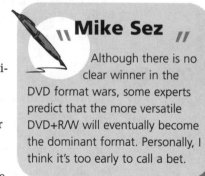

Mike Sez

Although there is no clear winner in the DVD format wars, some experts predict that the more versatile DVD+R/W will eventually become the dominant format. Personally, I think it's too early to call a bet.

Shopping for a CD or DVD Drive

When you're shopping for a new CD or DVD drive, you need to pay attention to a few key specifications. I'll discuss the three major specs next.

Speed

The speed spec measures how fast the data is read to and from the drive. This specification measures how fast the drive is in relation to the speed of the very first CD drive. The first drive is classified as 1X; a drive that is 10 times as fast would be classified as 10X.

If you're looking at a CD-R/RW drive, there will be three speed specs, the first one for *write*, the second for *rewrite*, and the third for *read*. For example, a 40X/12X/48X drive writes to CD-R media at 40X speed, rewrites to CD-RW media at 12X speed, and reads normal CDs at 48X speed.

If you're looking at a combo CD burner and DVD drive, you'll see a *fourth* speed spec tacked on to the end, like this: 40x/12x/48x/8x. This new number measures the read performance of the DVD drive.

tip

If you're looking to add DVD capability to your system, know that all DVD drives are also CD drives—so you don't need separate drives to your system for CD and DVD playback.

Naturally, faster is better—especially when it comes to burning your own discs. For example, an 8X drive takes about 10 minutes to burn a disc; a 16X drive does the same task in less than five minutes.

Format

If you're looking at a CD or DVD burner, make sure it records and writes in the formats you want to use—CD-R, CD-RW, DVD-RW, DVD+RW, and so on.

Interface

Internal CD/DVD drives, like hard drives, use a specific type of interface to communicate with your computer. As with hard drives, you can choose either an IDE or SCSI interface. IDE is more common, and easier to configure. Using SCSI will probably require that you also install a separate expansion card to provide SCSI capability. For that reason alone, stick to IDE.

If you're installing an external drive, you can choose from USB or FireWire drives. FireWire is faster, although USB 2.0 comes darn close. (Avoid USB 1.1 if you can; it's considerably slower than the other two interfaces.)

CD and DVD Drive Manufacturers

There are numerous manufacturers of both CD and DVD drives. These companies include the following:

- BenQ (www.benq.com)
- Iomega (www.iomega.com)
- LaCie (www.lacie.com)

- Micro Solutions (www.micro-solutions.com)
- Pacific Digital (www.pacificdigital.com)
- TDK (www.tdk.com)

Upgrade #1: Adding an External CD or DVD Drive

As with just about every type of peripheral, the easiest type of installation is the external one. Choose a USB- or FireWire-compatible CD or DVD drive, and all you have to do is follow these simple steps:

1. If your CD/DVD drive has its own power supply, plug the new drive into a live electrical outlet.

2. Connect the drive to an open USB or FireWire port on your PC.

3. When the new drive is detected by Windows, follow the onscreen instructions to install the proper device drivers.

It doesn't matter which type of optical drive you're adding; the steps for installing a CD-ROM, CD-R/RW, or CD/DVD drive are all the same.

Upgrade #2: Adding an Internal CD or DVD Drive

Adding an internal CD or DVD drive is just a tad more complex than installing an external model—physically, it's more like installing a hard drive. Naturally, you have to find an open drive bay and connect the appropriate data and power cables. Plus—and this is a new wrinkle—you have to make separate analog and (optionally) digital audio connections. Figure 5.2 shows the back of a typical IDE CD/DVD drive.

Follow these steps to install an internal CD or CD/DVD drive in your PC:

caution

Making the separate audio connection is crucial, as sound data is not transmitted via the CD's drive's standard data output. You have to connect the audio separately to the sound card, or you won't hear a thing.

FIGURE 5.2

All the various connections on the back of a CD/DVD drive.

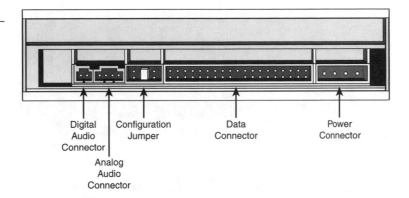

Digital Audio Connector | Configuration Jumper | Data Connector | Power Connector

Analog Audio Connector

1. Close Windows and power off your PC.

2. Disconnect your PC from its power source.

3. Open the system unit case.

4. Set the drive selection jumper on your CD/DVD drive to the slave position—or, if your system uses it, to the cable select position. (Try the slave position first; if this doesn't work, go with cable select.)

5. Locate an empty drive bay in your system unit and position the drive next to the bay. *Don't* slide the drive into the bay just yet.

6. Connect an internal power cable to the drive.

7. Connect a data cable to the drive. If you're replacing an existing CD/DVD drive, use that drive's connector. If you're adding a second CD/DVD drive, connect this new drive to the open (slave) connector on the cable.

8. Connect a 4-pin cable from the analog audio out connector on the drive to the analog audio in connector on your sound card (see Figure 5.3).

note

If this is your system's first CD/DVD drive, you might need to connect a brand new data cable inside the system unit. You'll need to purchase an IDE ribbon cable. One end of the cable will connect to your CD/DVD drive and the other to your system's motherboard. Look for an existing ribbon cable plugged into your motherboard, most likely running to your hard drive; there should be another IDE connector (sometimes labeled Secondary IDE) right next to it. Plug the new ribbon cable into this secondary IDE connector.

FIGURE 5.3

Be sure to connect the audio connector to the back of your optical drive and to your sound card.

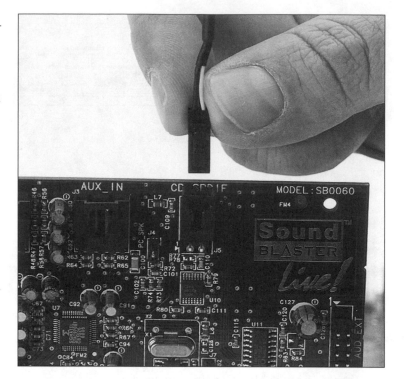

9. If your sound card has digital audio capability, connect a 2-pin cable from the digital audio out connector on the CD or DVD drive to the digital audio in connector on your sound card.

10. Slide the drive into the bay and fasten it securely with the screws either shipped with your PC's case or with the drive you are installing.

11. Reconnect your PC to an AC power supply, power it up, and let Windows recognize the drive and install the appropriate drivers. (If your new drive came with its own installation program on disk or CD, now is the time to run the program.)

12. Test the new drive. Assuming everything works okay, reinstall the system unit cover.

note

Whether you use the analog or digital audio connections depends on your PC's sound card. All sound cards should have an analog audio connector; newer and higher-end sound cards should also have a digital audio connector. You should use the digital connection if you can, as it provides much better sound.

The Absolute Minimum

- CDs can hold up to 700MB of audio or digital data; DVDs can hold 4.7GB or more of audio/video or digital data.

- All DVD drives can also play back audio and data CDs.

- Recordable (CD-R) discs let you record *once*; rewriteable (CD-RW) discs let you record and rerecord multiple times.

- There are multiple competing DVD recording formats (DVD-RAM, DVD-R, DVD-RW, DVD+RW, and so on), with no clear winner at this point in time.

- If you must buy a DVD burner today, look for a drive that can read/write multiple formats.

- The easiest way to add a CD or DVD drive to your system is with an external USB or FireWire model.

- Installing an internal CD or DVD drive is similar to installing a hard disk drive, but with the addition of making analog and digital audio connections to your PC's sound card.

IN THIS CHAPTER

- Understanding computer memory
- Adding RAM to a desktop PC
- Adding RAM to a portable PC

6

YOU MUST REMEMBER THIS: UPGRADING SYSTEM MEMORY

Every computer comes with a boatload of built-in electronic memory. This memory is called *random access memory*, or RAM, and is where your computer temporarily stores program instructions, open files, and other data while it's being used.

The more memory your computer has, the faster your applications will run—and the more applications (and larger files) you can have open at one time. If you don't have enough memory in your system, your computer will appear sluggish and possibly freeze up from time to time. The solution is simple: Add more memory!

Understanding Computer Memory

The easy part of increasing your computer's memory is performing the installation. The hard part is determining what type of memory you need to buy. That's because there are many different types of memory available; you need to figure out what type of memory your computer uses to buy the right RAM for your system.

> **Mike Sez**
>
> How much memory is enough? With Windows 98 and Windows Me, I recommend at least 128MB of RAM. If you're running Windows XP, however, you need even more memory; I find that 256MB works well for most users—although 512MB is much better.

Types of RAM Modules

All memory today comes on modules that contain multiple memory chips; the capacity of each chip adds up to the total capacity of the memory module. The memory modules plug into memory sockets located on your PC's motherboard; installation is actually quite easy.

Your computer could be using one of three different types of memory modules—SIMMs, DIMMs, or RIMMs. You'll need to consult your PC's instruction manual (or look up your PC's model number in a manufacturer's cross-listing) to determine the type of module your machine uses. See Figure 6.1 for a comparison of the various types of memory modules.

FIGURE 6.1
Most systems in production today use DIMMs, though you will find some that use RIMMs; SIMMs are found only in older computers.

SIMM   DIMM   RIMM

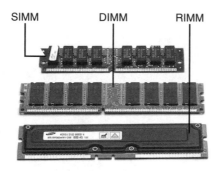

SIMM

SIMM stands for *Single Inline Memory Module*. Chips were originally mounted on only one side of a SIMM (hence the "single" in the name), although newer modules have chips on both sides. SIMMs use either 30-pin or 72-pin connectors.

DIMM

DIMM stands for *Dual Inline Memory Module*. Unlike single-sided SIMMs, DIMMs have memory chips mounted on both sides of the module. They come in both 168-pin and 184-pin versions. (DIMMs are the most popular memory modules in use today.)

RIMM

RIMM stands for *Rambus Inline Memory Module*. RIMMs use 184-pin or 232-pin connectors and are slightly faster than comparable DIMMs. RIMMs also cost at least twice as much DIMMs; for that reason, they're not widely used in most consumer-oriented PCs.

note

Although it's important to get the right type of module for your specific PC, you shouldn't worry about accidentally inserting the wrong module into the wrong type of slot. It's physically impossible to insert a module into a slot that doesn't match it, pin-wise—so you can't insert a 184-pin RIMM into a 232-pin slot, for example.

Types of Memory Chips

Not only do you have to specify what type of memory module your system uses, you also have to specify what type of RAM chip is installed on the module. There are five primary types of memory chips in use today:

- Synchronous Dynamic RAM (SDRAM)
- Double-Data-Rate SDRAM (DDR SDRAM)
- Rambus DRAM (RDRAM)
- Fast-Page-Mode DRAM (FPM DRAM)
- Extended Data Out DRAM (EDO DRAM)

The differences between these chip types are technical and not of interest to most users. The key thing is to recognize what type of chip is used in your particular PC.

SIMM modules typically use either FPM or EDO DRAM chips. Most DIMM modules use either SDRAM or DDR DRAM chips. RIMM modules use RDRAM chips. Consult with your PC's instruction manual to determine what type of RAM your system uses.

Specifying Memory

When you shop for a new memory module, you not only need to know the type of module and chip, but also a variety of other specifications. Table 6.1 details what you need to know in order to buy the right type of RAM for your system.

Table 6.1 RAM Specifications

Type of Module	Need to Specify
SIMM	Size (MB)
	Memory chip type (FPM or EDO)
	Speed (ns)
	Type of connector (gold or tin)
DIMM (SDRAM)	Size (MB)
	Speed (MHz)
	Voltage (3.3 volts for most PCs)
	Buffered, unbuffered, or registered memory
	CAS Latency (CL2, CL2.5, or CL3)
DIMM (DDR SDRAM)	Size (MB)
	Speed (MHz)
	ECC or non-ECC
RIMM	Size (MB)
	Speed (MHz)
	ECC or non-ECC

About some of the new specs presented in the table. *Speed* for DIMMs and RIMMs is measured in megahertz, typically with a PC or DDR in front of the number. (For example, a module with a 133MHz access speed is referred to as PC133.) *Voltage* is important only for SDRAM DIMMs; most IBM-compatible PCs use 3.3-volt modules, whereas Apple computers use 5-volt modules. *Registered memory* uses special circuits to amplify memory signals; you can't mix buffered, unbuffered, and registered types. *CAS Latency* measures how quickly a memory module can prepare data for use by your PC; lower latency is better. And *ECC* (*Error Correcting Code*) is used in some chips to correct certain types of memory errors. As with all these specs, check with your PC's instruction manual to determine the right options for your system.

RAM is typically available in 32MB, 64MB, 128MB, 256MB, or 512MB increments. So, for example, if you want to add 256MB of RAM to your system, you could buy one 256MB module, two 128MB modules, four 64MB modules, or eight 32MB modules. To make the most efficient use of your system's vacant memory slots, it's always best to add the smallest number of larger-capacity modules possible.

note

Some types of memory modules have to be installed in pairs. Check with your PC instruction manual (or the manufacturer's Web site) to determine the exact type of memory you need.

Memory Manufacturers

Memory modules are available from a variety of manufacturers, including the following:

- Crucial Technology (www.crucial.com)
- Kingston (www.kingston.com)
- PNY (www.pny.com)
- Viking Components (www.vikingcomponents.com)

Most of these manufacturers provide lots of charts and tables (and, in Viking's case, an interactive guide called a "configurator") to help you find the right type of memory for your particular PC model.

Upgrade #1: Adding RAM to a Desktop PC

After you've figured out what type of memory to buy, it's time for the actual upgrade. Fortunately, this is pretty much a "plug-and-go" installation, with no undo configuration necessary.

Just follow these steps:

1. Close Windows and power off your PC.
2. Disconnect your PC from its power source.
3. Open the system unit case.
4. Locate your system's empty memory slots.
5. Plug the new memory module into an open memory slot.
6. Reinstall the system cover, reconnect your PC to an AC power supply, and power it up.

Most newer PCs will automatically recognize the new additional memory when you reboot your PC. If your system displays any sort of error message when you start it up, you'll need to enter the BIOS setup program and reconfigure your system settings manually for the proper amount of memory now installed.

caution

More than any other type of internal upgrade, it's important to protect against electrostatic discharge while you're installing memory. Use an antistatic wrist band or take other precautions to make sure you don't fry your new RAM before you get to use it.

Note that each type of module inserts into its slot a little differently. DIMMs and RIMMs insert fairly traditionally, as you can see in Figure 6.2. You release the clips at either end of the slot, line up the module, press it firmly down into the slot, and then flip the end clips back into place.

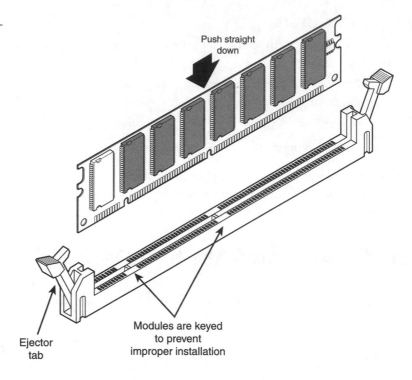

FIGURE 6.2

Inserting a
DIMM module.

Push straight
down

Ejector
tab

Modules are keyed
to prevent
improper installation

SIMMs, however, insert into the slot at a 45-degree angle, as shown in Figure 6.3; after the module is in place, you then push it up to lock it into a vertical position.

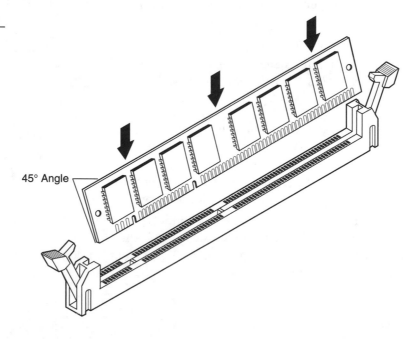

FIGURE 6.3

SIMMs insert at
an angle, and
then click
upward into
place.

45° Angle

Upgrade #2: Adding RAM to a Portable PC

Upgrading memory on a portable PC is a little different than with a desktop system. On one hand, it's easier; memory is typically added through an easily accessible compartment on the bottom of the unit. On the other hand, it's more complicated; every manufacturer (and seemingly every model) uses different non-standard memory types and form factors.

When shopping for laptop memory, you do it by manufacturer and model number. Some portable RAM comes in modules, some on units that look like little credit cards. You have to get the exact type of memory used by your particular PC, whatever that might happen to be.

Installing the memory, however, should be a snap—literally. On most models you use a screwdriver to open a small compartment on the bottom of the unit, and then snap the new memory into place. Just follow these steps:

caution

When you're installing RIMM modules, you cannot leave any RIMM sockets empty. Any empty slots must be occupied by a *continuity module* (sometimes called a *continuity RIMM*), which looks like a standard RIMM but with no memory chips installed.

1. Close Windows and power off your PC.
2. Locate and open your PC's memory compartment.
3. Insert the new memory module or card, per the manufacturer's instructions.
4. Reinstall the cover to the memory compartment and power up your portable.

As with desktop systems, your portable should automatically recognize the new memory on startup.

note

On some portables you may need to remove an old lower-capacity memory card to add a new higher-capacity one.

THE ABSOLUTE MINIMUM

Increasing system memory is one of the most popular upgrades for all levels of computer users. Just remember these key points:

- The more memory you have installed, the faster and smoother your system will run.

- If you're running Windows 98 or Windows Me, consider installing at least 128MB of RAM; if you're running Windows XP, go with at least 256MB—and 512MB is even better.

- RAM chips come preinstalled on memory modules. There are three primary types of modules: SIMMs, DIMMs, and RIMMs.

- There are five primary types of RAM chips in use today: SDRAM, DDR SDRAM, RDRAM, FPM DRAM, and EDO DRAM.

- You have to buy the specific kind of memory (module and chip type) that is used by your computer system—and there are a lot of variations in use by different PC manufacturers.

- Installing more memory is as simple as powering off your computer, inserting the new module into an empty memory slot, and then restarting your PC.

7

POINT AND CLICK: UPGRADING MICE AND KEYBOARDS

This is going to be a short chapter.

That's because installing a new mouse or keyboard is just about the easiest upgrade you can make to your computer system. You don't need to take the case off the system unit, you don't need to use your screwdriver, all you have to do is plug in the new device.

That's all.

Upgrade #1: Installing a New Mouse

The mouse is an indispensable part of the modern computer system. Although it's theoretically possible to perform most operations with the arrow keys on your keyboard, for all practical purposes you need your mouse to move your cursor and click the appropriate screen element.

Choosing a Mouse

There are two basic types of mice in use today. The older type is mechanical in operation, using a small hard rubber ball to roll around the desktop along the X (vertical) and Y (horizontal) axes. The newer type is optical, with no moving parts; the mouse uses an LED sensor to perform the X and Y positioning. As you might suspect, an optical mouse is a tad more expensive than a mechanical one, but it will also last a little longer, and won't require you to open up the unit and clean the mouse ball. (And there's nothing more disgusting than cleaning mouse balls....)

You don't have to spend a fortune for a new mouse. A simple mechanical mouse will cost you less than $20; a fancy optical one not more than that. Or, if you prefer your ball on the top instead of on the bottom, you can pay a little extra for a trackball device. A trackball works like an upside-down mouse—the device stays put on your desktop, and you roll the ball with your hand to move the cursor.

"Mike Sez"

The first thing I do when I buy a new PC is throw away the cheap mouse that comes with the computer and buy a new one with better feel and more buttons. It's the most affordable upgrade you can make, and a better mouse makes computing that much more tolerable over time.

Mouse Makers

When you go shopping at your local computer store, you'll find a lot of different mice from a lot of different companies—including a lot of "store brands" and no-name manufacturers. It's probably worth the money to upgrade to a mouse from a name company, such as one of the following:

- Belkin (www.belkin.com)
- Kensington (www.kensington.com)
- Logitech (www.logitech.com)
- Microsoft (www.microsoft.com/hardware/)

Connecting the Mouse

Whichever type of mouse you choose, they all hook up pretty much the same. Today, most mice use a PS/2-type connector, shown in Figure 7.1, the same as most keyboards use. Some older mice connect to a serial port, and some newer ones connect via USB. When you go mouse shopping, make sure you have the right connector on the back of your PC for the mouse you want to buy.

FIGURE 7.1

A typical two-button mouse with PS/2 connector.

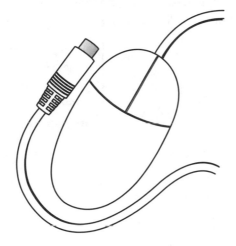

After you get your new mouse home and unpacked, here's how you install it on your PC:

1. Close Windows and power off your computer. (You don't need to unplug it, just turn it off.)

2. Disconnect your old mouse.

3. Connect the new mouse to the appropriate port on the back of your computer.

4. Turn your computer back on.

5. Windows should automatically recognize your new mouse and prompt you to install the appropriate driver software. (If your mouse came with an installation CD, now is the time to run the installation program.)

note

If you're installing a USB mouse, you don't need to turn off your computer; USB devices are hot-swappable.

Configuring Your Mouse

After you have your mouse installed, you can configure any special features by way of the Mouse Properties dialog box. You access this dialog box by opening the Control Panel and selecting Printers and Other Hardware, then Mouse.

As you can see in Figure 7.2, different tabs direct you to different configuration options; you can use this dialog box to adjust pointer speed, double-click speed, cursor shapes, and which button does what. Because each brand of mouse offers different features, the available options will vary from model to model.

caution

If you try to install a non-USB mouse without first powering off your PC, you'll find that the mouse port quits working altogether. You have to reboot your system to recognize any new mouse you connect.

FIGURE 7.2

Configure your mouse from the Mouse Properties dialog box.

Upgrade #2: Installing a New Keyboard

A keyboard is a keyboard is a keyboard—well, pretty much, anyway. Let's look at a few differences.

Choosing a Keyboard

If you do a lot of typing, you should definitely test drive any new keyboard you add to your system; some keyboards have an intolerable mushy touch, whereas others have a nice, firm, satisfying click. It pays to buy a keyboard that feels right to you.

In addition, ergonomic keyboards (like the one shown in Figure 7.3) are popular with some users. If you engage in long typing sessions, this type of keyboard can be a little easier on the wrists.

FIGURE 7.3

The "broken keyboard" design of an ergonomic keyboard.

All of the companies who manufacture mice also manufacture keyboards. (See the previous list for names and Web sites.) Also popular are keyboards from Keytronic (www.keytronic.com), one of the older companies in the computer accessory business.

Connecting the Keyboard

Almost all keyboards today connect via a PS/2 adapter, although some newer models are USB-compatible. Connecting a new keyboard is a simple process:

1. Close Windows and power off your computer. (You don't need to unplug it, just turn it off.)
2. Disconnect your old keyboard.
3. Connect the new keyboard to the appropriate port on the back of your computer.
4. Turn your computer back on.
5. Windows should automatically recognize your new keyboard and prompt you to install the appropriate driver software. (If your keyboard came with an installation CD, now is the time to run the installation program.)

tip

If you're installing a USB keyboard, you *technically* don't need to turn off your computer—although I always do, just to make sure that Windows properly recognizes the new device.

Upgrade #3: Installing a Wireless Mouse or Keyboard

There's another connection option when it comes to both mice and keyboards—going wireless. Wireless mice and keyboards are nice in that they let you roll away from your desk and do your computing (and Web surfing) from your easy chair.

Although some older wireless devices used the somewhat-limited infrared (IR) technology, most wireless mice and keyboards today work via radio frequency (RF) transmission. Some more expensive models use Bluetooth technology, which is a bit more reliable and secure than general RF; if you can find an affordable Bluetooth model, it's not a bad way to go.

caution

If you try to install a non-USB keyboard without first powering off your PC, you'll find that the keyboard port quits working altogether. You have to reboot your system to recognize any new keyboard you connect.

Installing a wireless mouse or keyboard is pretty much like installing a wired one, except that you're connecting the wireless receiver—not the mouse or keyboard itself—to the PS/2 or USB port on your system unit. Remember to insert fresh batteries into both the wireless receiver and the mouse or keyboard, then power down your PC, make the new connection, and reboot. Install the necessary software and you're ready to roll—without wires!

Upgrade #4: Installing a New Joystick or Game Controller

There's one last type of controller you might need for your computer system—a *game controller*. Although a mouse or keyboard might be fine for playing simple games, fast action games demand some type of dedicated game controller. That might mean a joystick or Nintendo-like game pad, or maybe even a steering wheel (for racing games) or airplane yoke (for flight simulators).

How you connect a game controller system depends on the type of controller you buy. Most newer controllers connect via USB, which is as easy as it gets. Older controllers are more likely to connect via a fifteen-pin connector to the game port on the back of your system unit.

If you're connecting a USB controller, all you have to do is plug it in and then run the installation software that came with the controller. If you're connecting a controller through the game port, you'll probably need to power down your computer before you connect the new device, and then power up your system and run the installation software.

After you install the controller you may want to calibrate for your own personal touch. You do this by opening the Control Panel and selecting Printers and Other Hardware, and then Game Controllers. This opens the Game Controllers dialog box; select your controller from the list and click the Properties button. From here you can calibrate the action specific to your controller.

THE ABSOLUTE MINIMUM

When it comes time to upgrade your input device, here are the key points to consider:

- Mice and keyboards both connect in the same fashion, typically using a PS/2 connector on the back of your PC.

- Unless you're connecting a USB mouse or keyboard, you have to power down your computer before you connect the new device.

- Mice come in two flavors, mechanical and optical; optical mice cost more but are more reliable (no moving parts).

- Another option is to go with a wireless mouse or keyboard; with this type of setup, you connect the wireless receiver (not the mouse or keyboard) to your PC.

- Joysticks and other game controllers come with either USB or game port connectors; you can calibrate either type of controller from the Control Panel's Game Controller utility.

IN THIS CHAPTER

- Understanding printers
- Installing a printer
- Installing a scanner

8

THE PAPER CHASE: UPGRADING PRINTERS AND SCANNERS

You've heard the old adage, garbage in, garbage out. Well, the garbage that comes out of your PC is reproduced by your system's printer—sometimes in living color! Every computer system needs at least one printer, and sometimes two, especially if you print both text-heavy documents and colorful graphics or photographs. And, although some types of printers might be expensive, at least they're easy to hook up.

As to the garbage in part of the equation, one way to get garbage into your system is by scanning it. A scanner is pretty much the opposite of a printer; it takes printed copies of documents and pictures and converts them into digital format for storage on your PC's hard disk.

Interestingly, both printers and scanners connect to your system in a similar fashion. In fact, there are many all-in-one devices that combine printing and scanning (in many cases, faxing and copying, too) in a single unit. (And there's nothing wrong with having one less thing to connect to your PC!)

Understanding Printers

There is an overwhelming variety of printers available today. Some print in black and white, some in color; they all connect to your computer via either the parallel or USB port.

Different Types of Printers

When it's time to choose a new printer for your system, you should consider how you want to use the printer. If all you're printing is memos, letters, and similar documents, go with a black and white printer—you don't need to pay extra (in both cost and printing time) for a color model. If, on the other hand, you'll be printing out a lot of children's projects, greeting cards, and the like, go for color. And if printing photos is your goal, adding a separate photo printer is a serious option.

Let's take a quick look at the different printing technologies you can choose from.

Inkjet

The lowest-priced printer available today is the *inkjet printer*. Inkjet printers produce printout by spraying ink through holes in a matrix onto single sheets of paper. These printers are lower-priced than laser printers, and the best of the bunch have print quality indistinguishable from laser quality. They're also slower than laser printers, and not quite up to task if you have a large printing volume.

If you want a color printer, you're pretty much limited to inkjet technology. (Color laser printers are too expensive for most consumers.) Just make sure you get a model with a separate black cartridge, so that when you do print black and white, you're not wasting your color ink.

Laser

The highest-quality (and highest-priced) printers available today are *laser printers*. Popularized by Hewlett-Packard's LaserJet models, these printers work much like copying machines, using a small laser to transfer *toner* (a kind of powdered ink) to paper. Like inkjet printers, laser printers print on single-sheet paper, with the only moving parts being in the paper-feed mechanism.

Laser printer output is extremely high quality, and the process is fast and quiet. If you print in large volume, laser printers are the only way to go. For this reason alone, these are the kinds of printers you see in most businesses.

Photo

A photo printer is optimized to create high-quality photo prints, typically on special photo print paper. Most consumer photo printers use inkjet technology.

Note, however, that photo printers are notoriously slow (five minutes or more to make a single print) and drink ink like it's Gatorade on a hot summer day. When you add up the cost of ink cartridges and the special photo paper you have to use, you'll find that a single print will cost you ten cents or so, on average.

Combo

One of the hottest trends today is the combo printer/fax/copier/scanner machine—sometimes called an *all-in-one*. These units are very efficient, both in terms of cost and in desktop footprint. They essentially hook up and configure like normal printers, but with additional functions.

You'll find that different manufacturers offer combo printers in a variety of configurations. Some combo units include inkjet printers; some use laser printing technology. Some feature sheet-fed scanners, others flatbed. You get the picture; shop around for the unit that best meets your particular needs.

Buying a Printer

There are several big companies that offer printers of all different shapes and sizes. These manufacturers include the following:

- Brother (www.brother.com)
- Canon (www.usa.canon.com)
- Epson (www.epson.com)
- Hewlett-Packard (www.hp.com)
- Lexmark (www.lexmark.com)

Upgrade #1: Installing a Printer

Hooking up your printer is a piece of cake. Most older printers connect to your PC's parallel port—which is why this connection is often called a printer port. Some newer printers (and almost all of the combo machines) connect via USB. Both types of connections are relatively easy to make.

Follow these steps:

1. Connect your printer to a power source and turn it on.
2. Fill the printer's paper tray and install the ink or toner cartridge.

3. If you're connecting to a parallel port, close Windows and power down your PC. If you're connecting to a USB port, skip this step and leave your PC running.

4. Connect your printer to the appropriate port on your PC.

5. If you connected to the parallel port, power up your PC. (Naturally, if you connected to a USB port, skip this step.)

6. Windows should automatically recognize your new printer and attempt to install the appropriate driver; you might need to insert your printer's installation disk at this point. Now is also the time to run any installation program that came with your printer.

tip

If you can't find your printer's driver listed in the Windows printer list, there are some generic drivers you can use. For example, if you have a laser printer, you can select the HP LaserJet driver because most laser printers can emulate the original Hewlett-Packard LaserJet printer. If worse comes to worst, choose the Generic Generic/Text Only driver, which will provide basic text printing for virtually any printer.

If Windows, for any reason, doesn't automatically recognize your new printer, you can use the Add Printer Wizard to add the device to your system. To launch the wizard, click the Start button, and then select Printers and Faxes. When the Printers and Faxes window appears, select Add Printer in the Printer Tasks pane. Follow the onscreen instructions to choose your printer brand and model, and then install the appropriate drivers.

By the way, Windows lets you install multiple printers on your system, and choose between them when it comes time to print—which is great if you want one unit for heavy-duty document printing and another for fancy color printing. Just repeat these instructions to install additional printers.

note

In Windows XP the Printers and Faxes utility is accessible directly from the Start menu. In previous versions of Windows (and XP, too) you can get to the utility from the Control Panel.

Configuring Your Printer

After the printer is installed, you can then configure a myriad number of options within Windows that will affect the way your printer prints. To open the Windows printer configuration utility, click the Start button and select Printers and Faxes; when the Printers and Faxes window appears, right-click the icon for your printer, and then select Properties from the pop-up menu.

The Properties dialog box, shown in Figure 8.1, contains a half-dozen tabs of settings for you to play with, including options for print sharing and port assignments and color management (on color printers). Because each type of printer has different options, I can't tell you exactly what you'll see in your specific Properties dialog box. I will tell you, however, that the default options are generally acceptable, unless you have some really unique printing needs.

FIGURE 8.1

Configuring your printer's properties.

Setting Your Default Printer

If you have multiple printers installed on your system, you need to select one of them as your main, or *default*, printer. The default printer is the printer that your applications automatically use for printing, unless instructed otherwise.

To set one of the printers as your default printer, open the Printers and Faxes window, right-click on that printer's icon, and select Set as Default from the pop-up menu. The default printer will always appear with a large black check mark in the Printers Window, and come up first in your printer list when you go to print from any Windows program.

Upgrade #2: Installing a Scanner

A scanner is useful if you want to convert your old photo prints to digital format. They're also good if you want to store your printed documents electronically. And they're cheap; you can get a decent scanner for around $100–$150.

Different Types of Scanners

A scanner works pretty much like a photocopier, but with the final result being a digital computer file, not a printed copy. The computer file actually contains a digital image of whatever you scanned; with some scanners, you have the option of extracting text information via optical character recognition (OCR) software.

There are two primary types of scanners available for home and small business use. The most popular type is the *flatbed* scanner. This type of scanner is great for scanning papers, photos, books, and anything else you can lay flat between the scanner's glass bed and its top cover. The image is scanned via a scan head that moves across the face of the original document. Most flatbed scanners scan in color.

The other type of scanner is the *sheet-fed* model. These work just like flatbed scanners, except the scan head is fixed and the original document moves across the head. Sheet-fed scanners are limited to scanning flat pieces of paper—and most scan in black and white only. (However, if they're part of an all-in-one printer/scanner machine, the scans are probably in color.) Their big selling point is that they take up less desk space than the larger flatbed models.

Shopping for Scanners

If you're looking to add a scanner to your computer system, look for models from these manufacturers:

- Epson (www.epson.com)
- Hewlett-Packard (www.hp.com)
- Microtek (www.microtekusa.com)
- Visioneer (www.visioneer.com)

Making the Connection

Scanners typically connect to your computer via the parallel or USB port. Some higher-end scanners (such as drum models) connect via SCSI. Look for a USB model for the easiest connection.

Here's how you connect a scanner to your PC:

1. If your scanner came with a "lock" to keep the moving parts from getting damaged during shipping, unscrew or undo the lock.

2. Connect the scanner to a power source and turn it on.

3. If you're connecting to a parallel port, close Windows and power down your PC. If you're connecting to a USB port, skip this step and leave your PC running.

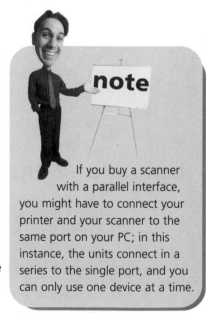

note

If you buy a scanner with a parallel interface, you might have to connect your printer and your scanner to the same port on your PC; in this instance, the units connect in a series to the single port, and you can only use one device at a time.

4. If your scanner will share a parallel port with your printer, power off your printer and connect (in order) the printer to the scanner to the PC, as directed in the scanner's instructions. If your printer connects directly to your PC, connect it now.

5. If you connected to the parallel port, power up your PC. (Naturally, if you connected to a USB port, skip this step.)

6. Windows should automatically recognize your new scanner and attempt to install the appropriate driver; you might need to insert your scanner's installation disk at this point. Now is also the time to run any installation program that came with your scanner.

If Windows, for any reason, doesn't automatically recognize your new scanner, you can use the Scanners and Cameras Wizard to add the device to your system. To launch the wizard, open the Control Panel and select Printers and Other Hardware, and then Scanners and Cameras; when the Scanners and Cameras window opens, select the Add Imaging Device option from the Imaging Tasks pane. Follow the onscreen instructions to choose your scanner brand and model, and then install the appropriate drivers.

caution

Some high-end scanners might require a manual calibration on installation. This is typically done by scanning a special shaded card that comes with the scanner, and then configuring various settings on the scanner's software control panel. This calibration is important if you need good color accuracy for your scans.

THE ABSOLUTE MINIMUM

Connecting a printer or scanner is a relatively easy task. Just remember these key points:

- Printers are available in a variety of flavors and colors; choose a black and white laser for heavy business use, or a color inkjet for home projects.
- Photo printers use inkjet technology to print on special photo print paper.
- Printers typically connect to a parallel or USB port.
- The most popular types of scanners are flatbed or sheet-fed.
- The easiest connection for your scanner is via the USB port; if you choose a scanner with a parallel interface, it might have to share the same port with your printer.

9

THE BIG PICTURE: UPGRADING VIDEO CARDS AND MONITORS

Probably the most important peripheral in your computer system is that thing you stare at all day—the computer monitor. A good monitor can reduce eyestrain and display stunning 3D-like images; a bad monitor will hurt your eyes and have trouble displaying realistic graphics, especially with today's high-octane PC games.

An easy way to enhance your computing experience is to upgrade your system's video display. That might mean going with a bigger monitor, or a thinner one, or even upgrading the video card that drives your monitor.

How important is a video upgrade? I'll tell you this—every single one of my desktop PCs is connected to a different monitor than it initially shipped with. That's right—I've upgraded *all* my monitors, and I'm very pleased with the results.

Understanding PC Video

The images you see on a computer monitor are generated inside your computer, via a specialized *video card* (sometimes called a *video adapter* or *graphics adapter*). This card generates video images at a specified *resolution*, which is a measurement of how detailed your picture is. (The higher the resolution, the sharper the picture—and the more items you can fit onscreen.) These video images then are displayed on your monitor. The resolution of the card must match the resolution of the monitor, or you get gibberish onscreen.

Monitor Options

Most users upgrade their monitors to get a bigger display. The move from a 14-inch monitor to a 17-inch monitor is literally eye-opening—whether you're working with numbers in a spreadsheet or shooting alien mutants in a PC game.

There are two different display technologies used in today's computer monitors. The older technology uses a big *cathode ray tube* (*CRT*) to display the images. The newer technology uses a thin *liquid crystal display* (*LCD*) instead of a CRT—and is quickly becoming the display of choice.

A CRT monitor, like the one in Figure 9.1, works and looks pretty much like a television set, but specialized to handle computer data. CRT monitors are big (depth-wise) but fairly low priced; you can get 14-inch CRT monitors for as little as $100, and even larger 17-inch models are relatively affordable.

FIGURE 9.1

A traditional CRT monitor—big screen, big cabinet.

LCD monitors, in contrast, give you the same size picture in a much thinner package. Most LCD monitors, like the one in Figure 9.2, are only a few inches thick, which makes them ideal for portable PCs and desktop systems where space is at a premium. LCD technology is more expensive than CRT technology, however, which is why you'll pay at least twice as much for a comparable LCD monitor over a CRT model—although the price is coming down.

FIGURE 9.2

A space-saving LCD monitor.

In addition to choosing whether you want a CRT or LCD monitor, you also need to focus on a few core specifications. Chief among these specs are size and available resolution, as discussed next.

Size

The size of all computer monitors, like all television sets, is measured in terms of diagonal inches. That is, you measure the distance from the lower-left corner to the upper-right corner of the display.

The problem, though, is that this diagonal measurement differs between CRT monitors and LCD monitors. How is that, you ask? Just compare a 15-inch CRT monitor and a 15-inch LCD monitor, and you'll see that their screens really aren't the same size. The 15-inch LCD monitor is bigger, despite the identical specification. That's because an LCD display offers a larger viewable area; the picture goes to the very edge of the frame. In contrast, CRT monitors typically have a black fringe around the edge of the tube, which decreases the viewable area.

> **" Mike Sez "**
>
> If you're looking at LCD monitors, you'll notice a big price difference between similar-sized models. For example, you can find 17-inch models for as little as $400 or as much as $800. This price difference reflects a significant difference in picture quality. The fact is, whereas picture quality between different CRT monitors varies a little, picture quality between different LCD monitors varies a *lot*—which is a good reason to demo all the different models you're looking at.

So when you're comparing screen sizes, you have to do a little math in your head to recognize that a 15-inch LCD monitor offers the same size display as a 17-inch CRT monitor. Or, if you don't want to do the math, just consult the comparison information in Table 9.1.

Table 9.1   Screen Size Comparison

CRT Monitor	LCD Monitor
12-inch	10-inch
14/15-inch	12-inch
17-inch	15-inch
21-inch	17-inch

An additional source of confusion is the new type of widescreen monitor offered by Sony and other manufacturers. These monitors eschew the traditional 4:3 horizontal-to-vertical screen ratio in favor of a more cinematic 16:9 dimension. If you look at a 15-inch traditional monitor and a 15-inch widescreen monitor, you'll notice that the widescreen monitor is actually less tall than the traditional monitor—the diagonal measurement is stretched over a wider area. So if you want a widescreen monitor, you'll need to get a bigger screen size just to keep the same display height.

Resolution

The resolution of a display is measured in pixels, which are the small dots that combine to make up the total display. The more pixels displayed, the higher the resolution—and the more information you can display onscreen.

The pixel level is specified by horizontal and vertical measurements. For example, a resolution of 640×480 displays 640 pixels horizontally (left to right) and 480 pixels vertically (top to bottom).

Over the years there have been several different resolution standards for personal computers. You'll sometimes see these standards listed on monitors, video cards, and some software applications. Table 9.2 details these resolution standards.

Table 9.2   Video Resolutions

Standard	Resolution	Colors
CGA	320×200	4
EGA (Extended Graphics Adapter)	640×350	16
VGA (Video Graphics Array)	640×480	256
SVGA (Super Video Graphics Array)	1280×1024	16.7 million
UXVGA (Ultra Extended Graphics Array)	1600×1200	16.7 million

Practically, there are resolutions that exist between and above these formal standards. For example, I'm writing this book on a new PC with an 18-inch LCD monitor running at 2048×1536 resolution—well above the current USVGA "standard." The old PC I have in my spare room has a smallish 12-inch monitor that runs best at 800×600 resolution. The key is to pick a resolution that works with your particular monitor—and the bigger the monitor, the higher the resolution you can choose.

Note that resolution is independent of screen size; you can have a very large monitor running a low resolution, or a very small monitor running a high resolution. In general, though, if you buy a larger monitor, you'll want to make sure that it's capable of displaying a higher resolution; if not, you won't be able to see more things on your screen, just bigger things.

Dot Pitch and Refresh Rate

There are two more technical specifications you want to be aware of when you're shopping for a new monitor. These are *dot pitch* and *refresh rate*.

The dot pitch, quite simply, measures the distance between the red, green, and blue phosphor dots that create the onscreen image. A smaller dot pitch should produce a sharper picture.

The refresh rate is the rate, measured in Hertz (Hz), at which the screen is refreshed with new information. A faster refresh rate reduces screen flicker—although setting too high a refresh rate on a low-end display can result in fuzzy text.

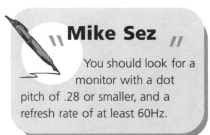

Mike Sez

You should look for a monitor with a dot pitch of .28 or smaller, and a refresh rate of at least 60Hz.

Connections

CRT monitors all connect to the standard video (sometimes called *VGA*) port on the back of your system unit. LCD monitors come with either analog or digital connectors. An LCD monitor with an analog connector plugs into the same VGA video port as a CRT monitor. An LCD monitor with a digital connector requires a special digital video port (called a *Digital Video Interface*, or DVI port) on your PC. (Figure 9.3 shows both connectors.) If you're buying an LCD monitor, make sure you have the matching port on your PC.

FIGURE 9.3
VGA and DVI video connectors.

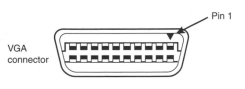

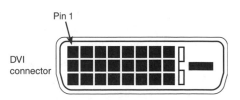

Shopping for a New Monitor

When you're shopping for a new monitor—CRT or LCD—it's easy to get stuck with a cheap, low-performance model. For that reason, you should stick to monitors from the following major manufacturers:

- KDS (www.kdsusa.com)
- NEC-Mitsubishi (www.nec-mitsubishi.com)
- Samsung (www.samsungusa.com)
- ViewSonic (www.viewsonic.com)

Video Card Options

Although changing monitors is a very popular (and relatively easy) upgrade, there are also some very good reasons for many users to upgrade their video cards. Many low-end PCs come with (surprise!) low-performance video cards, which just aren't up to snuff when it comes to displaying high-resolution graphics, fast-moving game images, and moving video from DVDs and digital movies. If your display has a tendency to shudder and jerk, it's time to think about getting a higher-performance video card.

Upgrading your video card is pretty much as easy as removing the old one and replacing it with a new one. You do, however, want to pay attention to some key specifications when you're shopping.

Resolution

Just as your monitor displays images at a specific resolution, your video card generates images at a specific resolution. Make sure the resolution of your card matches the resolution of your monitor; if you generate a higher resolution than your monitor is capable of, all you see onscreen is gibberish.

Memory

All video cards contain some amount of RAM, which is used to temporarily store graphics information while images are being assembled for display. The more memory on your video card, the faster high-resolution images (moving images, in particular) can be displayed.

note

The following specs are useful for the average home or business user. However, if you're a really hardcore PC gamer or a graphics professional, there are even *more* video specifications that you need to look at—much more technical than I can go into here.

If you're upgrading your video for gaming purposes, you want a card with at least 64MB of video memory. Some high-end video cards carry 128MB or even 256MB RAM, which provide extremely speedy rendering of 3D graphics.

3D Acceleration

A *graphics accelerator* is a special chip on the video card that assumes the task of drawing shapes onscreen. This enables faster rendering of graphics objects; a graphics accelerator specifically designed to render 3D graphics is sometimes called a *3D accelerator*. If you're an avid gamer, you need a card with a 3D accelerator to handle the graphics demands of today's graphics-intensive games.

You can tell a 3D video card by looking at the card's *frame rate* spec, which measures the number of frames per second of 3D animation that the card can reproduce. Cards with 3D accelerator chips have faster frame rates than other types of video cards.

Connectors

As explained earlier, different types of monitors use different types of connectors. All CRT monitors and some LCD monitors use a traditional analog video (VGA) connector. Some LCD monitors use a digital (DVI) connector. Most video cards include a VGA connector; some include both VGA and DVI connectors.

In addition, if you want to display your computer information on a traditional television set, you'll need a card with a video output jack. This output can be a fairly low-resolution composite video jack (a single RCA connector), or the higher-resolution S-video connector.

Figure 9.4 shows a video card with all three types of connectors: analog (VGA), digital (DVI), and video out (S-video).

Slots

You'll find video cards that insert into either PCI or AGP expansion slots. Low-priced video cards typically use PCI slots, whereas higher-priced cards use AGP slots.

If you want speedy video—for gaming or graphics editing—you want an AGP card. PCI slots let your

note

Some really high-end video cards—those capable of decoding high-definition television signals—include even higher-resolution component video connectors. Component video outputs aren't common, however.

video card transfer data at a maximum rate of 132MB/second, whereas AGP slots transfer data at up to 2.12GB/second. (That's right, 2.12 *gigabytes*—that's almost 20 times faster than a pokey old PCI card.) If you decide on an AGP card, note that there are four different AGP standards; AGP 1X transfers at 266MB/second, AGP 2X transfers at 533MB/second, AGP 4X transfers at 1.06GB/second, and the new AGP 8X standard transfers data at that blazing 2.12GB rate.

FIGURE 9.4

A video card with VGA, DVI, and S-video connectors.

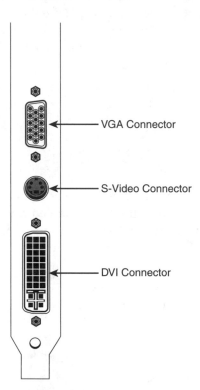

VGA Connector

S-Video Connector

DVI Connector

For gaming purposes, you should look for a video card running at least AGP 2X, and completely avoid PCI video cards; PCI won't deliver fast-enough graphics for the latest generation of PC games.

Shopping for a Video Card

When you're shopping for a new high-performance video card, look for models from the following companies:

caution

If you have an older PC, know that not all AGP slots are compatible with all AGP cards. Make sure the AGP slot supports the card speed you want to install; also check the electrical requirements of the card versus what your PC's motherboard supplies to the card slot. Fortunately, newer PCs feature universal AGP slots that will work with just about any AGP card out there.

- ATI Technologies (www.ati.com)
- BFG Technologies (www.bfgtech.com)
- Mad Dog Multimedia (www.maddogmultimedia.com)
- PNY Technologies (www.pny.com)
- VisionTek (www.visiontek.com)

Upgrade #1: Replacing Your Monitor

Replacing your monitor isn't much more complex than disconnecting your old one and reconnecting the new one. Just follow these steps:

1. Close Windows and power off your system.

2. Power off your old monitor and remove it from its power source.

3. Disconnect the video cable running from your old monitor to your system unit, and then set your old monitor aside.

4. Set your new monitor in place.

5. Use the supplied video cable to connect your new monitor to the video connector on the back of your system unit.

6. Connect your new monitor to a power source.

7. Power on your new monitor.

8. Power on your computer, and then restart your computer.

9. If your new monitor came with an installation program, run it now. Otherwise, you're done.

" Mike Sez "

If you're a hardcore gamer, your choice of video card is simple: go with any card that uses an nVidia chipset. nVidia makes the highest-performing video chips out there, and many game designers optimize their software to work best with the nVidia chipset. To learn more about nVidia chips—and which cards use them—check out the nVidia Web site, at www.nvidia.com.

tip

If you upgraded to a larger monitor, you might want to switch to a higher screen resolution. See "Configuring Your Display Properties," later in this chapter, for instructions.

Upgrade #2: Replacing Your Video Card

Changing video cards is more complicated than changing monitors, only because you have to fiddle around inside your PC's system unit. After you have the case opened up, all you have to do is pull out the old card and insert the new one.

Of course, you also have to tell Windows that you're changing cards—and then reconfigure your system to get the most out of your new card.

Making the Installation

With your replacement video card in hand, follow these steps:

caution

Before you buy a new video card, make sure that you can actually upgrade your system's video. Some low-end PCs come with the video adapter integrated into the motherboard—which means there's no video card to change out. Fortunately, most systems with on-board video still let you add a separate video card, which then disables the built-in video capabilities. (You might have to enter your PC's CMOS BIOS setup to disable the onboard video.)

1. From within Windows, open the Control Panel and select Performance and Maintenance, and then System. When the System Properties dialog box appears, select the Hardware tab and click the Device Manager button to open the Device Manager.

2. From the Device Manager, click the Display Adapters item, select your video card, and click the Uninstall button (or select Action, Uninstall).

3. Close Windows and power off your system.

4. Power off your monitor.

5. Disconnect both your PC and your monitor from their power sources.

6. Open the system unit case.

7. Locate your existing video card.

8. Disconnect the cable running from your monitor to the existing video card.

9. Remove the screw (on the back of the system unit) holding the old video card in place. Save the screw—you'll need to use it again.

10. If there are any cables running to the video card from other devices (such as your sound card or DVD drive), label them with masking tape or a sticker, and then disconnect them.

11. Remove the old video card from its slot and set it aside.

12. Insert the new video card into the now-open slot.

13. Reconnect any cables you disconnected previously (in step 10).

14. Use the screw you saved in step 9 to fasten the new card into place.

15. Reattach the cable that connects your monitor to the new video card.

16. Reinstall the system unit cover and reconnect the PC to its power source; while you're at it, go ahead and plug your monitor back in, too.

17. Power on your monitor and then restart your computer.

18. Run the installation software that came with your new video card, or use the Windows Add Hardware Wizard to install the proper drivers for the new card.

Configuring Your Display Properties

Your new video card now needs to be configured to run at the desired screen resolution. You configure your video card from the Display Properties dialog box. You access this dialog box by selecting the Display icon in the Windows Control Panel, or by right-clicking on any empty space on the Windows desktop and selecting Properties from the pop-up menu.

The settings you want to configure are on the Settings tab, shown in Figure 9.5. Use the Screen Resolution slider to select the desired resolution, and then pull down the Color Quality list to select the desired color level. The sample display will change to reflect your new settings.

FIGURE 9.5

Configure your video card from the Display Properties dialog box.

Choosing resolution is simple enough; just pick the one that puts enough stuff on your screen without everything being too small to read. As to color level, you might have to do a bit of bit conversion. That is, the higher the color bit-rate, the more colors displayed, as shown in Table 9.3.

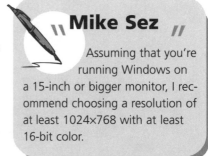

Mike Sez

Assuming that you're running Windows on a 15-inch or bigger monitor, I recommend choosing a resolution of at least 1024×768 with at least 16-bit color.

Table 9.3   Color Levels

Color Depth	Number of Colors Displayed
16-color	16
256-color	256
16-bit	65,536
24-bit	16.7 million
32-bit	16.7 million

Note that 24-bit and 32-bit settings display the same number of colors; the difference is that 32-bit color provides for a faster redraw of the screen. Choose 32-bit color for 3D gaming and other high-performance graphics applications.

Upgrade #3: Adding a Second Video Card and Monitor

Here's something different—you can actually run two different monitors from the same PC. Why would you want to do this? Depending on the software you use, you might be able to run two programs simultaneously on different monitors, display data on one monitor and menus on another, work on a presentation on one monitor and view the show on another, or write program code on one monitor and view the results on another.

Of course, you might not need to add a second video card to your system in order to use a second monitor. Some video cards come with dual-monitor support. These cards contain two sets of video connectors, so you can connect two monitors at the same time.

If you have a standard single-monitor card installed in your PC, you'll need to install a second video card to use a second monitor. You install the second card just like you did the first one; Windows will automatically detect the new card and install the appropriate drivers.

tip

While you have the Display Properties dialog box open, you can use it to change a number of other display-oriented settings, such as your Windows desktop background, color scheme, and such. Just select the appropriate tab to make specific adjustments.

note

Dual-monitor support was first introduced in Windows 98. Using two monitors, however, is a lot easier to do in Windows XP than it is in any older version of Windows.

After you have the second video card and monitor installed and connected, you need to configure your system for dual-monitor use. To do this, open the Display Properties dialog box and select the Settings tab; as you can see in Figure 9.6, the display should include icons for two different monitors. To activate the second monitor, select its icon and then select the Extend My Windows Desktop Onto This Monitor option. With the second monitor icon still selected, you can configure its screen resolution and color quality, as well as drag the icon to match the physical arrangement of your monitors. Click OK to register the new configuration.

FIGURE 9.6

Configuring your system for dual-monitor use.

With your system thus configured, you can now drag items across your screen from one monitor to another, as well as resize a window to stretch across more than one monitor. Just remember that the monitor designed as your primary monitor will be the one that displays the logon screen when you start your computer; in addition, most programs will display on the primary monitor when you first launch them.

Upgrade #4: Adding a TV Tuner Card

Most users don't know they can use their PCs to watch television programs. All you have to do is install a TV tuner card in your system unit; this card operates independent of your video card and contains a fully functioning television tuner. Connect your TV antenna, cable, or satellite signal to the card's input jack and you can watch television broadcasts on your computer monitor, either full-screen or in a resizable TV window.

Of course, if you don't want to go through all the rigmarole of installing a card, there are plenty of external TV tuners available, as well. These devices connect via

USB (no surprise there), and typically include a remote control unit for channel switching.

When you're shopping for a TV tuner card or device, look for models from these companies:

■ ATI Technologies (www.ati.com)

■ AVerMedia (www.aver.com)

■ Hauppauge (www.hauppauge.com)

■ Pinnacle Systems (www.pinnaclesys.com)

Installing a tuner card is as easy as installing any other type of expansion card. Just follow these steps:

1. Close Windows and power off your system.

2. Disconnect your PC from its power source.

3. Open the system unit case.

4. Locate an open expansion slot, and then unscrew and remove the slot's cover. Save the screw.

5. Insert the tuner card into the now-open slot.

6. Use the screw you saved in step 4 to fasten the new card into place.

7. Reinstall the system unit cover and reconnect the PC to its power source.

8. Connect your antenna, cable, or satellite dish to the tuner card's RF or S-video input. (If you already have a cable modem connected to your PC, you can split the cable—before the modem—to run the cable signal to your tuner card.)

9. Restart your computer.

10. Run the installation software that came with the tuner card, or use Windows' Add Hardware Wizard to install the proper drivers.

" Mike Sez "

If you want to upgrade your video card *and* add a TV tuner *and* add video capture, you don't have to buy and install three different cards. Check out ATI's All-in-Wonder cards, which combine all three functions into a single expansion card.

caution

If, after you install your TV tuner card, you don't get any sound when watching television programs, there's another installation step you need to take. Some TV tuner cards require connection of an internal cable to your system's sound card; check your instruction manual to see if this needs to be done.

Upgrade #5: Adding a Video Capture Card or Device

If you plan on using your PC to edit home movies, there's another upgrade you might need to make. To connect a non-digital camcorder to your PC, you'll need to install an *analog-to-digital converter* (ADC) card—also called a *video capture card.* You plug your camcorder into the jacks in this card, typically using standard RCA connectors, and the card converts the analog signals from your recorder into the digital audio and video your computer understands.

If you don't want to go to all the trouble of installing a new card, you can use an external video capture device instead. Most of these devices connect via USB or Firewire, which means they're easy to install and configure—just plug the unit into your USB or Firewire port and you're ready to roll. Performance is no different from an internal card.

Here are some of the major manufacturers of video capture cards and devices:

- ADS Technologies (www.adstech.com)
- AVerMedia; (www.aver.com)
- Dazzle Multimedia (www.dazzle.com)
- Hercules (www.hercules.com)
- Pinnacle Systems (www.pinnaclesys.com)

note

If you have a Digital8 or MiniDV camcorder, you don't need to install a video capture card. These digital camcorders connect directly to your PC via either Firewire or USB.

To install an internal video capture card, follow the steps in Upgrade #4. To install an external video capture device, just connect it to the appropriate port on your computer.

THE ABSOLUTE MiNiMUM

When you want to upgrade your system's video, keep these points in mind:

- Upgrading a monitor is as easy as disconnecting the old one and reconnecting the new one.

- You can choose from deep-but-cheap CRT monitors, or thin-but-expensive LCD models.

- A bigger monitor lets you display more stuff onscreen—as long as it's capable of displaying a higher-resolution picture.

- To speed up the display of moving and high-resolution images, consider upgrading your video card.

- For game use, go for a card with 3D acceleration—and make sure it connects to an AGP slot in your computer.

- If you want to use your PC to watch television broadcasts, you'll need to add a TV tuner card—which operates independently of your normal video card.

- To connect a non-digital camcorder to your PC, you'll need to add a video capture card or external video capture device.

10

PET SOUNDS: UPGRADING SOUND CARDS AND SPEAKERS

If you're like me, you like to listen to music—even (if not especially) when you're working. Being able to pop a music CD into your PC's CD-ROM drive is a great thing, as is being able to download your favorite music from the Internet.

The problem is, your PC was designed to be a computer, not an audio system. So the sound you get when listening to music on your PC often leaves a lot to be desired.

This chapter will help you beef up your PC for better playback of your favorite songs—as well as DVD soundtracks and the sound effects and background music of today's most bombastic PC games. Whether you choose to invest in a new speaker system or go with a completely different sound card, these upgrades will get your system pumping!

Understanding PC Audio

Sound on a computer system is generated by a dedicated audio circuit. On most older PCs, this circuit was contained on a separate expansion board, called a *sound card*. On some newer PCs the audio function is built into the motherboard. In either case, you can upgrade a PC's built-in audio by adding a new, higher-performance sound card.

Your PC's audio circuit or sound card only generates the electrical signals behind the sound; to hear this audio, you need to connect a set of speakers, or a pair of headphones. As with your home audio system, the better your speakers, the better the sound.

Understanding Sound Cards

Sound cards reproduce sound via two related processes: sampling and synthesis. Sampling converts an analog sound to digital format; synthesis creates a sound from scratch, by generated computer-synthesized waveforms. It's all very complex, but it's what a sound card does.

Higher-end sound cards are capable of reproducing higher-quality audio samples and more complex waveforms. The more bits in a sample, the more realistic the sound, so if you want really good sound, look for a 64-bit sound card. The lower-priced 16- and 32-bit cards just don't sound as good.

Note, however, that all these bits don't matter a whit when you're playing CDs or listening to DVD movie soundtracks. Your sound card doesn't have a thing to do with CD or DVD sound; your CD-ROM or DVD drive generates its own sound, which is then passed through the sound card to your PC's motherboard. (If you remember back in Chapter 5, "Optical Tricks: Upgrading CD and DVD Drives," you had to connect a cable from the CD/DVD drive to the sound card; that was the audio pass-through cable.) So upgrading your sound card won't affect your audio CD playback at all.

When you're looking at sound cards, pay close attention to the type of connections available. Most low-end sound cards are fairly simple in what they provide—typically a single speaker out jack, a single audio line out jack (to connect to an external audio amplifier or receiver), a game port (that also functions as a MIDI port—more on MIDI later), and a microphone (in) jack. Figure 10.1 shows a card with these standard connections.

More expensive sound cards provide a greater variety of connections. It's not uncommon for a higher-end card to include audio input as well as output jacks, separate connectors for each speaker (or for front and rear right/left pairs), and dedicated MIDI connectors. Figure 10.2 shows the connections available on a typical high-end sound card.

FIGURE 10.1

Typical audio connections on a low-end PC or sound card.

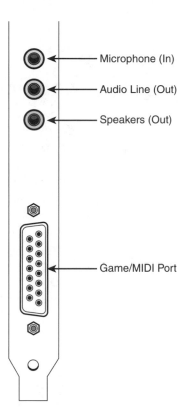

Microphone (In)

Audio Line (Out)

Speakers (Out)

Game/MIDI Port

FIGURE 10.2

The type of connections you might find on a high-end sound card.

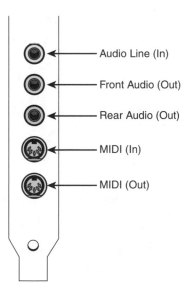

Audio Line (In)

Front Audio (Out)

Rear Audio (Out)

MIDI (In)

MIDI (Out)

Some high-end cards also include S/PDIF and digital DIN connectors, which are used for digital audio output, typically for playback of surround-sound DVD soundtracks or sophisticated PC games. Some *really* high-end cards include a separate "daughter" card with additional connectors. These cards take up just one slot internally, but two openings on the back of your PC—or one 5.25" drive bay on the front of your PC.

When shopping for a sound card, make sure you get one that connects to a PCI slot in your computer, rather than the older ISA type of card. ISA sound cards can cause all sorts of conflicts with other resource-heavy devices; PCI cards are much easier to configure and relatively trouble-free.

Here are the major sound card companies to look for:

- Creative Labs (www.americas.creative.com)
- Hercules (www.hercules.com)
- Mad Dog Multimedia
  (www.maddogmultimedia.com)
- Turtle Beach (www.turtlebeach.com)

Understanding Speakers

Now, a sound card in and of itself won't do you much good. You need to hook up a set of external speakers to get the most out of your system's new sound capabilities.

The most basic add-on speaker systems consist of just two speakers—right and left. Given the small size of most computer speakers, this type of low-end system won't cut the mustard for serious music and game playback. You'll either want to upgrade to larger speakers, or—more likely—go with a three-speaker system that includes a separate *subwoofer* for low-frequency sound reproduction.

Because you can't tell how a speaker sounds by how it looks, try to listen to any speaker system before you buy it. Some systems with deceptively small speakers actually have a very big sound, especially when mated with a powerful subwoofer. There's no way to tell what kind of sound you'll get without taking the system for a test listen.

Some of the most popular PC speaker brands include the following:

- Advent (www.adventaudio.com)
- Altec Lansing (www.altecmm.com)
- Creative Labs (www.americas.creative.com)
- JBL and Harman Kardon (www.harman-multimedia.com)
- Klipsch (www.klipsch.com)

> **caution**
>
> Double-check your speakers to make sure they're shielded from generating stray magnetic fields. (Most are.) Unshielded speakers can mess up the picture on CRT monitors, as well as damage data on any type of magnetic disk—including your system's hard disk!

Understanding Surround Sound

Some PC games and most DVD movies feature an added audio dimension—surround sound. Naturally, to listen to surround sound you need more than two speakers.

For DVD listening, you'll want to invest in a speaker system with a minimum of two front and two surround speakers, plus a subwoofer. This type of system is called a *4.1* system because you have four main speakers (the "4") and one subwoofer (the "1"). Even better is a *5.1* system, like the one in Figure 10.3, which adds a speaker for the front middle. Most surround-sound PC speaker systems connect via a digital DIN or S/PDIF connector, so make sure your sound card has this type of connection before you invest in a comparable speaker system.

Understanding 3D Audio

If you're big into PC gaming, you probably know all about 3D audio. This type of surround sound attempts to position individual elements in the game's sound image in a three-dimensional space, to better envelope you in the game environment.

Some 3D audio cards can do their magic with just two speakers, using sophisticated software-based algorithms. If you're a serious gamer, however, you'll want to invest in a surround sound system designed specifically for gaming purposes. These systems contain a minimum of four speakers (two front and two rear) and a subwoofer; some high-end systems include one or two additional surround speakers, for 6.1 or 7.1 sound.

FIGURE 10.3

A 5.1 surround
sound speaker
system.

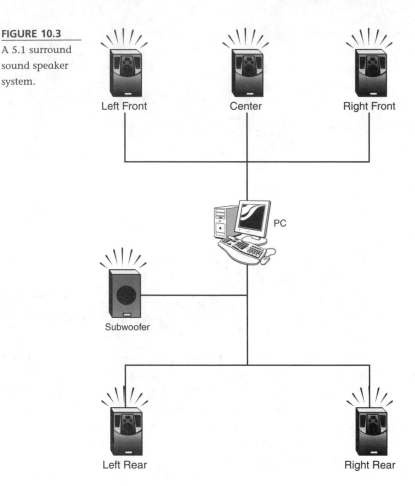

Understanding MIDI

If you *really* want to get into high-quality audio, look into something called MIDI. MIDI, which stands for *musical instrument digital interface*, is a standard used by professional musicians to record and play back music digitally. With a MIDI setup, you can connect your computer to digital keyboards and other synthesized instruments—and use your computer to "sequence" and play back music through the attached musical instruments.

All sound cards come with basic MIDI capabilities, but the low-priced ones don't include separate MIDI connectors. Instead, the MIDI function works through your PC's game port, so you'll need a MIDI-to-game port converter to connect your MIDI instruments.

Pro musicians (and serious hobbyists) can opt for a higher-end sound card with separate MIDI ports, or even a dedicated MIDI expansion card. Alternately, some audio interface boxes connect to your PC (typically via USB) and provide a slew of audio inputs and outputs, including multiple MIDI in and out connectors.

Upgrade #1: Connecting New Speakers

You'd think that installing a new set of speakers would be as simple as disconnecting your old speakers and then reconnecting your new ones. In the most basic sense, it is—but the non-standard nature of PC speaker connections can complicate things.

Let's start with the easy steps first:

1. Open the Windows Control Panel, select Sounds, Speech, and Audio Devices, and then Sounds and Audio Devices. When the Sounds and Audio Devices Properties dialog box opens, mute your PC's sound.

2. Disconnect your existing speakers from your PC.

3. If your existing speakers are powered, disconnect them from their power source.

4. Connect your new speakers to your PC, as directed in the speaker system's instruction manual.

5. If your new speakers are powered, connect them to a power source and turn them on.

6. Return to the Windows Sound utility and unmute your PC's sound

Simple enough. But exactly *how* you connect your speakers to your PC depends on the type of sound card and the type of speakers you have.

Computer systems that have motherboard-based audio, as well as some low-end sound cards, are incredibly simple in terms of their connections. In most instances, you're likely to encounter a single speaker out jack—and that's all.

In this type of setup, you typically connect the primary or *lead* speaker to the speaker out jack, and then connect the secondary speaker to the lead speaker. Sometimes you connect the subwoofer to the speaker out jack, and then connect the other speakers to the subwoofer. Other times you connect a kind of Y adapter to the speaker out jack, and then connect the left and right speakers to this adapter. Consult your speaker instructions for more specifics—then make sure the speakers are positioned for the best possible sound.

Higher-end sound cards will have separate output jacks for each channel—or, in some cases, combo jacks for front left/right and rear left/right. How you connect your speakers to this type of card depends on the specific connectors you have on your speaker system. Again, it's best to consult your speaker instructions.

The challenge in working with high-end speakers and sound cards is matching the output jacks on the sound card with the corresponding connectors on your speaker system. The best advice I can give you is to read all your manuals thoroughly, and be prepared for a trip to your local Radio Shack for whatever additional adapters you might need.

Upgrade #2: Replacing Your Sound Card

After you've decided on what type of new sound card to buy, it's time to install it. You install a sound card the same way you install any other expansion board—open up your system's case and slide the card into an open slot. The only thing to watch out for is any internal cables attached to your card, typically connected to your CD/DVD drive. You'll need to disconnect the cables from your old card and reconnect them to your new one.

You also need to determine whether your PC currently uses a removable sound card or whether it incorporates its audio functions on the motherboard. This is easy enough to see after you get the case off the system unit; a separate sound card will be installed in a normal expansion slot. Look for the audio connections on the back of your PC, and if they *don't* lead to a removable card—if they're hardwired to some spot on the motherboard—you don't have an existing sound card to remove. If this describes your system, skip ahead to the "Upgrading from Motherboard Audio" section *before* you attempt to install your new card.

Installing the Card

To install an internal sound card, follow these instructions:

1. From within Windows, open the Control Panel and select Performance and Maintenance, and then System. When the System Properties dialog box appears, select the Hardware tab and click the Device Manager button to open the Device Manager.

2. From the Device Manager, click the Sound, Video, and Game Controllers item, select your current sound card, and click the Uninstall button (or select Action, Uninstall).

3. Close Windows and power off your system.

4. Disconnect your PC from its power source.

5. Disconnect any cables currently connected to your sound card, such as speaker, headphone, or microphone cables.

6. Open the system unit case.

7. Locate your existing sound card. (If your PC has the audio integrated onto the motherboard, there won't be a separate sound card; in this instance, skip ahead to step 11.)

8. Remove the screw (on the back of the system unit) holding the old sound card in place. Save the screw—you'll need to use it again.

9. If there are any cables running to the sound card from other devices (such as your CD/DVD drive), label them with masking tape or a sticker, and then disconnect them.

10. Remove the old sound card from its slot and set it aside.

11. Insert the new sound card into the now-open slot (see Figure 10.4).

FIGURE 10.4

Holding the card by the edges, carefully insert it into the slot and press firmly to seat it.

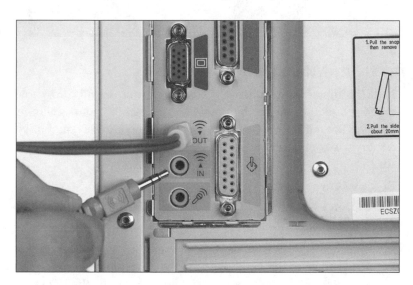

12. Reconnect any cables you disconnected previously (in step 9). See Figure 10.5.

13. Use the screw you saved in step 8 to fasten the new card into place.

14. Reattach the cable that connects your speakers to the new sound card. While you're at it, reconnect any other cables you disconnected back in step 5.

15. Reinstall the system unit cover and reconnect the PC to its power source; while you're at it, go ahead and plug your monitor back in, too.

16. Restart your computer.

17. Run the installation software that came with your new sound card, or use the Windows Add Hardware Wizard to install the proper drivers for the new card.

FIGURES 10.5
Reconnect all
the internal
cables—
fortunately, most
newer PCs use
color-coded
cables.

Upgrading from Motherboard Audio

If your computer system doesn't have an existing sound card, that means that the audio is built into the motherboard. If this describes your system, not only do you have to disregard steps 7 through 10 in the previous section, but you also have to disable your onboard audio. You should do this *before* you install your new sound card.

Here's what you need to do:

1. Shut down and restart your computer.

2. While your computer is booting up, press the appropriate key to enter the BIOS setup utility.

3. Navigate to the setup page used to configure your system's built-in audio. (This varies from system to system; it might be the I/O Device Configuration page, or something similar.)

4. Find the settings for audio, legacy audio, game port, MIDI, and SB (Sound Blaster) devices. Disable these devices.

5. Save the changes and restart your system.

With these changes you made, you can then proceed to install your new audio card.

Upgrade #3: Upgrading to a New External Sound Box

Here is an even easier way to upgrade your system's sound. Scratch all that internal sound card stuff and, instead, add an external sound box via your system's USB port. These devices, such as Creative Labs' Sound Blaster Extigy, function just like an internal sound card and include a slew of audio input and output connectors; they're just easier to install. (Unfortunately, they also cost more than a simple internal card.)

Here's how you upgrade to an external sound card/box:

1. Connect the sound box to a power source and power it on.
2. Connect the sound box to an open USB port on your system unit.
3. Run the sound box's installation program.

That's it—a whole lot simpler than adding a new internal card!

Upgrade #4: Adding an Audio Interface Box

If you're into home recording, you'll want more inputs than you get with a typical consumer-grade sound card. For example, if you want to connect a couple of MIDI keyboards, a guitar, and some microphones, you're pretty much out of luck with your standard Sound Blaster-type card.

What you need, in this instance, is a professional-quality audio interface box— sometimes called a *breakout box*. These boxes connect to your PC (typically via the ubiquitous USB port; sometimes via Firewire) and provide a variety of different audio inputs—line level RCA, XLR, 1/4-inch, S/PDIF digital, MIDI, and so on.

You won't find these devices in your local computer store; instead, you want to shop at a music store that caters to pro musicians. Look for models from the following companies:

- Digidesign (www.digidesign.com)
- Emagic (www.emagic.de)
- Frontier Design Group (www.frontierdesign.com)
- MOTU (www.moto.com)

Assuming that you purchase a USB-compatible interface box, installation is as easy as upgrading to a consumer-grade external sound box, as described in Upgrade #3. Non-USB interface boxes typically require the installation of a companion sound card; the box then connects to the new sound card.

The Absolute Minimum

When you want to improve the sound of your computer system, keep these points in mind:

- The best way to improve music playback is with a better speaker system—preferably one that uses a separate subwoofer.

- For serious gaming, consider a speaker/sound card combo that supports 3D audio.

- A better sound card won't improve CD or DVD playback—but will beef up the synthesized sounds of your PC games.

- If you don't mind spending a few extra bucks, the easiest way to upgrade your sound card is via an external sound box, like the Sound Blaster Extigy, that connects via USB.

- If you're a computer-based musician, consider a sound card with dedicated MIDI connectors—or a pro-level audio interface box.

PART III

Upgrading for Specific Applications

11

Play It Loud: Upgrading for Digital Music Playback and Recording

Your personal computer can do more than just compute. It can also serve as a fully functional audio system and CD replication factory!

That's right, you can use your PC to listen to your favorite audio CDs, download digital audio files from the Internet, and burn your own custom CDs. You can even convert your PC into the nucleus of a high-tech digital home recording studio.

For many of these applications you don't even need to upgrade your system; most new PCs come with the hardware and software you need for basic digital audio playback and recording. For more advanced applications, however—and to get the best-quality sound—there are some simple upgrades you can make.

Understanding Digital Audio

Before you consider which upgrades to make, it helps to know a little about digital audio. You see, there are many different ways to store, play back, and record audio on your computer system.

All computer audio files are digital in nature—hence the umbrella term, *digital audio*. The two most popular digital audio formats are *MP3* and *WMA*, and most digital media player programs can play and record files in either format.

MP3 was the first widely used digital audio format, and remains the most popular format today. It was the first audio file format that combined near-CD quality sound with reasonably small file sizes. Before MP3, a CD's worth of music took up 600MB or more on your hard disk. With MP3, the same amount of music might only use 60MB of hard disk space.

Of course, MP3 isn't the only digital audio file format in use today. Microsoft is waging a strong campaign for its Windows Media Audio (WMA) format, which offers similar quality to MP3, but with slightly smaller files. Unfortunately, WMA also offers something that you might not want—copy protection. Files encoded in the WMA format can be configured to play back only on the system that recorded the files. This means you're likely to stumble onto WMA files that were recorded on other computers that won't play back on your PC—or were recorded on your computer, but won't play back on your portable audio player.

Application #1: Listening to CDs and Digital Music Files

To listen to digital audio files, you need a piece of software called a digital media player. These programs let you play back digital audio files stored on your hard disk, as well as audio CDs you insert into your PC's CD-ROM drive. Many media players also let you record your own digital audio files, which we'll get into later in this chapter.

There are a number of digital media players available, most for free and almost all downloadable over the Internet. The most popular audio player programs include the following:

- MusicMatch Jukebox (www.musicmatch.com)
- RealOne Player (www.real.com)
- WinAmp (www.winamp.com)
- Windows Media Player (www.microsoft.com/windows/windowsmedia/)

Most new PCs come with at least one of these programs pre-installed. In fact, Windows Media Player (WMP), shown in Figure 11.1, is included as part of the Windows operating system.

FIGURE 11.1

Windows Media Player—the free digital media player included with Microsoft Windows.

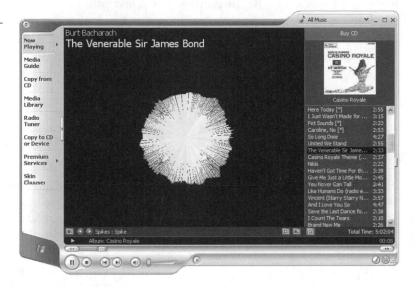

When it comes to playing CDs or digital audio files, you *can* use the existing speaker system that came with your PC—but, in most cases, the stock speakers leave a lot to be desired, sonically. If you plan to listen to a lot of music—and you have good ears—you should consider upgrading to a better set of speakers, ideally a system that includes full-range left and right speakers and a separate subwoofer for low bass reproduction. You probably don't need to upgrade your sound card; even today's least expensive sound cards do a good job reproducing digital music.

The following checklist details what you need to upgrade your system for optimal CD and digital audio playback.

Upgrade Checklist for CD and Digital Audio Playback

- [ ] Fast (48X) CD-ROM drive (see Chapter 5, "Optical Tricks: Upgrading CD and DVD Drives")
- [ ] High-quality speakers, preferably with separate subwoofer (see Chapter 10, "Pet Sounds: Upgrading Sound Cards and Speakers")
- [ ] Digital media player software, such as Windows Media Player or MusicMatch Jukebox

Application #2: Downloading Music from the Internet

If you're a music lover, the capability to download your favorite songs from the Internet—in the form of digital music files—is a big deal. Want to check out the latest single from a new band you've been hearing about? Then download it. Want your own copy of a big top forty hit from your teenage years? Download it. Or how about digging up an obscure album track from some long out-of-print vinyl LP? Chances are, you can download that, too.

There are a number of both "official" and "unofficial" digital audio archive sites and services on the Web. The official sites typically charge some sort of subscription fee to download a certain number of songs per month; the unofficial sites offer an unlimited selection of music for free.

All you need to download music from the Web is your PC and a fast Internet connection—and a big hard disk to hold all those files. Here's the upgrade checklist:

> **caution**
>
> Downloading or copying copyrighted material without permission is against the law and deprives musicians of their hard-earned income. Let your conscience be your guide.

Upgrade Checklist for Downloading Digital Music

- [ ] 40GB or larger hard disk (see Chapter 4, "Bigger Is Better: Upgrading System Storage")
- [ ] Broadband Internet connection (see Chapter 15, "Connect the Dots: Upgrading to a Wired or Wireless Network")
- [ ] Digital media player software, such as Windows Media Player or MusicMatch Jukebox
- [ ] Subscription to an online music service—or software to share files over a file-sharing service

Application #3: Ripping Music from a CD

If you have a decent compact disc collection and a CD-ROM drive in your computer system, you can make your own MP3 or WMA files from the songs on your CDs. You can then listen to these files on your computer, download the files to a portable audio player for listening on the go, share them with other users via a file-swapping service, or use these files to burn your own custom mix CDs.

This process of copying files from a CD to your hard disk, in either MP3 or WMA format, is called *ripping*. You use an audio encoding program to rip your files; most of the major digital media players, such as Windows Media Player and MusicMatch Jukebox, also function as audio encoders.

The ripping process is fairly simple. You start by inserting the CD from which you want to copy into your PC's CD-ROM drive. Then you launch your encoder program and select which songs on your CD you want to rip. You'll also need to select the format for the final file (MP3 or WMA) and the *bit rate* you want to use for encoding; the higher the bit rate, the better the sound quality. (And the larger the file size!) After you've set everything up, click the appropriate button to start the encoding process.

After you start encoding, the song(s) you selected will be played from your PC's CD drive, processed through the encoder program into a WAV-format file, encoded into an MP3- or WMA-format file (your choice), and then stored on your hard disk.

Here's the upgrade checklist:

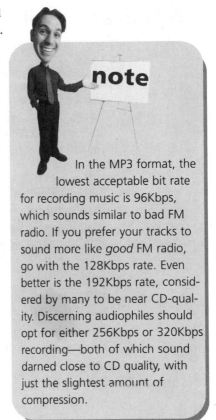

note

In the MP3 format, the lowest acceptable bit rate for recording music is 96Kbps, which sounds similar to bad FM radio. If you prefer your tracks to sound more like *good* FM radio, go with the 128Kbps rate. Even better is the 192Kbps rate, considered by many to be near CD-quality. Discerning audiophiles should opt for either 256Kbps or 320Kbps recording—both of which sound darned close to CD quality, with just the slightest amount of compression.

Upgrade Checklist for Ripping Music from CDs

- [ ] Fast (48X) CD-ROM drive (see Chapter 5)
- [ ] 40GB or larger hard drive (see Chapter 4)
- [ ] Audio encoding software or digital media player with audio encoding features, such as Windows Media Player or MusicMatch Jukebox

caution

After you've started the encoding process, do *not* use your computer to do anything else while encoding; you may even want to disable any background applications, such as antivirus software. Any other use of your PC during encoding runs the risk of adding "skips" to your MP3s.

Application #4: Burning Your Own Music CDs

CD burning is the opposite of CD ripping. When you burn a CD, you record an audio CD from the digital audio files stored on your computer's hard disk—which means you need to upgrade your system with a CD-R/RW drive.

Unlike CD ripping, CD burning doesn't require you to set a lot of format options. That's because when the original file gets copied to CD, it gets encoded into the CD Audio (CDA) format. All music CDs use the CDA format, so whether you're burning an MP3 or WMA file, your CD burner software translates it to CDA before the copy is made.

You can record up to 74 minutes or 650MB worth of music on a CD-R disc, whichever comes first. (Or, with the newer 700MB discs, up to 80 minutes of music.) Just load a blank disc into your computer's CD-R/RW drive, launch your CD burner software, and then follow the program's instructions to start translating and copying the song files. After the ripping begins, the digital audio files on your hard drive are converted and copied onto a blank CD-R in standard CD Audio format.

tip

To play your new CD in a regular (non-PC) CD player, record in the CD-R format and use a blank CD-R disc specifically certified for audio use. (CD-RW discs will not play in most CD players.)

Of course, you can also record your songs to CD in MP3 or WMA format. All computer CD drives will be able to play back these discs, as will *some* home and car CD players—newer models, especially. Most older CD players, however, can only play audio CDs, not data CDs, so make sure your player can play MP3s before you choose this option.

Here's what you need to burn your own audio CDs:

Upgrade Checklist for Burning Audio CDs

☐ Fast CD-R/RW drive (see Chapter 5)

☐ Digital media player software with CD-burning features, such as Windows Media Player or MusicMatch Jukebox

Application #5: Transferring Digital Music to a Portable Audio Player

One of the cool things about digital audio files is that they're portable. You can listen to them on your desktop PC, burn them to an audio CD, or download them to a portable audio player—and take your music anywhere.

Most portable audio players (sometimes called *MP3 players*, though they'll also play WMA-format files) connect to your PC via the USB port. Just connect the USB cable between your player and your PC, fire up the file transfer software (typically included with your audio player), and download your music of choice.

Here's what you need to transfer digital audio files to a portable audio player:

tip

Some digital media player programs—such as Windows Media Player and MusicMatch—also include a file-transfer function, which makes copying music from your computer to your digital media player a snap. (You may need to download a plug-in from the manufacturer's Web site to make this function work, however.)

Upgrade Checklist for Transferring Digital Music to a Portable Audio Player

- ☐ Open USB port (see Chapter 3, "Ports Ahoy: Upgrading System Inputs")
- ☐ Portable audio player and connecting cable
- ☐ File transfer software or digital media player program with file-transfer features, such as Windows Media Player or MusicMatch Jukebox

Application #6: Listening to Internet Radio

Although most music lovers use the Internet to download digital audio files, there's another good source of music online—real-time audio "Webcasts," commonly referred to as *Internet radio*.

Many real-world radio stations broadcast over the Internet using a technology called *streaming audio*. Streaming audio is different from downloading an audio file. When you download an MP3 or WMA file, you can't start playing that file until it is completely downloaded to your PC; with streaming audio, however, playback can start before an entire file is downloaded. This also enables live broadcasts—both of traditional radio stations and made-for-the-Web stations—to be sent from the broadcast site to your PC.

The two most popular players for streaming audio are Windows Media Player and RealOne Player. These programs play back streaming audio recorded in competing formats, so you might need to have both players installed on your PC. In addition, you'll need a fast and persistent Internet connection; dial-up connections don't work very well for this application, so you'll want a broadband connection of some sort.

The following checklist details my recommended upgrades for listening to Internet radio.

Upgrade Checklist for Internet Radio

- ☐ Broadband Internet connection (see Chapter 15, "Connect the Dots: Upgrading to a Wired or Wireless Network")
- ☐ High-quality speakers, preferably with a separate subwoofer (see Chapter 10)
- ☐ Streaming media player software, such as Windows Media Player or RealOne Player

Application #7: Playing a Digital Piano or Synthesizer

This might seem like a niche application, but it's becoming more and more popular—thanks to the number of interactive piano-instruction programs available for today's PCs. Most digital pianos and synthesizers come equipped with built-in MIDI capabilities, and can be connected to any standard home PC.

To connect a musical keyboard to your PC, you either need a high-end sound card with MIDI connectors, an expensive audio breakout box, or (the preferred approach for most users) an inexpensive MIDI-to-game port adapter. This adapter, like the one shown in Figure 11.2, connects between the game port on the back of your system unit or sound card and the MIDI cable running from your instrument.

Here's what you need, then, to upgrade your system for musical instrument playback:

Upgrade Checklist for Connecting a Musical Keyboard

- ☐ Open game port on your system unit or sound card (see Chapter 3)
- ☐ MIDI/game port adapter
- ☐ Digital piano or synthesizer with MIDI Out jack
- ☐ Audio instruction, sequencing, or recording software

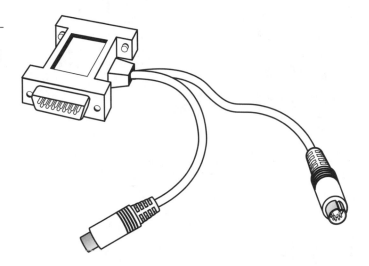

FIGURE 11.2

Use a MIDI/game port adapter to connect your musical instrument to your PC's game port.

Application #8: Setting Up Your Own Home Recording Studio

This is really a niche application, but one with appeal to a lot of musicians out there—turning your home computer into a digital recording studio. Whether you play in a band or are a budding composer, this is the low-cost way to put your songs on disc. (Setting up a complete home studio is a *lot* less expensive than even a single day in a professional recording studio.)

In this type of setup, you use your PC as both a mixing console and hard disk recorder. As shown in Figure 11.3, You connect your instruments or outboard mixers to your PC, typically through a MIDI or USB port. You then use digital studio software—such as Cakewalk (www.cakewalk.com) or Cubasis (www.steinberg.net)—to create the mix and record the sounds on your hard disk. After you've created the final mix, you burn your music to CD. It's really as simple as that.

Well, actually, it's not that simple. First, you'll need to upgrade to a high-end sound card that can handle high-speed, high bit-rate audio recording. Then you'll need to add one or more MIDI interfaces to your PC. Your new sound card might include a MIDI interface, or you might need to buy a separate audio interface box, which adds a variety of MIDI and audio connectors in a separate unit, typically connected via a separate card or USB port. (Audio interface boxes were discussed in Chapter 10.)

FIGURE 11.3

A typical home studio setup— centered around your personal computer.

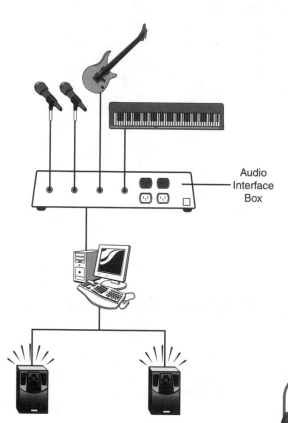

Audio
Interface
Box

You'll also need to beef up your PC, to some degree. Recording large digital files in real time is processor-intensive, so you'll need a fairly fast system to ensure error-free recording. Any newer machine running at 1GHz or better should do the trick, and you'll want to have at least 256MB of RAM on board, as well.

Another necessity for home recording studios is a very large, very fast hard disk. I recommend at least 40GB of storage with spin rate 7,200 RPM. (Most professionals go for a SCSI drive, as well— although that isn't necessary for most home studios.)

tip

You won't find sound cards, interfaces, and software for musicians at your local computer store. A better place to shop for these professional audio products is the electronics department at any large musical instrument retailer, such as Guitar Center or Sam Ash Music, or at an online music retailer specializing in recording gear, such as Midi Warehouse (www.midiwarehouse.com), MTLC.net (www.mtlc.net), or Sweetwater (www.sweetwater.com).

You might also want an external mixer, a signal processor or two, and at least one MIDI keyboard/synthesizer. In addition, some digital recording programs can utilize a second monitor; they display the recording data on one monitor, and the mixing controls on the second.

Still, it's not as expensive as it sounds, especially if you already have a MIDI keyboard. Here's an upgrade checklist:

Upgrade Checklist for a Home Recording Studio

- ☐ 40GB or larger hard disk, with 7,200 RPM spin rate (see Chapter 4)
- ☐ Fast CD-R/RW drive (see Chapter 5)
- ☐ 256MB or more RAM (see Chapter 6)
- ☐ High-speed, high bit-rate sound card with MIDI connectors (see Chapter 10)
- ☐ Audio interface box (optional, see Chapter 10)
- ☐ Outboard USB mixer (optional)
- ☐ Studio-quality powered speakers (optional)
- ☐ Second video card and monitor (optional; see Chapter 9, "The Big Picture: Upgrading Video Cards and Monitors")
- ☐ Digital piano or synthesizer with MIDI Out jack
- ☐ Home recording and mixing software

" Mike Sez "

Although there are all sorts of equipment available for home PC recording, I particularly like those units that connect to your PC via USB—such as the Tascam US-428 mixer (www.tascam.com). These units supercede your PC's internal sound (eliminating the need for a new sound card) and provide a MIDI interface, all through a single, easy-to-configure USB connection.

The Absolute Minimum

When it comes to upgrading your system for digital audio playback and recording, here's what you need to remember:

- Most newer PCs come with all the hardware and software you need for basic audio playback and recording—no upgrading necessary.

- Whether you're downloading music from the Web or listening to live Internet radio, you need a broadband Internet connection for fast downloading and optimal playback.

- The best digital media players let you listen to digital music, rip songs from CD, and burn your own music CDs.

- To burn your own CDs, you need a fast CD-R/RW drive and a large supply of CD-R discs—the kind that are certified for audio playback.

- To connect a digital keyboard or audio recording equipment to your PC, you need a sound card with a MIDI connector—or a low-cost MIDI adapter to connect to your PC's game port.

12

Slides and Prints: Upgrading for Digital Photography and Picture Editing

One of the hottest pieces of gear today is the digital camera. Digital cameras work like normal film cameras, except they capture images electronically, instead of on film. These digital images are stored within the camera on flash memory cards. You can then connect your camera to your PC and transfer your digital photos to your computer.

That's when the fun starts.

After you've transferred a digital photo from your camera to your PC, you have lots of options available to you. A digital picture file is just like any computer file, which means you can store it, copy it, delete it, or whatever. You can also use photo editing software to manipulate your photos—to touch up bad spots and red eye, crop the edges, and apply all sorts of special effects.

To use your PC as a digital darkroom, you might need to perform a few simple upgrades. Naturally, you'll need some way to get your digital photos into your PC—a USB or FireWire connection, or maybe a memory card reader. (Or, if you're working with photo prints, you'll need to connect a scanner.) A bigger monitor is nice, especially if you're retouching your photos. And all those digital files take up disk space, which makes a bigger hard drive a necessity.

After you have beefed up your system, however, working with digital photographs is a snap—no pun intended.

Application #1: Downloading Photographs from a Digital Camera

Connecting a digital camera to your new PC is extremely easy, especially if you're using Windows XP and have a relatively new camera. Most new cameras connect to a PC via either USB or FireWire, and are Plug and Play–compatible. Just use the cable that came with your camera to connect the camera to one of your PC's USB or FireWire ports, as shown in Figure 12.1.

FIGURE 12.1
Connecting a digital camera to your PC via USB.

Digital camera

PC

When you turn on your camera (and switch it to "PC" or "transfer" mode), Windows should automatically recognize your camera and install the appropriate drivers. If Windows doesn't recognize your camera, you can use the Windows Scanners and Cameras utility to install the camera on your system. Or, better yet, just run the PC setup program that came with your camera.

For many users, a better approach is to not connect your camera to your PC at all. Instead, you can add a memory card reader to your system (typically via USB connection) and download photos directly from your camera's memory card. This approach has the advantage of treating your memory card as another drive on your system, with the attendant ease of operation.

> **" Mike Sez "**
>
> If you have a choice, go with a camera that offers a FireWire or USB 2.0 connection. USB 1.1, although completely functional, is a tad slow when it comes to downloading megapixel digital photographs from your camera to your PC.

Here's what you need, then, to prepare your system for digital photo downloading:

Upgrade Checklist for Digital Camera Downloading

- [ ] USB or FireWire connector (see Chapter 3, "Ports Ahoy: Upgrading System Inputs")

  or

- [ ] Memory card reader (see Chapter 4,"Bigger Is Better: Upgrading System Storage")
- [ ] 40GB or larger hard disk (see Chapter 4)
- [ ] Digital camera

Application #2: Scanning Photo Prints

If you don't have a digital camera—or if you have a lot of old photo prints lying around that you'd like to work with—there's another way to get your photos into your computer. All you need is a low-cost flatbed scanner. Just connect the scanner to your PC, place a print on the scanner bed, and get down to business.

Upgrade Checklist for Scanning Photo Prints

- [ ] Flatbed scanner (see Chapter 8, "The Paper Chase: Upgrading Printers and Scanners")
- [ ] 40GB or larger hard disk (see Chapter 4)

Application #3: Editing Digital Photographs

Not all the pictures you take are perfect. Sometimes the image might be a little out-of-focus or off-center, or maybe your subject caught the glare of a flash for a "red eye" effect. The nice thing about digital pictures is that you can easily edit them to correct for these and other types of flaws.

To fix the flaws in a picture, you use a photo editing program. Some of these programs are quite simple to use, others offer more features but have a steeper learning curve. The most popular of these programs include Adobe Photoshop Elements (www.adobe.com), Jasc Paint Shop Pro (www.jasc.com), Microsoft Picture It! Photo (pictureitproducts.msn.com), and PhotoSuite (www.roxio.com).

You don't have to tweak your computer much to use any of these programs. Just make sure you have a big hard disk and plenty of memory; an oversized monitor is also nice.

Upgrade Checklist for Editing Digital Photographs

- [ ] 40GB or larger hard disk (see Chapter 4)
- [ ] 256MB or more RAM (see Chapter 6, "You Must Remember This: Upgrading System Memory")
- [ ] 17-inch CRT or 15-inch LCD monitor (see Chapter 9, "The Big Picture: Upgrading Video Cards and Monitors")
- [ ] Digital photo editing software, such as Adobe Photoshop Elements or Microsoft Picture It! Photo

Application #4: Printing Digital Photographs

If you have a color printer, you can make good-quality prints of your image files. Even a low-priced color inkjet can make surprisingly good prints, although the better your printer, the better the results.

As you learned in Chapter 8, most manufacturers sell printers specifically designed for photographic prints. These photo printers use special photo print paper and output prints that are almost indistinguishable from those you get from a professional photo processor. If you take a lot of digital photos, one of these printers is a good investment.

Interestingly, some photo printers don't even need to be connected to your PC. These printers either connect directly to your digital camera via USB, or have slots to accept all the popular memory card formats, as shown in Figure 12.2. This type of setup is particularly recommended for computer-phobic family members.

> **tip**
>
> Whichever type of printer you choose, the quality of your prints is significantly affected by the type of paper you use. Printing on standard laser or inkjet paper is okay for making proofs, but you'll want to use a thicker, waxier paper for those prints you want to keep. Check with your printer's manufacturer to see what type of paper is recommended for the best quality photo prints.

Upgrade Checklist for Making Photo Prints

- ☐ Photo printer (see Chapter 8)
- ☐ Photo print paper

FIGURE 12.2
A photo printer that prints directly from memory cards.

Card slots

Application #5: Sharing Digital Photos Over the Internet

The nice thing about digital photos is that you don't have to print them to share them. If you and your friends and family are all connected to the Internet, it's extremely easy to share your pictures online—either via email or through one of the many photo processing Web sites.

The big challenge with emailing photographs is file size. If you shoot at a high megapixel resolution, you create very large graphics files. We're talking files in the multiple megabyte range—much too large to email, for all practical purposes. If you're intent on emailing your photos, either shoot at a lower resolution, or use a photo editing program to reduce the picture size and resolution, thus creating more easily managed files.

Another option is to use a photo processing site to store copies of your pictures for the viewing pleasure of your online visitors. These services will also print your photos for you, if you don't have your own printer. Just remember that low-res photos are best for online viewing (they download faster), whereas high-res photos are best for creating prints. Shoot or edit accordingly.

If you do a lot of online photo sharing, you'll really appreciate a fast Internet connection. Suffering through a slow dial-up session might be tolerable on occasion, but if you're an active photographer, spend the bucks for a broadband connection.

Upgrade Checklist for Sharing Photos Online

☐ Broadband Internet connection (Chapter 15, "Connect the Dots: Upgrading to a Wired or Wireless Network")

THE ABSOLUTE MINIMUM

Here's what you need to keep in mind when using your PC to work with digital photographs:

■ Most digital cameras connect to your PC via USB or FireWire; alternatively, you can transfer photos directly from your camera's memory card by adding a memory card reader to your system.

■ If you have a lot of existing photo prints to work with, invest in a good flatbed scanner.

■ Graphics files are big, so you'll probably want to invest in a large hard disk.

■ When you want to create your own photo prints, a photo printer is a necessity.

■ If you do a lot of photo editing, a bigger monitor might prove useful—and easier on your eyes.

■ When sharing your photos over the Internet, a broadband Internet connection significantly speeds up the process.

IN THIS CHAPTER

- Viewing television programs
- Watching DVD movies
- Editing movies from a digital or analog camcorder
- Creating your own digital movies

13

EVERYONE'S GONE TO THE MOVIES: UPGRADING FOR TV VIEWING AND DIGITAL VIDEO EDITING

For many users, the personal computer is becoming the center of a full-featured audio/video center. Not only can you use your PC to listen to CDs and digital music, you can also use your computer to watch television programs and movies on DVD.

In addition, if you have a camcorder and make your own home movies, you can use your computer system to make those movies a lot more appealing. With the right hardware and software, you can turn your PC into a video editing console—and make your home movies look a *lot* more professional.

Read on to learn how to upgrade your system for all of these video applications.

Application #1: Viewing Television Programs

Let's face it; your computer monitor is just a glorified television display, but without a built-in tuner. Add a tuner (in the form of a television tuner card) and you can use your PC to watch all your favorite television broadcasts. Of course, a PC is kind of an expensive television set, but it's nice to have all that functionality in a single system.

Here's all you need:

Upgrade Checklist for PC-Based Television Viewing

- [ ] Television tuner card (see Chapter 9, "The Big Picture: Upgrading Video Cards and Monitors")
- [ ] Large CRT or LCD monitor (see Chapter 9)

Application #2: Viewing DVD Movies

If you have a DVD drive in your PC, you can use your computer to watch DVD movies. To optimize your viewing experience, of course, you'll want a big monitor (and maybe one of those nifty new widescreen models from Sony and other manufacturers) and a sound system designed for surround sound. Even a low-cost PC can do the trick, when it's equipped with the right upgrades.

Upgrade Checklist for DVD Viewing

- [ ] DVD drive (see Chapter 5, "Optical Tricks: Upgrading CD and DVD Drives")
- [ ] Large CRT or LCD monitor—possibly a widescreen (16:9) model (see Chapter 9)
- [ ] Sound card with digital output (see Chapter 10, "Pet Sounds: Upgrading Sound Cards and Speakers")
- [ ] Surround sound speaker system (see Chapter 10)

Application #3: Editing Movies from a Digital Camcorder

Do you make your own home movies? Then you'll want to turn your PC into a video editing studio—which is especially easy if you have a digital video (DV) camcorder, in either the Digital8 or MiniDV formats. Just install a desktop video editing program and beef up your hardware as necessary; the results can be truly amazing.

Understanding Digital Video Editing

PC-based video editing software performs many of the same functions as the professional editing consoles you might find at your local television station. You can use this software to cut entire scenes from your movie, rearrange scenes, add fancy transitions between scenes, add titles (and subtitles), and even add your own music soundtrack. Go with an all-digital video system—from DV camcorder to DVD output—and you can do all this without degrading the quality of the original footage.

Another advantage of using a DV camcorder is that you don't need to install a separate video capture card in your PC, as you would with older types of camcorders. What you *do* need is a FireWire or USB 2.0 port on your PC. (FireWire is preferable; the faster connection is necessary to handle the huge stream of digital data pouring from your DV recorder into your PC in real time.)

Necessary Upgrades

Whether you're using a DV camcorder or an analog model (discussed in Upgrade #4), you definitely need to beef up your computer, as video editing is one of the most taxing applications you can perform. You'll need a fairly powerful computer just to get started—a Pentium III or (better still) a Pentium 4 machine, running at no less than 1.5GHz, is the bare minimum configuration necessary.

note

Don't confuse the Digital8 and MiniDV digital recording formats with the new High Definition Television (HDTV) digital broadcast format. HDTV is a broadcast standard with higher resolution and a wider 16:9 aspect ratio; DV camcorders record digitally, but employ the older NTSC low-resolution broadcast standard.

Assuming you have this type of computing horsepower, the first thing to upgrade is your hard disk. Raw digital video takes up about 3.6MB for each second of footage; work with an hour-long movie, and you'll fill up two-thirds of a 20GB disk. So a big—no, make that a *huge*—hard disk is a necessity. Some users simply add a second hard drive to their system, dedicated solely to video editing. Whatever you do, make sure it's a *fast* disk; choose an IDE drive with a 7,200 RPM spin rate, or (if you're flush) a SCSI drive. And when you install the drive, format it with the NTFS file system if you can. (You can if you're running Windows XP; you can't if you're running an older operating system.)

Memory is also important. Lots of it. Like 512MB worth. Any less and you'll find your system slows down considerably when processing all that digital video data.

While we're on the subject of memory, it helps to have a video card with lots of onboard memory. For best performance, look for a card with 64MB or 128MB video RAM.

Finally, consider going with a big monitor—the easier to view your movies with. In fact, you might think about a dual-monitor system, so you can edit on one screen and view your results on the other.

As to software, if you're running Windows XP, you have Windows Movie Maker (shown in Figure 13.1) pre-installed on your machine. This is a good basic editing program (and it's free—always a good thing!), but you might want something a little more powerful. For real video editing power, check out Adobe Premiere (www.adobe.com) or Ulead VideoStudio and MediaStudio Pro (www.ulead.com).

FIGURE 13.1

Windows Movie Maker— Windows XP's video editing program.

So here's all you need to do to upgrade your system for digital video editing:

Upgrade Checklist for Digital Video Editing

- ☐ FireWire or USB 2.0 port (see Chapter 3, "Ports Ahoy: Upgrading System Inputs")

- ☐ 80GB or larger dedicated hard disk (see Chapter 4, "Bigger Is Better: Upgrading System Storage")

- ☐ 512MB or more RAM (see Chapter 6, "You Must Remember This: Upgrading System Memory")

☐   64MB or 128MB video card (see Chapter 9)

☐   Large CRT or LCD monitor (see Chapter 9)

☐   Optional second monitor (see Chapter 9)

☐   Digital8 or MiniDV camcorder

Application #4: Editing Movies from an Analog Camcorder

If you have a VHS, VHS-C, SVHS, 8mm, or Hi8 camcorder, you're working old school—and creating analog, not digital, video. Because you can't connect an analog camcorder to a digital input, you'll need to install a video capture card or an outboard video capture device. You connect your camcorder to this card or device, as shown in Figure 13.2, and it converts your camcorder's analog video signals into digital audio and video, all ready for editing.

FIGURE 13.2

Connecting an analog camcorder for video editing.

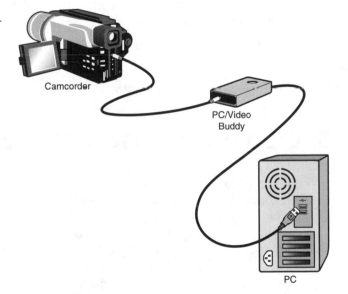

Camcorder

PC/Video Buddy

PC

When it comes to connecting your analog camcorder, most video capture cards provide a variety of different inputs; which input you use depends primarily on which outputs your camcorder has. If your camcorder offers them (and most don't), use *component video* connectors; this is a grouping of three RCA-type jacks, typically labeled Y, Pr, and Pb, that delivers extremely high-quality video signals with improved color accuracy and reduced color bleeding. Next in order of preference (and more common) is an *S-video* connection, followed by *composite video* (normally labeled simply as "video"). The least preferable connection is the *RF* or antenna connection; most video capture equipment doesn't even support this type of connection because the image quality is very low.

Of course, you'll also have to make all the system upgrades discussed in Application #3. Here's the list of what you need to do:

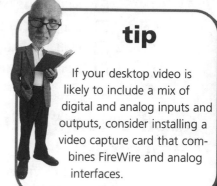

tip

If your desktop video is likely to include a mix of digital and analog inputs and outputs, consider installing a video capture card that combines FireWire and analog interfaces.

Upgrade Checklist for Digital Video Editing

- ☐ Video capture card or external video capture device (see Chapter 9)
- ☐ 80GB or larger dedicated hard disk (see Chapter 4)
- ☐ 512MB or more RAM (see Chapter 6)
- ☐ 64MB or 128MB video card (see Chapter 9)
- ☐ Large CRT or LCD monitor (see Chapter 9)
- ☐ Optional second monitor (see Chapter 9)
- ☐ VHS, VHS-C, SVHS, 8mm, or Hi8 camcorder

Application #5: Creating Your Own DVD Movies

After you've edited your home movie into a cinematic masterpiece, you need to share your work with the world. The easiest way to do this is to burn your movie to DVD discs. All you need is a DVD burner and enough RAM to make the process more speedy (or less sluggish)—and a big enough hard disk to store your movie during the process.

tip

For optimal compatibility, you'll want to record your movies in the DVD-R format.

Upgrade Checklist for Burning DVD Movies

- ☐ DVD-R burner (see Chapter 5)
- ☐ 80GB or larger dedicated hard disk (see Chapter 4)
- ☐ 512MB or more RAM (see Chapter 6)

THE ABSOLUTE MINIMUM

When you want to use your PC for video purposes, keep these facts in mind:

- Just about any fancy video application you can think of will require upgrading your system in some fashion.
- To watch TV on your PC, you'll need to install a television tuner card.
- To watch DVD movies on your PC, you'll need a DVD drive.
- To edit home movies on your PC, you'll need to upgrade almost all your components—you need lots of memory, a big (and fast) hard disk, a 64MB video card, and either a FireWire connection (for DV camcorders) or a video capture card or device (for older analog camcorders).
- To burn your movies to DVD, you'll need a DVD burner compatible with the DVD-R format.

14

FUN IS GOOD: UPGRADING FOR ENHANCED GAME PLAY

Most people use their PCs, even just a little, for playing games. It's nothing to be ashamed of; everybody does it.

The part about PC gaming that many users have trouble believing is that playing a game is probably the most demanding application you can perform on your computer. It's true; all those fancy graphics and gee-whiz sound effects definitely put your computer system through its paces.

In fact, to get the *best* game play possible, you need a truly state-of-the-art computer system. If you purchased a low-end computer, you might find that it doesn't play the latest games quite as fast or as smoothly as you might have expected—which means that it's time to upgrade!

Application #1: PC Gaming

What can you do to beef up your system for better game play?

First, you'll want to start with a fairly high-powered microprocessor. It may seem excessive but trust me when I say you'll want a Pentium 4 running at 2.4GHz or more. If you have an older, less-powerful PC, no upgrade in the world will make the most-demanding games play smoothly on your system.

Assuming you have enough horsepower, you should consider upgrading almost everything else in your system. You should go with a fairly large hard disk, lots of memory, and a 3D sound card connected to a kick-ass surround sound speaker system. You'll also need a CD-ROM drive, and possibly a DVD drive—many of the new games come on a single DVD rather than multiple CDs.

As to video cards, you want to get the newest and most expensive one you can afford. For new games like Doom III and Half-Life 2, you'll need a card with 3D graphics acceleration, 256MB of video RAM, and compatibility with Microsoft's new DirectX 9 technology, which allows enhanced shading effects and the layering of different textures. Expect to pay up to $500 for one of these cards.

The result of these upgrades is a state-of-the-art gaming system, as shown in Figure 14.1.

> **"Mike Sez"**
>
> If you're running an older PC, I'll recommend another upgrade—your operating system. Windows XP is far and away the best operating system for running both newer and older PC games. If you haven't yet upgraded to XP—and you're a serious gamer—do it now!

> **tip**
>
> For reviews of the hottest video cards for gamers, visit the AnandTech (www.anandtech.com) or sharkeyextreme.com (www.sharkeyextreme.com) Web sites.

FIGURE 14.1
A state-of-the art PC gaming system.

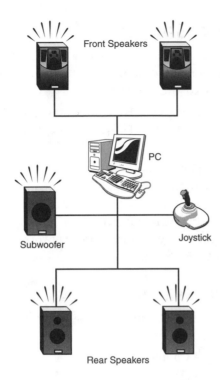

Front Speakers

PC

Subwoofer

Joystick

Rear Speakers

Upgrade Checklist for PC Gaming

☐ 80GB or larger hard disk (see Chapter 4, "Bigger Is Better: Upgrading System Storage")

☐ CD/DVD drive (see Chapter 5, "Optical Tricks: Upgrading CD and DVD Drives")

☐ 512MB or more RAM (see Chapter 6)

☐ 256MB video card with 3D graphics accelerator and DirectX 9 compatibility (see Chapter 9, "The Big Picture: Upgrading Video Cards and Monitors")

☐ 19-inch CRT or 17-inch LCD monitor (see Chapter 9)

☐ 3D sound card (see Chapter 10, "Pet Sounds: Upgrading Video Cards and Monitors")

☐ 4.1 surround sound speaker system with subwoofer (see Chapter 10)

☐ Joystick or other game controller (see Chapter 7, "Point and Click: Upgrading Mice and Keyboards")

Application #2: Network Gaming

Most PC games sold at retail today include a multiplayer option, which lets you play the game against a human opponent. You can play another player on the Internet (discussed next), or on your own local area network.

To play games over your home or small-office LAN, you still need to beef up your system as you would for playing single-player PC games. The difference is the network connection.

The big consideration when setting up a small LAN is whether to go wired or wireless. As convenient as a wireless network might be, the wired variety is preferred by serious gamers. There's a simple reason for this—*speed*. WiFi wireless networks transfer data at 11Mbps, where wired Fast Ethernet networks hit 100Mbps speeds. When you're pumping that joystick in the heat of battle, a slow network connection can mean the difference between (virtual) life and death.

Upgrade Checklist for Network Gaming

- ☐ 100Mbps Fast Ethernet LAN (see Chapter 16, "The Faster the Better: Upgrading Your Internet Connection")
- ☐ 80GB or larger hard disk (see Chapter 4)
- ☐ CD/DVD drive (see Chapter 5)
- ☐ 512MB or more RAM (see Chapter 6)
- ☐ 256MB video card with 3D graphics accelerator and DirectX 9 compatibility (see Chapter 9)
- ☐ 19-inch CRT or 17-inch LCD monitor (see Chapter 9)
- ☐ 3D sound card (see Chapter 10)
- ☐ 4.1 surround sound speaker system with subwoofer (see Chapter 10)
- ☐ Joystick or other game controller (see Chapter 7)

Application #3: Online Gaming

Of course, you're not limited to playing games with other members of your household. Connect to the Internet and you can play games with opponents from all around the world!

As with network gaming, online gaming works best with a fast connection. That means a broadband connection (cable, DSL, or satellite), the faster the better. (Dial-up gaming just doesn't cut it these days.) Naturally, you'll need to beef up your PC in all other aspects, as well.

Upgrade Checklist for Internet Gaming

- ☐ Broadband Internet connection (see Chapter 15)
- ☐ 80GB or larger hard disk (see Chapter 4)
- ☐ CD/DVD drive (see Chapter 5)
- ☐ 512MB or more RAM (see Chapter 6)
- ☐ 256MB video card with 3D graphics accelerator and DirectX 9 compatibility (see Chapter 9)
- ☐ 19-inch CRT or 17-inch LCD monitor (see Chapter 9)
- ☐ 3D sound card (see Chapter 10)
- ☐ 4.1 surround sound speaker system with subwoofer (see Chapter 10)
- ☐ Joystick or other game controller (see Chapter 7)

THE ABSOLUTE MINIMUM

If you plan on using your PC to play the latest games, keep these points in mind:

- ■ Playing games is one of the most demanding applications for your PC.
- ■ To play the most-demanding PC games, you'll need to start with at least a 2.4GHz Pentium 4 machine.
- ■ For best game play, you'll need a big hard disk, CD/DVD drive, 512MB or more RAM, 256MB 3D video card, a big monitor, a 3D sound card with 4.1 surround sound speaker system, and a joystick or other game controller.
- ■ To play multiplayer games over a LAN, go with wired Fast Ethernet connections.
- ■ To play multiplayer games over the Internet, get a cable or DSL connection.

PART iV

Upgrading Your Entire System

15

CONNECT THE DOTS: UPGRADING TO A WIRED OR WIRELESS NETWORK

When you need to share files or printers or an Internet connection, you need to hook all your computers together into a *local area network*, or *LAN*. Networks have always been popular in the corporate environment, but they're becoming increasingly so in the home, as well. That's because more and more of us are living in multiple-computer households; you have a PC, your spouse has a PC, even your kids have a PC (or two or three). And even though you have three PCs, you don't want to invest in three printers or install three separate Internet connections. No, the thing to do now is to learn how to share—which is where the network comes in handy.

With all your computers connected together, you can share all your big peripherals—printers, scanners, you name it. You can also share that expensive broadband Internet connection. And you can share your data files and folders, so that someone on one computer can open and work with files stored on another PC.

Although installing a network used to be technically daunting, today's home and small business networks are relatively easy to set up and configure. The equipment involved has come down in price, and is a lot easier to use than it used to be. You can even skip running a bunch of cables and go with a wireless network; if you only have a handful of PCs, you shouldn't have to spend any more than $200–$300 for the whole network.

Understanding Networks

When it comes to physically connecting your network, you have two ways to go—wired or wireless.

Wired Versus Wireless

A *wired network* is the kind that requires you to run a bunch of cables from one PC to the next. In a wired network you install a *network interface card* (*NIC*) in each PC and connect the cards via Ethernet cable. Although this type of network is easy enough to set up and is probably the lowest-cost alternative, you still have to deal with all those cables—which can be a hassle if your computers are in different areas of your house.

Wired networks transfer data at either 10Mbps or 100Mbps, depending on what equipment you install. A 10Mbps network is called *10Base-T*; a 100Mbps network is called *Fast Internet*; networking equipment that can work at either 10Mbps or 100Mbps rates is labeled *10/100*.

The cable used in most home and small business networks is called Category 5, or CAT-5, Ethernet. The Ethernet connector, shown in Figure 15.1, looks a little like a telephone connector, but a little bit wider.

note

How quickly data is transferred across a network is measured in megabits per second, or Mbps. The bigger the Mbps number, the faster the network—and faster is always better than slower.

FIGURE 15.1
A CAT-5
Ethernet cable
and connector.

Ethernet connector

The alternative to a wired network is a *wireless network*. Wireless networks use radio frequency (RF) signals to connect one computer to another. The advantage of wireless, of course, is that you don't have to run any cables. This is a big plus if you have a large house with computers on either end, or on different floors. The most popular wireless networks, using the Wi-Fi standard (also known as IEEE 802.11b), transfer data at 11Mbps—slower than Fast Ethernet, but fast enough for most practical purposes.

If you want a faster wireless connection, you have a few options. Some companies are selling what they call "enhanced 802.11b," which transmits data at up to 22Mbps, or twice the normal Wi-Fi rate. In addition, there is a new version of Wi-Fi on its way. These new 802.11g networks are fully compatible with existing 802.11b devices, but transmit data at a blazing 54Mbps rate. If you tend to copy a lot of big files from one PC to another, consider upgrading to one of these faster wireless networks.

Connecting and Configuring

Whether you're going wired or wireless, you can probably find everything you need to create your network in a preassembled networking kit. These

note

Wi-Fi is short for *wireless fidelity*; learn more at the official Wi-Fi Alliance Web site (www.wi-fi.org).

Mike Sez

If you use your network primarily to share an Internet connection or a printer, wireless should work just fine. However, if you plan on transferring a lot of big files from one PC to another, or using your network for multiplayer gaming, you'll want to stick to a faster wired network.

kits contain all the cards, cables, and hubs you need to create your network, along with easy-to-follow instructions. (And if you don't want to open up your computer, you can even find kits that include external network adapters that connect via USB!)

After you get all your equipment installed and connected, you then have to configure all the PCs on your network. If you're running Windows XP, the configuration process is handled by the Network Setup Wizard. You launch the wizard by opening the Control Panel and selecting Network and Internet Connections, and then Network Connections; when the Network Connections utility opens, select Set Up a Home or Small Office Network from the Network Tasks panel.

You run the Network Setup Wizard on each PC that is connected to the network. During the process you provide details about your network connections, including any and all devices or connections you want to share—such as a printer or your broadband Internet connection. The wizard does all the hard work, and when it's done, your network is up and running and ready to use.

If you're running an older operating system, you'll want to use the configuration utility that comes with your network kit or hub.

Upgrade #1: Creating a Wired Network

Connecting multiple computers in a wired network is actually fairly simple. Just make sure you do the proper planning beforehand and buy the appropriate hardware and cables; everything else is a matter of connecting and configuration.

Wired Network Hardware and Topology

You need to install a network interface card, as shown in Figure 15.2, in each computer in your wired network. Each NIC then connects, via Ethernet cable, to the network *hub*, which is a simple device (like the one in Figure 15.3) that functions like the hub of a wheel and serves as the central point in your network. Then, after you make the physical connections, each computer has to be configured to function as part of the network and to share designated files, folders, and peripherals.

The whole thing, when complete, should look like the network in Figure 15.4.

If you're using your network to share a broadband Internet connection, you have a couple of options here. Most users will run the broadband modem directly into the network hub, which lets all computers share the connection even if one computer isn't turned on. An alternative setup connects the broadband modem to your main, or *gateway*, PC; this lets you use the gateway PC as a firewall to protect the other machines from unauthorized access. Another setup involves connecting your broadband modem to a *router* that functions both as a hub and as a gateway to the Internet (sometimes called a *residential gateway*).

FIGURE 15.2

A typical network interface card, complete with Ethernet connector.

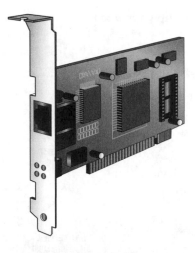

FIGURE 15.3

A typical network hub.

FIGURE 15.4

Setting up a wired Ethernet network.

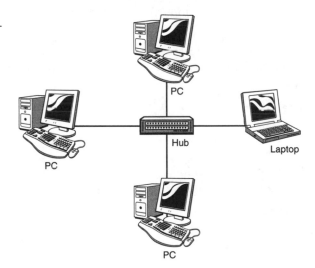

The best course of action is to follow the recommendation of your broadband service provider because some ISPs will need to assign multiple IP addresses if you're connecting multiple computers. Just ensure you properly configure each PC to share the Internet connection; in Windows 98 Second Edition and later, you can do this with Windows' Internet Connection Sharing (ICS) utility.

Here's the hardware you'll need to set up your wired network:

Upgrade Checklist for Wired Networking

- ☐ Network interface cards (one for each PC; possibly a second NIC for your gateway PC)
- ☐ Ethernet network hub (one for the entire network)
- ☐ Router or residential gateway device (optional, for sharing an Internet connection)
- ☐ Enough CAT-5 Ethernet cables to run from each PC to the hub

note

For more information on sharing a broadband connection, see Chapter 16, "The Faster the Better: Upgrading Your Internet Connection."

When you assemble this equipment, make sure you buy devices that all work at the same speed; there's no point buying a 100Mbps hub if all your NICs are 10Mbps. Along the same lines, you can save some headache by purchasing equipment from a single manufacturer. It's not that you can't mix and match devices from different companies, it's just that you're likely to have fewer configuration issues if you stick to a single supplier.

As to cost, you'll pay between $25–$50 for your network hub and $20 or less for each NIC. The cost for the Ethernet cables varies by length. Popular manufacturers include the following:

- ■ Belkin (www.belkin.com)
- ■ D-Link (www.dlink.com)
- ■ Linksys (www.linksys.com)
- ■ Microsoft Broadband Networking (www.microsoft.com/hardware/broadbandnetworking/)
- ■ Netgear (www.netgear.com)
- ■ SMC (www.smc.com)

Making the Connections

Naturally, you should follow the instructions that come with your networking hardware to properly set up your network. In general, however, here are the steps to take:

1. Power down your main computer and remove the system unit case.

2. Install a network interface card into an open expansion slot.

3. Close up the case, reboot the computer, and run the NIC installation software.

4. Connect your network hub to a power source.

5. Run an Ethernet cable from your main computer to the network hub.

6. Run the network configuration utility (or the Windows XP Network Setup Wizard) to set up your network.

7. Move on to the second computer in your network and repeat steps 1–3.

8. Run the network configuration utility on the second computer to connect it to your new network.

9. Repeat steps 7 and 8 for each computer on your network.

note

If your host PC has built-in Ethernet networking, you can skip steps 1–3.

After you've connected all the computers on your network, you can proceed to connect your broadband modem, as well as configure any devices (such as printers) you want to share over the network. For example, if you want to share a single printer over the network, it connects to one of the network PCs (*not* directly to the hub), and then is shared through that PC.

Upgrade #2: Creating a Wireless Network

If you don't want to run all those cables, you need a wireless network. The most popular wireless technology is Wi-Fi, which is the same type of wireless network used in large corporations—it's very stable and robust. Wi-Fi lets you connect to wireless network access points up to 150 feet away from your PC, at up to 11Mbps (or 22Mbps for the newer enhanced 802.11b).

Wireless Network Hardware and Topology

In a wireless network, the hub function is performed by a *wireless router*, sometimes called a *base station* or an *access point*. This device, like the one shown in Figure 15.5, can make both wireless and

note

Another type of wireless network is one that works through your home phone lines. Known as *HomePNA*, this type of network is losing popularity in favor of the faster Wi-Fi standard.

wired connections; most base stations include four or more Ethernet connectors, in addition to wireless capabilities.

FIGURE 15.5

A typical wire-less base station.

As shown in Figure 15.6, you connect your main PC directly to the base station using an Ethernet cable. All the other PCs in your network can connect either wire-lessly or via Ethernet.

FIGURE 15.6

Setting up a wireless network.

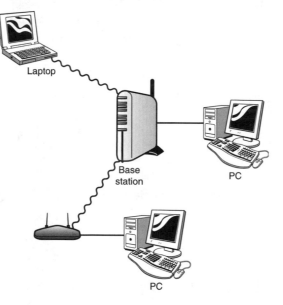

Laptop

Base station

PC

PC

The wireless PCs on your network must be connected to or contain *wireless adapters*. These devices function as mini-transmitters/receivers to communicate with the base station. Wireless adapters can be small external devices that connect to the PC via USB; expansion cards that install inside your system unit; or PC cards that insert into a portable PC's card slot.

To share a broadband connection over a wireless network, you connect your broadband modem to your wireless base station, using an Ethernet cable. The connection is then available to any PC connected to your network, wired or wireless.

Here's the hardware you'll need to set up your wireless network:

Upgrade Checklist for Wireless Networking

- ☐ Network Interface card (one for the host PC)
- ☐ Wireless network adapters (one for each client PC)
- ☐ Wireless network router/base station (one for the entire network)
- ☐ Two CAT-5 Ethernet cables (one to connect your host PC to the wireless base station, the other to connect from your broadband modem to the wireless base station)

Many newer portable PCs come with wireless functionality built in. Intel's new Centrino chip set was designed around this mobile technology.

You'll pay around $100–$150 for the wireless base station, $40–$80 for the wireless adapters, and $20 or less for the NIC. The necessary Ethernet cables are priced according to length.

The same companies who manufacture wired networking equipment also manufacture wireless networking equipment.

Making the Connections

Just as when you're setting up a wired network, you should follow the instructions that came with your wireless base station to properly set up your wireless network. In general, however, here are the steps to take:

1. Power down your main computer and remove the system unit case.
2. Install a network interface card into an open expansion slot.
3. Close up the case, reboot the computer, and run the NIC installation software.

If your host PC has built-in Ethernet networking, you can skip steps 1–3.

4. Connect your wireless base station to a power source.

5. Run an Ethernet cable from your main computer to the wireless base station.

6. Run the network configuration utility (or Windows XP's Network Setup Wizard) on your main computer to set up your network.

7. Move on to the second computer in your network and install a wireless networking adapter—either internally, via an expansion card, or externally via USB. (Or, if your second PC is a portable, insert a wireless networking PC card.)

8. Run the installation software to properly configure the wireless adapter.

9. Run the network configuration utility on the second computer to connect it to your new network.

10. Repeat steps 7 and 8 for each additional computer on your network.

After you've connected all the computers on your network, you can proceed to connect your broadband modem, as well as configure any devices (such as printers) you want to share over the network. For example, if you want to share a single printer over the network, it connects to one of the network PCs (*not* directly to the router), and then is shared through that PC.

caution

Most wireless networks include some sort of wireless security to prevent outsiders from tapping into your network computers and illicitly accessing your PCs and computer files. In many cases this security consists of a rather long and involved encrypted password or security key that must be applied to each authorized computer. Make sure you know where this setting is stored on your main PC, so that you can write it down and enter it when prompted when configuring the other computers on your network.

THE ABSOLUTE MINIMUM

When it's time to connect your computers in a network, remember these key points:

- You can use a local area network to connect all your computers, for the purpose of sharing peripherals, an Internet connection, and important files and folders.

- A wired network is your fastest option (up to 100Mbps), but involves running Ethernet cables between all your PCs and a network hub.

- A wireless network is slower (11Mbps) but easier to connect because there are no cables to run.

- In any network, all the PCs in your network connect to a central device called a hub; your broadband modem can connect directly to the hub, or through your system's gateway PC.

- The easiest way to set up a network—wired or wireless—is to purchase an all-in-one upgrade kit, which should contain all the cards, cables, and devices you need to connect two or more computers together.

16

THE FASTER THE BETTER: UPGRADING YOUR INTERNET CONNECTION

When most users say they want to speed up their computer system, what they really mean is that they want to speed up their Internet connection. Speeding up your surfing and downloading is the goal, which has nothing to do with how fast your computer is running. Upgrading to more memory or a bigger hard disk—or even buying a new system with a faster microprocessor—will not speed up your Internet sessions.

The only way to make the Internet speedier is to upgrade to a faster connection. A traditional dial-up connection just won't cut it—especially as more and more Web sites add more and larger graphics and multimedia files. Every single item on a Web page must be downloaded to your computer before you can view it, and a 56.6Kbps pipeline just isn't big enough to download everything instantaneously.

What you need, then, is what is called a *broadband* Internet connection. A broadband connection can speed up your Internet access by 10 times or more. The difference is truly amazing; with a broadband connection, surfing the Internet is actually pleasant!

Understanding Broadband Internet

Unlike connecting to the Internet via your old analog phone line, a broadband connection is an end-to-end digital connection. When you don't have to modulate and demodulate the data from digital to analog (and back again), the all-digital data can travel much faster from your computer to other points on the Web.

There are five types of digital broadband connections available today. When you want to speed up your connection, you can choose from:

- **ISDN (Integrated Services Digital Network)**. ISDN was the first digital connection technology available to home and small business users, offering speeds of 128Kbps—twice as fast as traditional dial-up. In most areas of the country, ISDN has been supplanted by the much faster (and lower-cost) DSL technology.

- **DSL (Digital Subscriber Line)**. DSL piggybacks on your existing telephone lines and provides speeds of at least 384Kbps—more typically, 500Kbps–1Mbps.

- **Digital cable**. Digital cable is the most popular form of broadband in the U.S. today. Cable modems easily connect to digital cable lines and typically offer speeds between 1Mbps–2Mbps.

- **Digital satellite**. The same company that offers DIRECTV digital satellite service via an 18-inch dish also offers DIRECWAY satellite-based Internet access. Download speeds average 400Kbps.

- **Broadband wireless access**. Also known as fixed-wireless connections, wireless broadband systems use microwave technology to transmit and receive Internet data at up to 1Mbps. Unfortunately, this technology has not been widely adopted outside of a few major cities.

Of these broadband options, three are in widespread use today: DSL, digital cable, and digital satellite. ISDN is an older technology no longer widely used; broadband wireless, at this point in time, appears to be a failed experiment with few providers and even fewer subscribers.

Choosing a Broadband Technology

Which of these broadband technologies are the best for your particular needs? You need to consider *availability* (not all types of broadband are available in all areas); *ease of installation* (you can install a cable modem yourself; DSL and satellite connections require professional installation); and *speed* (cable is fastest—although the more people in your neighborhood with cable modems, the slower your connection will be). Table 16.1 compares the basic features of the three major broadband technologies: DSL, cable, and satellite broadband.

Table 16.1   Comparison of Major Broadband Technologies

Feature	DSL	Cable	Satellite
Typical connection speed (downstream)	384Kbps–1.5Mbps	512Kbps–2Mbps	400Kbps
Typical connection speed (upstream)	384Kbps–768Kbps	128Kbps–384Kbps	128Kbps–256Kbps
Hardware required	DSL modem, network card (optional)	Cable modem	Satellite dish, modem card
Professional installation required?	Yes	Optional	Yes
Initial installation cost	0–$150	0–$100	$500–$600 (includes cost of dish)
Monthly subscription cost	$35–$50	$20–$50	$60–$100
Availability	Selected areas	Selected areas	Most areas

DSL

DSL is a phone line-based technology that doesn't require a dedicated telephone line. Most providers offer DSL service for a flat fee of $35–$50 per month, which includes standard ISP service. This gives you a high-speed broadband connection for about what you'd pay for a second phone line and a subscription to a traditional ISP.

DSL service piggybacks onto your existing phone line, turning it into a high-speed digital connection. DSL technology splits your existing phone line into three frequency bands—one for standard voice communications, one for downstream data flow, and one for upstream data flow.

There are actually several different types of DSL, each using a variation of the basic DSL technology, and each with its own acronym. The DSL technology offered to most households and small businesses today is called *ADSL (asymmetric digital subscriber line) Lite*. With ADSL Lite you have a maximum downstream speed of 1.5Mbps, and a typical upstream speed of 384Kbps.

To get DSL, you have to be within 15,000 feet or so of a phone company's switch facility (called a *central office*, or *CO*). DSL access is spreading, however, so if you can't get DSL today, wait a bit—it will be in your neighborhood soon.

For additional comparisons and more information about all types of broadband services, visit the Broadband Reports Web site (www.broadbandreports.com).

Digital Cable

The most popular type of broadband connection today is available from your local cable company—*if* your local cable company offers digital cable service, that is. If you can get it, broadband cable access is a great deal, offering a high-speed Internet connection for between $20–$50 per month. It's also the easiest of all broadband installations, involving nothing more than connecting a cable modem between your cable line and your PC.

Where DSL piggybacks over your telephone lines, cable broadband occupies a defined space (called a *tunnel*) within the signal that travels through the cable company's coaxial or fiber-optic cable. Most cable companies assign Internet signals to a 6MHz slot within the cable signal, which enables downstream speeds as high as 5Mbps. (This theoretical maximum is seldom achieved; speeds in the 500Kbps to 2Mbps range are more common.) Upstream signals are assigned to a subset of the total data tunnel, which produces slower upstream rates—typically in the 128Kbps to 384Kbps range.

The data signals are extracted from the cable line via a cable modem, which feeds directly into your computer. The modem also serves to pack your computer's data signals back into the cable signal for upstream transmission.

Digital Satellite

If neither DSL nor cable broadband is available in your area, you have another option—connecting to the Internet via satellite. Any household or business with a clear line of sight to the southern sky can receive digital data signals from a geosynchronous satellite at a downstream speed of 400Kbps. Newer two-way systems also transmit data back via satellite, at upstream rates of 128Kbps–256Kbps. Although this is slower than digital cable, it's about what you'd expect from a moderate DSL connection.

The largest provider of satellite Internet access is Hughes Network Systems. (Hughes also developed and markets the popular DIRECTV digital satellite system.) Hughes' DIRECWAY system (www.direcway.com) enables you to receive Internet signals via an 18-inch round dish that you mount outside your house or on your roof. The installation package (including dish and modem card) will set you back around $500 (before any specials), with monthly subscription fees in the $60–$100 range, depending on which usage plan you pick.

Internet service via satellite works by beaming Internet data off an orbiting satellite down to a satellite dish that is connected to your PC. It's the same digital data you get via DSL or cable, it just has to travel a lot farther to get to you—in the neighborhood of 44,000 miles, from transmission point to your PC!

When you access a Web page, the request to view that page travels (via phone line in one-way systems, or via the satellite in two-way systems) to DIRECWAY's Network Operations Center (NOC) in Maryland. The NOC sends a request to the Web page's server, and the data that makes up that page is then sent from that server back to DIRECWAY's NOC. The NOC then beams the data for the Web page up to the DIRECWAY satellite (22,000 miles up); the signal bounces off the satellite back down to your DIRECWAY dish (22,000 miles down), at 400Kbps. The signal then travels from your dish to a broadband modem in your PC.

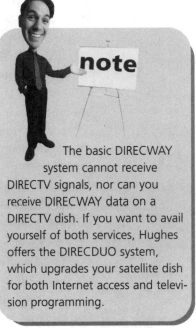

note

The basic DIRECWAY system cannot receive DIRECTV signals, nor can you receive DIRECWAY data on a DIRECTV dish. If you want to avail yourself of both services, Hughes offers the DIRECDUO system, which upgrades your satellite dish for both Internet access and television programming.

caution

Because of the huge distances involved in satellite transmission, there is some delay (called *latency*) in the receipt of the requested page. Typical latency is around 0.5 seconds, which is virtually unnoticeable when you're dealing with typical Web viewing or email communications. It could be a problem when you're playing real-time multiple-player online games, however.

Upgrade #1: Connecting to DSL Internet

Subscribing to a DSL service is one of the most complicated chores in all of computing. Not only is it something you can't do yourself, you'll probably end up dealing with three different companies to get everything up and running properly.

The reason for this is that the path from you to the Internet has been divided into three distinct areas, each of which can (and often is) provided by a different company.

The first step in this three-part path is provided by a *DSL service provider*, typically an ISP that either offers or specializes in DSL service. This company is your main contact throughout the installation process, and your only contact after you've established service.

The DSL service provider then contracts with a *Competitive Local Exchange Carrier* (*CLEC*) to obtain access to a DSL network. These companies provide a "middleman" function by bundling large volumes of DSL service to multiple ISPs.

Now it's time to get the third company involved. This happens when the CLEC contracts and coordinates with your *local telephone company* (telco) for the usage of the phone line that runs into your home or business.

So when you order an installation, you deal with the DSL ISP, who deals with the CLEC, who deals with the telco. This is why it often takes weeks or months to complete a DSL installation, and why any problems with the setup typically result in a substantial amount of finger pointing.

When your DSL line is installed (by the CLEC, after the telco confirms that your phone line is adequate for DSL service), the installer will connect a DSL modem to your computer. This is typically an external modem that connects via USB—although some companies still use DSL modems that connect via an Ethernet cable to a network interface card (NIC) installed inside your PC. The DSL line connects to this modem, installation software is run, and you should be ready to surf.

note

Some telcos, such as Verizon and SBC, offer their own DSL service and handle all steps in the process—which means you only have to deal with one company, not three.

Your part of a DSL installation? Call the DSL ISP and get the ball moving—then keep making phone calls until the process is complete.

Upgrade #2: Connecting to Digital Cable Internet

To establish a cable broadband connection, you might have to schedule a profes-sional installation from your local cable guy, although you can probably do the installation yourself. Most cable companies offer self-installation kits that include installation software, a USB cable modem, and easy-to-follow instructions. The basic installation is relatively simple, which is why you don't really need to spend $50–$100 for the cable guy to do it. (Of course, if your cable company offers the installation at no charge, there's no reason not to take advantage of their largesse!)

If you're making your own connection, follow these steps:

1. Connect a coaxial cable from the cable outlet on the wall to your cable modem.

2. Connect the cable modem to a power source.

3. Connect the cable modem to your PC's USB port, as shown in Figure 16.1.

4. Run the cable company's installation software (or run the Windows Add New Hardware Wizard) to configure the Windows network settings to recognize the new connection.

FIGURE 16.1

A typical cable
Internet
installation.

Wall
jack   Modem

PC

In a perfect world, the installation software con-figures the necessary network settings within Windows to recognize the new connection, and you're up and ready to surf—typically in less than a half hour.

Upgrade #3: Connecting to Digital Satellite Internet

Setting up a satellite connection requires the installation of a small pizza box-sized satellite dish outside your house, and the connection of a broadband modem to your PC's USB port. Although this entire installation is simple enough to be performed by

tip

You might need to install a low-cost coaxial splitter so that a single cable outlet can feed both your TV and your PC.

anyone with a minimal amount of technical and mechanical skills, you're forced into scheduling a professional installation. The FCC mandates that trained professionals (not you or me, sorry) install any two-way satellite system.

The installer will mount your dish on a wall or pole that has a clear view of the southern sky, unobstructed by trees or other objects. After the dish is aimed and tightened down, a special coaxial cable is run from the dish back inside your house. This cable connects to the broadband modem. After everything is properly connected, you run the DIRECWAY installation software to set up your system and start surfing.

Upgrade #4: Sharing a Broadband Connection

If you have more than one PC in your home, you probably want them both to be connected to your new broadband Internet connection. Fortunately, a broadband connection provides enough bandwidth to connect multiple computers to the Internet simultaneously.

There are several ways to share a broadband connection, and they all involve setting up some sort of a local area network (LAN). Which configuration you choose is dependant on how much work you want to take on, what kind of connections you want for each PC, and the type of service offered by your broadband ISP.

Home networking was covered in Chapter 15, "Connect the Dots: Upgrading to a Wired or Wireless Network."

The Bridge Configuration

The most common type of network configuration for sharing an Internet connection is called a *bridge*. In this configuration, the broadband connection is routed first to the broadband modem, and then to your network hub or router. Each PC on your network is also connected to the hub, as shown in Figure 16.2.

The chief advantage of the bridge configuration is that it's easy to set up and configure. It's also a popular configuration for users with wireless networks. (Most wireless base stations also function as network hubs or routers.)

The Combination Modem/Hub Bridge Configuration

If you have a DSL connection, some DSL modems also function as network hubs. To use a DSL modem/hub to connect multiple PCs, you create a modified bridge configuration. The broadband connection is routed directly to the modem/hub, and then each PC is connected to the modem/hub. This type of configuration is illustrated in Figure 16.3.

FIGURE 16.2

A bridge config-
uration for shar-
ing an Internet
connection.

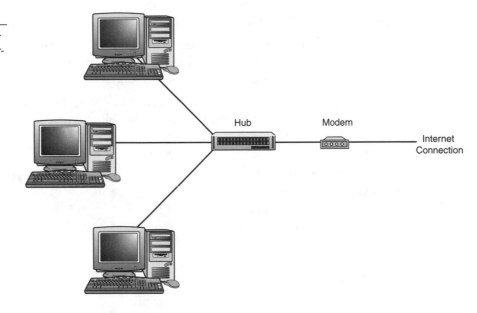

FIGURE 16.3

A bridge config-
uration using a
combination
modem/hub.

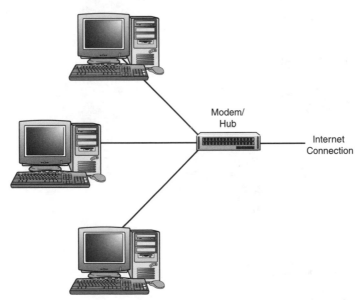

Using a modem/hub is a nice option, if offered by your DSL supplier. It's probably the easiest configuration possible, and it eliminates the need to purchase and install a separate network hub.

The Gateway Configuration

This configuration uses a lead computer as a "gateway" to the Internet. This gateway computer is the only computer on your network that is visible to the Internet, and it manages the connections for all the other PCs.

As you can see in Figure 16.4, you set up a gateway configuration by routing the broadband connection first to your broadband modem, and then to the gateway PC. The gateway PC then connects to your network hub; all your other PCs are also connected to the hub.

When you set up a small network with the Windows XP Network Setup Wizard, this is the type of network that you create. It's a very secure configuration; the gateway computer can serve as a type of firewall for the other PCs on your network. (It's also the only configuration you can use if you're sharing a dial-up connection; your dial-up modem has to be attached to a computer—*not* to a hub or router.)

caution

For a gateway configuration to work, the gateway computer has to have *two* network cards installed—one connected to the modem, and one connected to the network hub.

FIGURE 16.4

In the gateway configuration, a lead computer serves as a gateway to the Internet for all your other PCs.

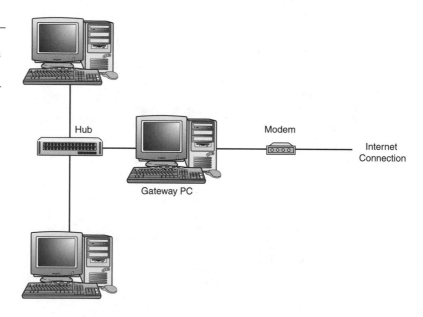

THE ABSOLUTE MINIMUM

When you want to speed up your Internet connection, keep these points in mind:

- The bottleneck in going online is your Internet connection, not your computer.

- Most users choose either a DSL or cable Internet connection, either of which is 10 times or more faster than traditional dial-up.

- Cable Internet is generally faster than DSL, and easier to install; in fact, it's the only broadband installation you can do yourself.

- DSL and digital cable aren't available everywhere, especially in rural areas; if you aren't serviced by either of these technologies, go with the DIRECWAY satellite Internet service.

- After you have broadband Internet installed, you can share your connection between multiple PCs by setting up a simple local area network.

17

OPENING NEW WINDOWS: UPGRADING TO WINDOWS XP

Microsoft updates its Windows operating system every few years—although the big releases only come once or twice a decade. The latest big release was Windows 95 (back in 1995), which was a total rewrite of the previous 3.X version of Windows. Windows 98 (which followed in 1998) was a less-significant upgrade, and Windows 98 Second Edition (in 1999) was really no more than a minor bug fix. Windows Me (released in 2000) added a few bells and whistles, but was still basically the same operating system released back in 1995.

All of these versions of Windows were targeted at individual computer users, and weren't terribly stable. (They tended to crash a lot, as you well know.) If you wanted better stability, you had to move up to the

32-bit Windows NT/2000 operating system, which was the version of Windows targeted at corporations. However, Windows NT/2000 cost a lot more than Windows 9X/Me, and wasn't as user-friendly.

Which brings us to Windows XP, which Microsoft released in 2001. Windows XP is built on the Windows 2000 engine, but includes an interface and driver support built on what was available in 9X/Me. This means that Windows XP is as stable and robust as Windows 2000, and as easy-to-use as Windows 9X/Me.

All this makes Windows XP the most important operating system release since Windows 95. Although you might not have had a good reason to upgrade to Windows 98 or Windows Me, the performance and usability improvements in Windows XP make upgrading a tempting proposition.

Why Windows XP?

The first thing you notice about Windows XP is that it looks different, as you can see in Figure 17.1. Compared to previous versions of Windows, XP features brighter colors, rounder edges, bigger buttons and icons, and a more three-dimensional look and feel. (Although, when you get past all the razzmatazz, it still looks and acts pretty much like all previous versions of Windows.)

FIGURE 17.1

The brighter, more three-dimensional look of Windows XP.

Windows XP offers some (but not a lot of) new functionality in the core of the operating system. A lot of operations that used to be accessible by right-clicking an object are now front-and-center via the context-sensitive task panes found in most folder windows. Just click a task when you want to get something done—which is much easier than right-clicking items or pulling down menus.

There are also a handful of new features in Windows XP, including a more robust media player, a digital video editor, a new instant messaging program that incorporates Internet telephony and video conferencing, and improved support for digital cameras and scanners. Most of these new features were previously available from third-party providers, but now they're built into the operating system.

But of all the changes in Windows XP, the biggest one is invisible to the eye. The guts of Windows XP aren't the same guts that were in Windows 9X/Me; instead, Windows XP uses the underlying engine that is used in the Windows 2000 operating system. The result of this switch to a 32-bit engine is that Windows XP has all the stability of Windows 2000—which means that Windows XP should crash a lot less frequently than Windows 9X/Me did.

Which Version for You?

Microsoft offers three different versions of Windows XP. *Windows XP Home Edition* is the version of XP for home and small business users. *Windows XP Professional* is designed for larger businesses and corporate users, and includes the more robust networking and system administration functions required for that environment. *Windows XP 64-Bit Edition* is designed for workstation-class applications, such as designing bridges and making professional movies.

Windows XP Home Edition includes all the functionality you need for typical home or small business use, including an improved Network Setup Wizard that makes it easy to set up small home networks or shared Internet connections. XP Home Edition is the version pre-installed on most consumer-grade PCs, and the most popular version for upgrades.

note

There's one more version of Windows XP, dubbed Windows Media Center. The Media Center is a separate interface that sits on top of the normal XP interface and makes it easier to play DVDs, listen to CDs, and the like. You can only get Windows Media Center when you buy a new Media Center PC; Microsoft won't let you upgrade your current system to the Media Center version. For more information on Windows XP Media Center, see *Absolute Beginner's Guide to Windows XP Media Center*, by Steve Kovsky, also published by Que.

Windows XP Professional is somewhat of a superset of XP Home Edition. Everything you can do with XP Home you can do with XP Pro—and then some. The additional features include things like administrative tools, group policy settings, a network monitor, Internet Information Services (IIS) Web Server, and support for the Encrypting File System (EFS)—nothing you're going to be using on a typical home or small business system.

With Windows XP 64-Bit Edition, you get support for Intel's new Itanium 64-bit processor. Suffice to say, you won't be running XP 64-Bit Edition unless you're using some sort of high-end professional workstation.

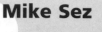

Mike Sez

Unless you're running a large network, stick to Windows XP Home Edition. Most home and small business users will never need the (few) additional features in the Professional version.

Can You Make the Upgrade?

As good as Windows XP might sound, the choice to upgrade isn't clear cut. This is primarily because Windows XP has fairly stiff system requirements, which is a result of using the Windows 2000 engine that has always required more powerful hardware to run.

To install Windows XP, you need a working CD-ROM drive hooked up to your PC, because the entire installation is done from CD. It also helps if you're connected to the Internet, as the software needs to activate itself to operate.

Mike Sez

If you have a relatively new, relatively powerful computer with a lot of memory and hard disk space, you're probably okay to upgrade. If you have a computer more than three years old, you should stick with your current operating system.

The installation itself takes about an hour. Fortunately, you don't have to stand by your PC for the entire process; after you get past the initial decision-making, you can walk away and let the installation program do its thing.

System Requirements

Like Windows NT and Windows 2000 before it, Windows XP requires some powerful hardware just to get up and running. If you have an older PC, you probably don't have the muscle to run XP. Even if you have a newer PC, you might need to add more memory to handle the overhead of the new OS.

Table 17.1 details Microsoft's recommended system requirements for Windows XP—along with my personal, more stringent recommendations.

Table 17.1   Windows XP System Requirements

	Microsoft Sez	Mike Sez
Processor type	Intel Pentium/Celeron family or AMD K6/Athlon/ Duron family	Intel Pentium III or Pentium 4, or AMD Athlon/Duron family
Processor speed	233Hz or higher	500MHz or higher
Memory	128MB	256MB
Available hard disk space	1.5GB	5GB
Video resolution	800×600	1024×768
Monitor size	No recommendation	17-inch CRT or 15-inch LCD

Fortunately, memory and hard disk storage are relatively cheap—as you know from reading this far in the book. If you have to do a little hardware upgrading to make XP run well, it won't cost you an arm and a leg.

Upgrade or Clean Install?

Installing Windows XP is much easier than installing any previous version of Windows. You have the choice of an *upgrade* installation or a *clean* installation; the latter actually reformats your hard drive before installing the new operating system. The upgrade installation is the only option available when you purchase the upgrade version of Windows XP. Both upgrade and clean installations are available when you purchase the full version of the software—which costs about twice as much.

Not every previous version of Windows has the same upgrade path, however. Check Table 17.2 to see if and how you can upgrade from your current operating system.

> **Mike Sez**
>
> For most users, the upgrade installation is the easiest—and definitely the lowest-priced—way to go.

Table 17.2   Upgrade Options for Windows XP

If you have this version of Windows	You can upgrade to this version of Windows XP
Windows 3.1	No upgrade possible; clean install required
Windows 95	No upgrade possible; clean install required
Windows 98 (first edition)	Windows XP Home Edition or Windows XP Professional
Windows 98 Second Edition (SE)	Windows XP Home Edition or Windows XP Professional

Table 17.2   (continued)

If you have this version of Windows	You can upgrade to this version of Windows XP
Windows Millennium Edition (Me)	Windows XP Home Edition or Windows XP Professional
Windows NT 3.51 Workstation	No upgrade possible; clean install required
Windows NT 4 Workstation	Windows XP Professional
Windows 2000 Professional	Windows XP Professional

In addition, you can easily upgrade from Windows XP Home Edition to Windows XP Professional.

Upgrade #1: Windows XP Typical Upgrade Installation

The upgrade installation is the easiest way to convert an old PC to Windows XP. When you make an upgrade, you install Windows XP on top of your previous version of Windows, and retain access to all your old applications and data.

Before You Upgrade

Before you upgrade to Windows XP, make the effort to download the latest version of all your key hardware drivers. Go to the manufacturer's Web site, or to DriverGuide.com (www.driverguide.com), and grab the Windows XP, Windows 2000, or Windows NT version of all your drivers. (Because XP is based on Windows NT/2000, it uses those drivers—*not* the drivers used in Windows 9X/Me.) Store these drivers in a handy folder on your hard drive, in case you need to install those drivers post-installation.

When you first start the Windows XP installation program, it runs a utility called the Windows Upgrade Advisor. This little program analyzes all the hardware and software on your system and prepares a report that lists any items that might cause problems under Windows XP.

Examine this report carefully before proceeding with the installation. If you see a critical component that Windows thinks might cause problems, cancel the installation and download any new drivers that might alleviate the problem. (Remember to get the Windows 2000 or NT drivers if specific Windows XP drivers aren't available.) If it looks like there will be more problems than you can deal with, delay the installation until you can discuss your situation with Microsoft technical support.

Installing the Software

When you've prepared yourself as best you can for any potential problems, you can proceed with the installation. Just follow these steps:

1. Insert the Windows XP CD into your CD-ROM drive. The installation program should launch automatically.

2. When the Welcome screen, shown in Figure 17.2, appears, select Install Windows XP.

FIGURE 17.2

Welcome to the Windows XP installation!

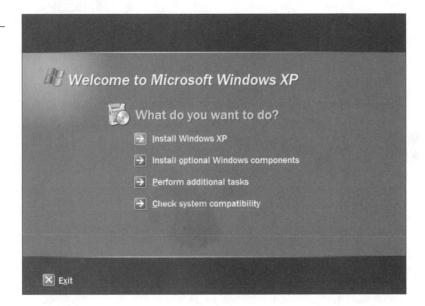

3. When the next screen appears, select Upgrade (Recommended), and then click Next.

4. When the License Agreement appears, read it (if you want), check the I Accept This Agreement option, and then click Next.

5. The next screen asks for your Product Key. This is the long, convoluted number affixed to the back of the Windows XP CD case. *Carefully* enter this number into the box, and then click Next.

6. Windows now prompts you to create an Upgrade Report, as discussed previously. Select the Show Me Hardware Issues option and click Next. Review the report to prepare yourself for any hardware-related issues that might occur.

7. When the next screen appears, you're ready to begin the installation process itself. Click Next to get things underway.

From here on out, the installation proceeds automatically; follow the onscreen instructions and make the appropriate choices when prompted. It's a slow and plodding process, but rather solid. You shouldn't run into many (if any) problems. Just be patient and wait for the entire operation to finish. Then you'll be up-and-running and ready to start using Windows XP.

After the Installation: Activating and Registering

In an attempt to discourage what Microsoft calls "casual" software piracy, the company now requires that each individual copy of XP be activated before it can be used. You're prompted to activate XP at the end of the installation process—although you can delay the activation for up to 30 days if you want. If you don't activate within 30 days, Windows will become mostly unusable, until you complete the activation.

When you follow the onscreen instructions, you'll have a choice of activating online or by phone. If you have a modem or Internet connection, choose the online option because this automates the entire procedure. No further action will be required on your part.

If you choose to activate by phone, you'll be given a 24/7 toll-free phone number to call. You'll have to provide Microsoft with the activation number that Windows XP has generated. In return, the operator will give you another number to enter into XP to complete the activation. As these numbers are extremely long, this process is a big pain in the rear. Again, choose the online activation option, if you can.

After you've activated Windows XP, you can then register the program. As with previous versions of Windows, registration is optional, and really

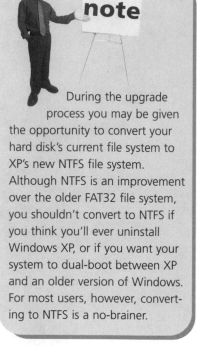

note

During the upgrade process you may be given the opportunity to convert your hard disk's current file system to XP's new NTFS file system. Although NTFS is an improvement over the older FAT32 file system, you shouldn't convert to NTFS if you think you'll ever uninstall Windows XP, or if you want your system to dual-boot between XP and an older version of Windows. For most users, however, converting to NTFS is a no-brainer.

note

To activate XP *after* the installation process, click the Start button, and then select All Programs, Accessories, System Tools, Activate Windows.

doesn't gain you much—other than access to Microsoft's technical support department. Unlike activation, if you don't register your copy of XP, it doesn't quit working.

Upgrade #2: Windows XP "Clean" Installation

As you saw in Table 17.1, some users have no choice but to do a "clean" installation of Windows XP. Other users might choose to install clean, to avoid any baggage (in terms of settings, and so on) associated with their previous operating system.

Understanding the Clean Install

What makes a clean installation so different? Simple—it wipes everything off your hard disk, reformats the disk, and then installs XP to what is now a completely clean disk. This is a rather drastic installation, as you can imagine. When you choose the clean install, you'll need to back up all your data beforehand, and reinstall all your old programs afterwards.

When is a clean installation a good idea? If your old system wasn't running right or was messed up in one way or another, a clean install makes sure that your old problems won't follow you to a new operating system. A clean installation is also called for if you were running Windows 3.1, Windows 95, or Windows NT 3.51. These versions of Windows can't be easily upgraded, so you have to start from scratch if you want to run Windows XP.

There's one other reason you might want to consider a clean installation. When you upgrade, you retain many of the files from the old operation. When you do a clean install, you don't have these old files sticking around to clutter up your hard disk. Compare the average 2.9GB size of Windows XP installed via upgrade to the 1.7GB size after a clean installation. That's a lot of wasted disk space you can recover by doing a clean install.

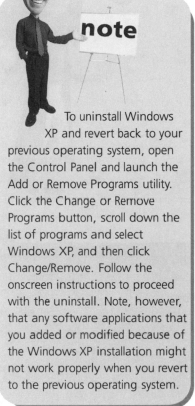

note

To uninstall Windows XP and revert back to your previous operating system, open the Control Panel and launch the Add or Remove Programs utility. Click the Change or Remove Programs button, scroll down the list of programs and select Windows XP, and then click Change/Remove. Follow the onscreen instructions to proceed with the uninstall. Note, however, that any software applications that you added or modified because of the Windows XP installation might not work properly when you revert to the previous operating system.

Making a Clean Installation

If you decide to perform a clean installation, follow these steps:

1. Close Windows and turn off your PC.

2. Insert the Windows XP CD into your CD-ROM drive and restart your PC.

3. When you see the onscreen message Press Any Key to Boot from CD, press any key on your keyboard.

4. After a minute, you'll see a list of onscreen options. Select Set Up Windows XP Now and press Enter.

5. When the License Agreement appears, read it (if you want), and then press F8 to proceed.

6. You'll now be asked how you want to partition your hard disk. Choose the Delete the Selected Partition option.

7. You're now presented with three more options. Select Setup Windows XP on the Selected Item to proceed.

8. Next, you're prompted to format the Windows XP partition. You have four options; choose Format the Partition Using NTFS. (NTFS is the new file system included with Windows XP; it's preferable to the older FAT file system.)

The installation program now begins to format your hard disk and then install the Windows XP operating system. At some point you'll need to make some configuration choices and input a variety of information—including that long Product Key located on the back of the Windows XP CD. Just follow the onscreen instructions and be sure you have a few thick magazines to read while the installation program does its thing.

caution

Be extra-sure you want to delete your partition—this step is the one that irretrievably deletes every program and piece of data on your hard drive!

caution

If you can't boot your system from the Windows XP CD, you need to reconfigure your CMOS BIOS so that your CD drive is the boot path. You do this by rebooting your PC, pressing the correct key to enter the BIOS Setup utility (see Chapter 2, "Preparing Your System for an Upgrade," for more information on getting to the BIOS), finding the boot sequence setting, and adding your CD drive to the boot sequence *before* the hard disk. With this reconfigured, you should now be able to boot from the Windows XP CD.

Upgrade #3: Updating Your Copy of Windows XP

Microsoft is constantly updating its products—so much so that the Windows XP you buy today is slightly different from the Windows XP that went on sale back in 2001. If you're running an older version of XP, you can update it to the new version by installing Service Pack 1. This software update upgrades your system to include all sorts of bug fixes and security patches, as well as adds the new features found on the version of XP currently distributed by Microsoft.

To see which version of Windows XP you have installed on your computer, open My Computer, and then select Help, About Windows. The About Windows dialog box shows the version number (it should be 5.1) and whether Service Pack 1 has been installed. (If it doesn't mention the Service Pack, it isn't installed.)

If you've purchased a new PC since fall 2002, you probably have the latest version of Windows XP with Service Pack 1 pre-installed. If you have an older version of XP, you can upgrade it with Service Pack 1 (SP1) by following these steps:

1. Click the Windows Start button and select Help and Support to open the Help and Support Center window.

2. Select Keep Your Computer Up-to-Date with Windows Update (in the Pick a Task section). Be sure you're connected to the Internet; this selection will take you online (to the Microsoft Windows Update Web site) to find out what updates are available that haven't yet been installed on your system.

3. If this is the first time you've used this feature, you'll be prompted to install Microsoft's update software before you can continue. Follow the onscreen instructions to do this.

4. Assuming you don't have Service Pack 1 installed, the Windows Update application will sense this and prompt you to

note

Service Pack 1 is the update available mid-year 2003. By the time you read this book, it's possible Microsoft might have a Service Pack 2 or 3 available; make sure you upgrade to the most recent version!

tip

You can also download SP1 directly by going to the Windows XP Service Pack 1 page, at www.microsoft.com/ WindowsXP/pro/downloads/ servicepacks/sp1/. This page is also where you order the SP1 update on CD.

download and install the Service Pack. Just follow the onscreen instructions to complete the upgrade.

THE ABSOLUTE MINIMUM

One of Microsoft's big themes for Windows XP is, "it just works." I'd have to agree with that statement. It's worth the time and effort to upgrade—if your system can cut the mustard. Just remember these key points:

- Windows XP is a 32-bit operating system that melds the stability of Windows NT/2000 with the user-friendliness of Windows 9X/Me.

- You need a relatively new and relatively powerful PC to run Windows XP— with at least a 500MHz Pentium III processor and 256MB memory.

- Three different versions of Windows XP exist. Windows XP Home Edition contains all the features you need for home and small business use and Windows XP Professional contains additional functionality for corporate networks. The third version, Windows XP 64-Bit Edition, isn't a consideration for most users—unless you have Intel's new Itanium 64-bit processor.

- You can choose to make a typical upgrade installation, or a "clean" installation—which deletes all the programs and data from your hard drive before it installs the operating system.

- Even if you're already running Windows XP, you need to keep your system updated with the latest Service Packs, which you can download and install (for free) from Microsoft's Web site.

- Choosing the right PC for your needs
- Where to buy
- Migrating your old files and settings to your new PC
- Getting rid of your old PC

18

THE BIG SWITCH: UPGRADING TO A NEW COMPUTER

Sometimes it's just not worth it to upgrade your old PC. Either the thing is too old to upgrade properly or too messed up to get straight. Or, more likely, you do the math and discover that it will cost less to buy a whole new machine than it would to upgrade your old one.

Whatever your motivation, every few years you'll find yourself upgrading your personal computer. When PC fever hits your household, you need to find the right system for your particular needs—and then figure out how to get all your old files over to the new machine.

The good news is that new PCs—even top-of-the-line models—are a lot less expensive than when you bought your last unit. The bad news is...well, there isn't a lot of bad news. Buying a new PC is a lot less painful than it used to be, as is the process of transferring all your old files and settings. In fact, the biggest challenge for most users is what to do with the old machine!

Choosing the Right PC for Your Needs

What type of PC you buy depends on how you want to use it. Using your computer to check email and surf the Web doesn't require near the horsepower than if you're playing the latest graphics-intensive multi-player games. You need to match your system requirements to the applications you plan to run.

Most computer users fall into one of the following categories:

- **Surfer**. You use your PC primarily to surf the Web and send and receive email. Your needs are minimal; a low-end (sub-$1,000) PC should suffice.

- **Worker**. You use your PC to access the Internet *and* to run traditional desktop applications, such as word processors, spreadsheets, and financial management programs. You don't need a real powerful PC for these purposes; a low-end PC should suffice—although you probably want to get a CD-R/RW drive for storing your application data.

- **Music Lover.** You use your PC as a high-tech audio system. You listen to music CDs, download music from the Internet, and even burn your own mix CDs. You need a machine with a good sound card (24-bit is nice), a quality stereo speaker system (including a subwoofer), a CD burner, and a big hard disk to hold all those MP3 files!

- **Student**. You're a blend of the surfer, the worker, and the music lover. You use the Internet to keep in touch with friends and family; use desktop applications to do homework and write reports; and listen to and burn a lot of music in your spare time. In addition, you probably use your PC to watch movies and play games when classes are done for the day. You don't need a lot of processing power for all this, but you do need a machine with a CD burner and DVD drive, and maybe even a PC camera (for all that after-school video messaging).

tip

If you're a student with a few extra bucks to spend, a PC running Windows XP Media Center is an interesting approach. This type of PC includes a built-in TV tuner and can function as an all-in-one entertainment center for the typically space-constrained dorm room.

■ **Audio/video enthusiast**. You use your computer to edit and store digital photographs, and to edit digital video movies. You want a fast processor, a big hard disk (two, ideally, with the second one dedicated to video editing), and lots of memory. You'll also want your new PC to include a FireWire connection, a DVD burner, a video capture card/device, a TV tuner, and a versatile memory card reader.

■ **Gamer**. You push your system to the limits playing all the latest PC games. You want to buy the best system you can afford, with particular attention to your video card, sound card, and speaker system. (Surround sound is a must—and the new 6.1 systems are better than old-fashioned 4.1 and 5.1 surround.) Style is probably important to you; many machines for gamers come in really cool shapes and colors.

Table 18.1 shows the type of system that best fits each of these users.

tip

Hard-core gamers should check out the ultra-high end machines available from specialty manufacturers such as Alienware (www.alienware.com), Falcon Northwest (www.falcon-nw.com), and Voodoo PC (www.voodoopc.com). A typical top-of-the-line model is tricked out with a 3GHz Pentium 4 or Athlon XP processor, 1GB RAM, multiple 120GB hard drives, 6.1 speaker system, 512MB nVidia video card, and 19-inch LCD monitor. You'll get incredible raw performance and truly unique styling, but at a price—expect to pay anywhere from $3,000 to $5,000 for one of these custom-built screamers.

Table 18.1 System Requirements for Different Users

	Surfer	Worker	Music Lover	Student	A/V Enthusiast	Gamer
Processor speed (min.)	1.5GHz	1.5GHz	1.5GHz	1.5GHz	3.0GHz	3.0GHz
Memory (min.)	256MB	256MB	256MB	256MB	512MB	512MB
Hard drive (min.)	40GB	40GB	80GB	80MB	120MB¥2	120GB
Optical drive	CD/DVD	CD-R/RW/ DVD	CD-R/RW/ DVD	CD-R/RW/ DVD	CD-R/RW/ DVD-R	CD-R/RW/ DVD
Monitor	17" CRT/ 15" LCD	17" CRT/ 15" LCD	17" CRT/ 15" LCD	17" CRT/ 15" LCD	19" CRT/ 17" LCD	19" CRT/ 17" LCD

Table 18.1   (continued)

	Surfer	Worker	Music Lover	Student	A/V Enthusiast	Gamer
Video card	Generic	Generic	Generic	64MB	128MB AGP	256MB AGP w/ 3D graphics acceleration
Sound card	Generic (16-bit)	Generic (16-bit)	24-bit	24-bit	24-bit w/ 5.1 digital output	24-bit w/ 3D audio
Speaker system	Generic	Generic	2.1 (w/ subwoofer)	2.1 (w/ subwoofer)	5.1 (w/ subwoofer)	6.1 (w/ subwoofer)
Ports	Serial, parallel, USB 2.0	Serial, parallel, USB 2.0	Serial, parallel, USB 2.0	Serial, parallel, USB 2.0	Serial, parallel, USB 2.0, FireWire	Serial, parallel, USB 2.0
Accessories	None	None	None	TV tuner card/device (optional); PC camera	Video capture card/device; TV tuner card/device; (optional) reader	Game controller; additional hard drives; memory card
Approx. price range	$500–$800	$600–$1,000	$800–$1,200	$800–$1,200	$2,000–$3,000	$2,000–$5,000

Naturally, you can add to any of these systems for your particular needs. You'll need some sort of printer (color for family use, black and white for work) and (ideally) a broadband Internet connection. In addition, if you intend to connect your new PC to a home network, you'll want to add an Ethernet card (for a wired network) or wireless network adapter (for a wireless network), along with the appropriate hub or router. Increase your budget accordingly.

> **" Mike Sez "**
>
> Keep down the purchase price of a new PC by only buying the pieces and parts that you need. If you have a perfectly serviceable monitor, purchase a new system without a monitor. Same with speakers and other peripherals; there's no reason not to reuse these parts of your old system.

Where to Buy

Just about every type of retailer carries computers these days, from Wal-Mart to CompUSA and everywhere in-between. You should buy at a retailer with which you're comfortable. Look for a decent selection of models from a variety of manufacturers, good pricing (of course), knowledgeable salespeople (harder to find), and after-the-sale service and support.

You shouldn't limit your shopping to the big-box stores, or to bricks and mortar merchants. There are lots of good deals to be had online, either direct from the manufacturer (think Dell and Gateway) or from mail-order or Web-specific retailers. You can even find good buys on brand-new (but often close-out) PCs on eBay (www.ebay.com).

If you want to stick to name brands (and why not—they're often just as low-priced as the no-names!), here are the big manufacturers to check out:

- Compaq (www.compaq.com)—owned by HP, but still a separate brand in the marketplace
- Dell (www.dell.com)—now the largest PC manufacturer in the world
- eMachines (www.emachines.com)—a good source for low-priced models
- Gateway (www.gateway.com)—like Dell, a big online/mail-order merchant
- Hewlett-Packard (www.hp.com)—offers both home and business PCs
- IBM (www.ibm.com)—specializes in PCs for large and small businesses
- Sony (www.sonystyle.com)—offers some truly innovative audio/video features
- Toshiba (www.toshiba.com)—portable PCs only

Mike Sez

When it's time to go PC shopping, do yourself a favor and do a little homework. Hit the Web for information direct from the manufacturers, and to price shop the online retailers. I recommend checking the professional equipment reviews at CNET (www.cnet.com) and the user reviews at Epinions.com (www.epinions.com). It's also worth your while to read some of the monthly computer magazines; if nothing else, browsing through the ads will give you an idea of what's available, and for how much.

Migrating Your Old Files and Settings to Your New PC

Have you ever bought a new PC, and then spent days—and *days*—trying to get your new unit configured the same way your old one was? Have you ever had to manually add all your favorites and contacts to a new installation? Have you ever searched all through your old hard disk, hunting for all the documents you created in the past few years that absolutely, positively have to be copied to your new system? Have you ever wished you'd just stuck with the old PC, because you'd spent so much time getting it configured *just so*?

Well, it isn't as hard as it used to be. There are now a number of easy ways to transfer all your files and settings from your old PC to your new one, so you won't spend an inordinate amount of time getting everything moved and configured.

Transferring Files Over a Network

If all you're concerned about is transferring your data files, the easiest thing to do is set up both your old and new PCs on a small network and manually copy the files from one machine to another. At 100Mbps speeds (for a wired network; 11Mbps for a wireless one), even the largest files transfer quickly. This is particularly easy if your old PC is already connected to the network; all you'll have to do is add your new machine to the network and you'll be ready to go.

If you're running a recent version of Windows and have adhered to Microsoft's folder management scheme, all your data files should be somewhere in the My Documents folder. Just copy this folder to your new PC, and you'll be ready to rock and roll.

Using a Commercial File Migration Program

An even better approach is to use a software program designed specifically for migrating your old files to your new machine. These programs find all your files and settings and automate the transfer process. Your part of the process involves clicking the mouse a few times; the migration program does the rest of the work.

Some of these programs require both your machines to be connected to a network; others provide the cables you need to create a direct connection between the two PCs. Make sure you understand the instructions before you buy.

When you're looking for a file and settings migration program, check out these products:

- IntelliMover (www.detto.com)
- PC Clone (www.synet.biz)
- Ultra WinLink (www.wincleaner.com)

Using Windows XP Files and Settings Transfer Wizard

If you're running Windows XP—and if you just bought a new PC, you are—then you might not need to make any additional purchase. Windows XP includes a new Files and Settings Transfer Wizard. This wizard lets you pick and choose which files and configuration settings you want to keep when you move to a new machine. It then copies those files, templates, and settings to a location on your network or to some form of removable storage (CD-R/RW or Zip disk), which you can take with you to your new machine. Then you run the wizard on the new machine, and copy your old files and settings to the new PC.

Using the Files and Settings Transfer Wizard is a two-part process. The first part involves gathering all the data and settings from your old computer; the second part is where you actually transfer those items to your new PC.

Gather Your Old Data and Settings

Start by gathering what you want to keep from your old PC:

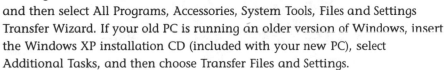

> **tip**
>
> The Files and Settings Transfer Wizard is also a good way to back up a single computer's key files and settings—just in case something goes haywire with your existing PC.

1. From your old PC, launch the Files and Settings Transfer Wizard. If your old PC is running Windows XP, click the Start button and then select All Programs, Accessories, System Tools, Files and Settings Transfer Wizard. If your old PC is running an older version of Windows, insert the Windows XP installation CD (included with your new PC), select Additional Tasks, and then choose Transfer Files and Settings.

2. When the wizard launches, click the Next button.

3. When the Which Computer Is This? screen appears, check the Old Computer option, and then click Next.

4. When the Select a Transfer Method window appears, select how you want to transfer the files—over a home network, on multiple floppy disks, or from some other removable drive (such as a Zip disk). Click Next.

5. When the What Do You Want to Transfer? screen appears (as shown in Figure 18.1), select whether you want to copy settings, files, or both.

FIGURE 18.1

Use the Files and Settings Transfer Wizard to copy all the important stuff from your old PC to your new PC.

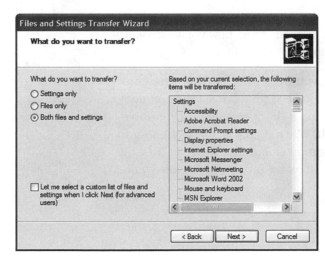

6. If you want to select specific files and settings to copy, check the Let Me Select a Custom List of Files and Settings option. When you click Next, you'll be able to select specific items to copy.

7. The wizard now collects everything it needs to copy to the new PC. This takes several minutes.

8. You'll now be prompted to insert a disk in your disk drive, or connect to the network, or do whatever is necessary to begin the transfer. Follow the onscreen instructions to complete the procedure.

Transfer Data and Settings to Your New PC

After you've gathered all these items, you have to transfer them to your new PC. Follow these steps:

1. Assuming that your new PC is running Windows XP, click the Start button and then select All Programs, Accessories, System Tools, Files and Settings Transfer Wizard.

2. When the wizard launches, click the Next button.

3. When the Which Computer Is This? screen appears, check the New Computer option, and then click Next.

4. When the Where Are the Files and Settings screen appears, select how you've stored the files, and then click Next.

The wizard now transfers the files and settings to your new computer. If you're asked to insert disks, do so. Otherwise, sit back and wait for the whole thing to finish. When it's done you might have to reboot your computer, but then it will be up and running—and looking and acting just like you're used to!

> **caution**
>
> The Files and Settings Transfer Wizard only transfers files and settings from the currently active user. So if you have more than one user assigned to your old PC, you'll have to run the wizard again for each user of the computer yo.

> **" Mike Sez "**
>
> If you're not sure what to transfer from your old PC, *transfer everything!* You can always delete stuff from your new PC if you don't need it; you can't recover something you didn't transfer, however. (And make sure that the files actually got transferred before you go deleting them from your old machine!

Getting Rid of Your Old PC

After you have your new PC set up and configured *just so*, you're faced with another problem—what to do with your old computer?

If your old PC is still working reasonably well, you might not want to get rid of it. I happen to have three working PCs in my household, with a fourth held back as a spare in case one of the others breaks down. There's no reason not to use an old PC as a dedicated Internet machine, or for your children to use for homework. And if you choose this option, it's easy to connect all your PCs together in a simple home network, as you learned in Chapter 15, "Connect the Dots: Upgrading to a Wired or Wireless Network."

If your old PC *isn't* working well, or if you just don't want to keep the boat anchor around the joint, you have a disposal issue. Although you can just throw the thing in the trash, there are a number of reasons to reconsider that decision. First, unless you've removed or reformatted the old PC's hard disk, it's possible (though unlikely) that someone could grab personal data off the old machine. Second, dumping a computer isn't environmentally sound; the monitor and circuit boards contain a number of toxic materials that need to be disposed of properly. And third, even though the old thing might be useless to you, someone less fortunate might have great use for a second-hand PC.

That said, if your PC isn't *too* old (at least a Pentium II), you should consider recycling or donating it to an appropriate organization. The first places to check are your local schools and churches; after that, there are a number of computer recycling services available, including the following:

> **caution**
>
> Before you give away your old PC, you should reformat the hard disk to make inaccessible all your old data and personal information. For instructions, see Chapter 4, "Bigger Is Better: Upgrading System Storage."

- ■ Computer Recycling Center (www.crc.org)
- ■ IBM Product Recycling Programs
    (www.ibm.com/ibm/environment/products/prp.shtml)
- ■ Share the Technology (www.sharetechnology.org)

In addition, the PEP National Directory of Computer Recycling Programs (www.microweb.com/pepsite/Recycle/recycle_index.html) offers a worldwide directory of recycling programs for old PCs.

THE ABSOLUTE MINIMUM

When your old system is no longer worth upgrading, it's time to buy a new one. Just remember these key points:

■ The type of system you buy is dependent on how you plan to use it.

■ Most casual users can get by with a relatively inexpensive model; only hard-core gamers and A/V enthusiasts have to shell out for top-of-the-line systems.

■ Transferring your old data to the new PC is facilitated by the use of third-party migration software, or the Windows XP Files and Settings Transfer Wizard.

■ When it comes to disposing of the old machine, you probably can't just throw it in the trash. Consider recycling or donating it to a worthy organization.

PART V

PREVENTING PC PROBLEMS

IN THIS CHAPTER

- Basic hardware maintenance
- Let Windows tune up your system
- Using third-party utilities
- Preparing a PC survival kit

19

SIMPLE STEPS TO KEEP YOUR SYSTEM IN TIP-TOP SHAPE

"An ounce of prevention is worth a pound of cure."

That old adage might seem trite and clichéd, but it's also true—especially when it comes to your computer system. Spending a few minutes a week on preventive maintenance can save you from costly computer problems in the future.

If you want to avoid problems with your PC system, you need to read this chapter. There are a ton of easy-to-use tools available that you can use in a regular maintenance routine—or, heaven forbid, if you ever experience problems with your computer.

Basic Hardware Maintenance

I'm a lazy guy. I think it's easier to *prevent* problems beforehand than it is to try to solve them after they occur. Let's face it—even if you're able to fix a problem, you would have saved yourself a lot of grief if you could have avoided that problem completely. It pays to spend a little time on preventive maintenance *now* if it saves you hours of problem-solving and disaster recovery *later*.

That said, let's look at some simple things you can do to reduce your chances of contracting computer problems.

System Unit

Your PC system unit has a lot of stuff inside—everything from memory chips to disk drives to power supplies. Check out these maintenance tips to keep your system unit from flaking out on you:

- Position your system unit in a clean, dust-free environment. Keep it away from direct sunlight and strong magnetic fields. In addition, make sure your system unit and your monitor have plenty of air flow around them, to keep them from overheating.

- Hook your system unit up to a surge suppressor to avoid deadly power spikes.

- Avoid turning your system unit on and off too often; it's better to leave it on all the time than incur frequent "power on" stress to all those delicate components. However...

- Turn off your system unit if you're going to be away for an extended period—anything longer than a day or two.

- Check all your cable connections periodically. Make sure all the connectors are firmly connected, and all the screws properly screwed—and make sure your cables aren't stretched too tight, or bent in ways that could damage the wires inside.

- If you're really adventurous, open up the system case periodically and vacuum or wipe the dust from the inside. (Just make sure the system unit is unplugged at the time!) Using a can of "compressed air" is also a good way to blast the dirt out of your system. You should also "dust" the inside of your CD-ROM drive, and even use a swab or commercial cleaner to clean the laser lens.

Keyboard

Even something as simple as your keyboard requires a little preventive maintenance from time to time. Check out these tips:

- Keep your keyboard away from young children and pets—they can get dirt and hair and Silly Putty™ all over the place, and have a tendency to put way too much pressure on the keys.

- Keep your keyboard away from dust, dirt, smoke, direct sunlight, and other harmful environmental stuff. You might even consider putting a dust cover on your keyboard when it's not in use.

- Use a small vacuum cleaner to periodically sweep the dirt from your keyboard. (Alternately, you can use compressed air to *blow* the dirt away.) Use a cotton swab or soft cloth to clean between the keys. If necessary, remove the keycaps to clean the switches underneath.

- If you spill something on your keyboard, disconnect it immediately and wipe up the spill. Use a soft cloth to get between the keys; if necessary, use a screwdriver to pop off the keycaps and wipe up any seepage underneath. Let the keyboard dry thoroughly before trying to use it again.

Mouse

If you're a heavy Windows user, you probably put thousands of miles a year on your mouse. Just like a car tire, anything turning over that often needs a little tender loving care. Check out these mouse maintenance tips:

If you have an optical mouse, you can skip these steps; there aren't any mouse balls to clean!

- Periodically open up the bottom of your mouse and remove the roller ball. Wash the ball with water (or perhaps a mild detergent). Use a soft cloth to dry the ball before reinserting it.

- While your mouse ball is removed, use compressed air or a cotton swab to clean dust and dirt from the inside of your mouse. (In extreme cases, you might need to use tweezers to pull lint and hair out of your mouse—or use a small knife to scrape packed crud from the rollers.)

- Always use a mouse pad—they really do help keep things rolling smoothly, plus they give you good traction. (And while you're at it, don't forget to clean your mouse pad with a little spray cleaner—it can get dirty, too.)

Monitor

If you think of your monitor as a little television set, you're on the right track. Just treat your monitor as you do your TV and you'll be okay. That said, look at these preventive maintenance tips:

- As with all other important system components, keep your monitor away from direct sunlight, dust, and smoke. Make sure it has plenty of ventilation, especially around the back; don't cover the rear cooling vents with paper or any other object, and don't set anything bigger than a small plush toy on top of the cabinet.

- Don't place any strong magnets in close proximity to your monitor. (This includes external speakers!)

- *With your monitor turned off*, periodically clean the monitor screen. Spray standard glass cleaner on a soft cloth (anti-static type, if possible) and then wipe the screen clean.

- Don't forget to adjust the brightness and contrast controls on your monitor every now and then. Any controls can get out of whack—plus, your monitor's performance will change as it ages, and simple adjustments can often keep it looking as good as new.

Printer

Your printer is a complex device with a lot of moving parts. Follow these tips to keep your printouts in good shape:

- Use a soft cloth, mini-vacuum cleaner, and/or compressed air to clean the inside and outside of your printer on a periodic basis. In particular, make sure you clean the paper path of all paper shavings and dust.

- If you have an ink-jet printer, periodically clean the ink jets. Run your printer's cartridge cleaning utility, or use a small pin to make sure they don't get clogged.

- If you have a laser printer, replace the toner cartridge as needed. When you replace the cartridge, remember to clean the printer cleaning bar and other related parts.

- *Don't* use alcohol or other solvents to clean any rubber or plastic parts—you'll do more harm than good!

Let Windows Tune Up Your System

Windows includes several utilities to help you keep your system running smoothly. These utilities are mainly unchanged since Windows 98, when Microsoft completely overhauled almost all the Windows system maintenance features.

One thing that *did* change in Windows XP is that some of these system tools are a little easier to get to. Although you can still find most of these tools by clicking Start, All Programs, Accessories, System Tools (which is how it works with Windows 98/Me), you can also find some of the key tools in the Help and Support Center, which is accessible from the Start menu. Just click the Use Tools to View Your Computer Information link in the main Help and Support window, and Windows displays a list of the most popular support tools.

The next few sections discuss these built-in system maintenance utilities. (And the best thing is— they're all free!)

> **tip**
>
> The Help and Support Center is the *only* place to find some of the most popular tools in Windows XP. If you're looking for a tool or utility that used to be on the System Tools menu and isn't there anymore, open the Help and Support Center and look for it there.

Make Your Hard Disk Run Better by Defragmenting

File fragmentation is sort of like taking the pieces of a jigsaw puzzle and storing them in different boxes along with pieces from other puzzles. The more dispersed the pieces are, the longer it takes to put the puzzle together. Spreading the bits and pieces of a file around your hard disk occurs whenever you install, delete, or run an application, or when you edit, move, copy, or delete a file.

If you notice your system takes longer and longer to open and close files or run applications, it's because these file fragments are spread all over the place. You fix the problem when you put all the pieces of the puzzle back in the right boxes— which you do by *defragmenting* your hard disk.

Use the Windows Disk Defragmenter utility to defragment your hard drive. In Windows XP, you should follow these steps:

1. Click the Start button and select All Programs, Accessories, System Tools, Disk Defragmenter to open the Disk Defragmenter utility, shown in Figure 19.1.

2. Select the drive you want to defragment, typically drive C:.

3. Click the Defragment button.

19.1

Use Disk Defragmenter to make your hard drive run faster.

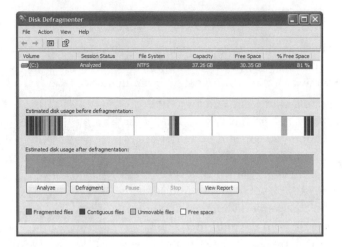

Defragmenting your drive can take awhile, especially if you have a large hard drive or your drive is really fragmented. So, you might want to start the utility and let it run while you are at lunch.

Performing a Hard Disk Checkup with ScanDisk

Any time you run an application, move or delete a file, or accidentally turn the power off while the system is running, you run the risk of introducing errors to your hard disk. These errors can make it harder to open files, slow down your hard disk, or cause your system to freeze when you open or save a file or an application.

> **caution**
>
> You should close all applications—including your screensaver—and stop working on your system while Disk Defragmenter is running.

Fortunately, you can find and fix most of these errors directly from within Windows. All you have to do is run the built-in ScanDisk utility.

To find and fix errors on your hard drive from Windows XP, follow these steps:

1. Open the My Computer folder and right-click the icon for the drive you want to scan, and then select the Properties option from the pop-up menu.

2. When the Properties dialog box appears, select the Tools tab.

3. Click the Check Now button to display the Check Disk dialog box, shown in Figure 19.2.

4. Check both the options (Automatically Fix File System Errors and Scan for and Attempt Recovery of Bad Sectors).

5. Click Start.

Windows now scans your hard disk and attempts to fix any errors it encounters.

Delete Unnecessary Files with Disk Cleanup

Even with today's humongous hard disks, you can still end up with too many useless files taking up too much hard disk space. Fortunately, Windows includes a utility that identifies and deletes unused files on your hard disk—automatically.

In older versions of Windows, you open ScanDisk by clicking the Start button and selecting Programs, Accessories, System Tools, ScanDisk.

Disk Cleanup is a great tool to use when you want to free up extra hard disk space for more frequently used files. To use Disk Cleanup in Windows XP, follow these steps:

1. Click the Start button and select All Programs, Accessories, System Tools, Disk Cleanup.

2. Disk Cleanup starts and automatically analyzes the contents of your hard disk drive.

3. When Disk Cleanup is finished analyzing, it presents its results in the Disk Cleanup dialog box, shown in Figure 19.3.

4. Select the Disk Cleanup tab.

5. You now have the option of permanently deleting various types of files. Depending on how your system is configured, this list might include downloaded program files, temporary Internet files, deleted files in the Recycle Bin, setup log files, temporary files, WebClient/Publisher temporary files, and catalog files for the Content Indexer. Select which files you want to delete.

6. Click OK to begin deleting.

Mike Sez

You can safely choose to delete all these files *except* the setup log and Content Indexer files.

FIGURE 19.3

Use Disk
Cleanup to
delete unused
files from your
hard disk.

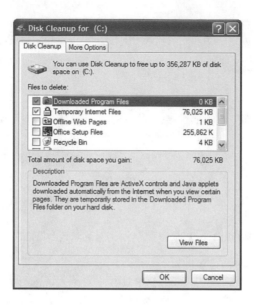

Scheduling Your Maintenance

If you can never seem to find time to run basic
system maintenance, you should be glad that
Windows includes a Scheduled Tasks utility. This
utility lets you automatically run various system
maintenance tasks—including Disk Defragmenter
and Disk Cleanup—while you're away from your
computer.

To use this utility in Windows XP, click the Start
button, and then select All Programs, Accessories,
System Tools, Scheduled Tasks. (In older version of
Windows, this utility is called the Maintenance
Wizard.) When the Scheduled Tasks window
opens, click the Add Scheduled Task icon. This
launches the Scheduled Task Wizard. Follow the
onscreen instructions to add a scheduled task.

caution

For a scheduled task to
run, your computer has
to be turned on during
the scheduled mainte-
nance periods. Windows
will not turn on your PC for you! If
your PC is turned off when maintenance is scheduled, the Scheduled
Task utility simply skips that scheduled activity.

Update Important Files with Windows Update

Windows is constantly changing. Microsoft often releases updated versions of critical
system files to improve performance or fix bugs; peripheral manufacturers often
issue updated versions of their driver files.

If you want to keep your operating system up-to-date, you can go online to Microsoft's official Web site every few days and look for bug fixes, patches, and other updates, and then manually download and install the new items as they come available.

Or you can let Windows do it for you.

Windows Update is the online extension of Windows XP that helps you to keep your operating system up-to-date. When Windows Update is activated, it will periodically go online and check in with the main Windows Update Web site. It will notify you if any new updates are available. You can choose to download the updates, and install them.

Getting Automatic Updates

By default, Windows Update will run in the background and use the Internet to check for updated system files. It will then automatically download and install those files on your PC.

Windows Update runs once a day, when it goes online and checks the Microsoft Web site for updates to the basic operating system. If it finds an update, it downloads the files automatically. After the files are downloaded, you'll be prompted to install them. (So it's not totally automatic—it's good to have at least a little choice in the matter!)

> **tip**
>
> You can turn off the automatic updating by opening the System Properties dialog box (from the Control Panel, select Performance and Maintenance, and then System), selecting the Automatic Updates tab, and making the appropriate changes.

Updating Manually

You also can choose to use Windows Update manually—just click the Start button and then select All Programs, Windows Update. You'll now be connected to the Internet and taken to the Windows Update Web site.

The site installs the latest version of its software on your PC, and then proceeds to scan your computer. Click the Scan for Updates option and you'll then be provided with a list of updates that are available for your particular system. Follow the onscreen instructions to install specific updates.

Using Third-Party Utilities

As neat as Windows' built-in utilities are, they don't do everything your system might need done. For those occasions where you need more specialized software help, you might need a third-party utility to get the job done.

I won't go into details about all the maintenance programs on the market today—there are just too many of them! I will, however, draw your attention to some of the most popular utility suites that offer a variety of different maintenance programs in a single package:

- CheckIt Diagnostics (www.smithmicro.com)
- Norton SystemWorks (www.symantec.com)
- System Mechanic (www.iolo.com)
- Ultra WinCleaner Utility Suite (www.wincleaner.com)
- VCOM SystemSuite (www.v-com.com)

Preparing a PC Survival Kit

If you're a worrisome type, you're probably convinced that a PC disaster is just around the corner—and you're wondering what in the world you can do to prepare for such a catastrophe. Well, one of the most important things you can do is to plan for that eventuality by preparing a PC Survival Kit.

The contents of your PC Survival Kit will prove indispensable if you are to recover your system after a complete or partial hard disk crash. In other words, these items are required accessories for every cautious PC user.

The good news is, you probably already have all of these items close at hand. What kinds of things are we talking about? Here's a checklist of the items you need to prepare:

PC Survival Kit Checklist

- ☐ Original Windows installation CD
- ☐ Windows Emergency Startup Disk
- ☐ Set of backup data
- ☐ Original installation CDs for all your software programs
- ☐ Disk utility software

Original Windows Installation CD

Your original Windows installation CD is the most important part of your PC Survival Kit—no matter which version of Windows you're running.

The reason is simple. If your hard disk gets trashed, you'll need to reinstall Windows. And the best way to reinstall Windows is from the original Windows installation CD. (This is preferable to spending the money for a new copy of Windows, of course.)

In addition, from Windows 98 on, you use the Windows installation CD to boot your computer, on the occasion where your hard disk is trashed or otherwise inaccessible. So if your computer can't start by itself, all you have to do is insert the Windows installation CD, restart your PC, and your system should boot up from there.

caution

Just having the Windows installation CD isn't quite good enough. You also need to have the CD case, in order to access the product key needed to reinstall the software. The CD without the product key is practically useless!

Windows Emergency Startup Disk

Okay, I know I just said that (from Windows 98 on) you can boot your computer from the Windows installation CD. That is definitely the preferred approach when you can't boot from your hard disk. However, if you for some reason can't access your CD-ROM drive, you need another option. (And if you have a pre-Windows 98 PC, booting from CD isn't an option, anyway.)

For that reason, you need to create a Windows Emergency Startup Disk. It's easy to do, and it could be a real lifesaver in the event of a catastrophic problem.

To create an Emergency Startup Disk, you must instruct Windows to format a bootable disk. Just follow these instructions:

1. Insert a blank disk into your PC's disk drive.
2. Open My Computer.
3. Right-click the disk drive icon and select Format from the pop-up menu.
4. When the Format dialog box appears, check the Create an MS-DOS Startup Disk option.
5. Click Start.

To use the Windows Emergency Startup Disk, insert it into your PC's A: drive, and then turn on your machine. Your PC should start and, after some simple system diagnostics, display an A:\ prompt. From here you can use simple disk utilities (such as ScanDisk) to diagnose problems and hopefully get your system up and running again.

Backup Data

Now we come to the part of the PC Survival Kit that requires a bit of work on your part—making backup copies of all your important data.

The best way to protect yourself against catastrophic data loss is to make backup copies of all your important files. That means all your Word and Excel documents, Quicken or Microsoft Money financial records, MP3 audio files, digital photographs, and so on—everything you have stored on your hard disk that you can't (or don't want to) re-create from scratch.

After you get in the habit of doing it, it's relatively easy to make backup copies of these files. All you need is a file backup program (such as Microsoft Backup, included free with Windows) and some sort of backup media. This type of storage needs to be large (because you'll be backing up *lots* of files) and relatively inexpensive. In the old days, serious users gravitated to removable tape cartridges as backup media; today, CD-RW discs are much preferred.

If your backup needs are more sophisticated than what Microsoft Backup can achieve, check out Handy Backup (www.handybackup.com), NTI Backup Now (www.ntius.com), or Retrospect Backup (www.dantz.com). Or you can use an *online backup* service, which lets you back up your files online to a separate Internet site; this way, if your house burns down, your key files are safely stored offsite. Some of the more popular online backup services include @Backup (www.backup.com), Connected (www.connected.com), IBackup (www.ibackup.com), and Xdrive (www.xdrive.com).

Making a Backup with Microsoft Backup

Microsoft Backup is a Windows utility that lets you store your backup files on floppy disks, backup tapes, Zip disks, or CD-RW discs. If you ever happen to have a hard drive crash, you can also use Microsoft Backup to restore your backed-up files from your backup copies, and thus minimize your data loss.

To back up your data with Microsoft Backup, follow these steps:

1. From within My Computer, right-click the drive you want to back up, and then select Properties from the pop-up menu.

2. When the Properties dialog box appears, select the Tools tab.

3. Click the Backup Now button to launch the Backup or Restore Wizard.

4. Click the Next button.

5. Check the Back Up Files and Settings option and click Next. This displays the What to Back Up screen, shown in Figure 19.4.

6. Select the files you want to back up: your personal documents and settings, everybody's documents and settings, all data on this computer, or specific files that you select (the Let Me Choose What to Back Up option). Most users back up either their own personal data or (if you've configured your system for multiple users) everyone's data. Click Next when you're done selecting.

7. Select the specific backup device, and then click Next.

8. You'll now be prompted to insert the appropriate backup media; follow the balance of the onscreen instructions to complete the backup.

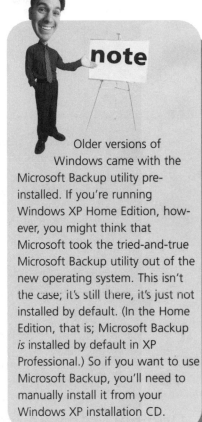

note

Older versions of Windows came with the Microsoft Backup utility pre-installed. If you're running Windows XP Home Edition, however, you might think that Microsoft took the tried-and-true Microsoft Backup utility out of the new operating system. This isn't the case; it's still there, it's just not installed by default. (In the Home Edition, that is; Microsoft Backup *is* installed by default in XP Professional.) So if you want to use Microsoft Backup, you'll need to manually install it from your Windows XP installation CD.

FIGURE 19.4

Use the Microsoft Backup utility to back up important data files from your hard drive.

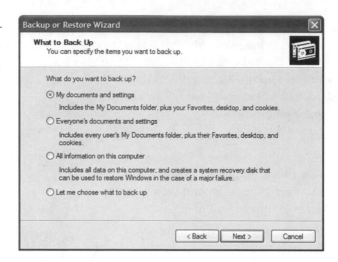

Restoring Files from a Backup

If you ever need to restore files from a backup, you do it from the same Backup or Restore Wizard. In this instance, when you get to the second screen, select the Restore Files and Settings option.

The wizard will now display the What to Restore screen. Select which files and folders you want to restore, and then click the Next button. You'll be prompted to insert your backup copies; follow the onscreen instructions to copy your backup files back to their original locations.

Original Software Installation Media

In the event of a hard disk crash, you'll lose everything on your hard disk—including all your software programs. Although you should be able to restore your data files from a backup (see the section previous), you probably didn't back up all the contents of your hard disk—in particular, your programs.

tip

Make sure you keep your backup copies in a safe place—and, ideally, in a *different* place from your computer, like in a safe deposit box or at a neighbor's house. This way, if your computer is damaged as part of a larger disaster (fire, flood, or something similarly dire), your backup data will still be safe.

This means that, if your hard disk crashes, you'll need to reinstall all your software programs. Of course, you can only do this if you hang on to all your old software installation CDs. And remember to keep the software packages and instruction manuals, as well—in case you need to access any appropriate installation codes or passwords.

Useful Disk Utilities

Now, if you really want to play it safe, include in your survival kit at least one of the third-party disk utility programs we talked about earlier in this chapter. You can use these utilities to repair most of the damage your hard disk might incur in a crash.

caution

The files you restore from a backup might not be the most recent versions of those files, especially if the original files were used anytime after your most recent backup. Still, recovering a slightly older version of a file is better than not having any version of that file at all.

THE ABSOLUTE MINIMUM

Here are the key points to remember from this chapter:

- Dedicating a few minutes a week to PC maintenance can prevent serious problems from occurring in the future.
- To delete unused files from your hard disk, use the Disk Cleanup utility.
- To defragment a fragmented hard disk, use the Disk Defragmenter utility.
- To find and fix hard disk errors, use the ScanDisk utility.
- Other useful third-party utilities include Norton SystemWorks and CheckIt Diagnostics.
- To prepare for any future problems, make sure you have a PC Survival Kit prepared, consisting of your original Windows installation CD, a Windows Emergency Startup Disk, a set of backup data, the original installation CDs for all your software programs, and appropriate disk utility software.

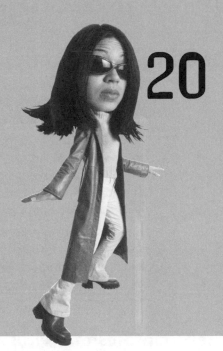

20

PROTECTING YOUR COMPUTER FROM VIRUSES AND INTERNET ATTACKS

When you connect your PC to the Internet, you open up your computer to a whole new world of potential dangers. That's because the Internet is how most computer viruses are transmitted today—and how unscrupulous hackers and crackers can attack your system from half a world away.

The good news is that most Internet users are well intentioned. The bad news is the few miscreants out there can cause a lot of damage. Read on to learn about the real dangers you might find online—and how to protect against them.

Dealing with Computer Viruses

A computer virus actually is similar in many ways to a biological virus. A biological virus invades your body's system and replicates itself; likewise, a computer virus invades your computer's system and also replicates itself—and, in the process, causes untold damage.

Unlike biological viruses, a computer virus is not a living thing. A computer virus is actually a rogue computer program that injects copies of itself into other programs on your computer system. Viruses typically invade executable program and system files—the very heart of your computer system.

Some viruses merely display an annoying message on your screen or send unwanted emails to everyone on your contact list; other more deadly viruses actually destroy your software programs or system information. The worst of this loathsome bunch are difficult both to detect and to dislodge, because they craftily conceal themselves from observation and doggedly defend against removal.

The Symptoms of a Virus

How do you know whether your computer system has been infected with a virus?

Maybe your system starts performing an action totally on its own—such as sending rogue email messages to people in your personal address book. Perhaps a normally well-behaved program starts to operate erratically or crash intermittently. Maybe a file or two turns up missing, or becomes somehow corrupted. Or maybe you notice that your system is acting a tad sluggish—or, even worse, it crashes or fails to start.

If your computer exhibits one or more of these symptoms—and if you've been online sometime in the past few days—the prognosis is not good. Your system has probably been infected.

How to Catch a Virus

Whenever you share data with another computer or computer user, you risk exposing your computer to potential viruses.

In the old pre-Internet days, viruses were most often spread by users swapping files on disks. The virus file hitched a ride on the disk, and was copied to the second PC when the user accessed the files on the disk.

Today, it's more likely that if you're going to get a virus, you'll get it from the Internet. You can catch a virus from files that you download from Web and FTP sites, or by opening attachments to email and newsgroup messages.

That said, the most likely way to catch a virus today is via email—specifically, email attachments. Users unknowingly infect their systems when they open executable files attached to email messages; the message itself is harmless, as is the attached file—until you click the attachment and run the program. If you ignore the attachment, no harm is done. If you delete the attachment, no harm is done. Harm only ensues when you activate the .EXE or .VBS or .COM or .BAT or .PIF file attached to the message.

Different Types of Viruses

Literally thousands of different viruses have been detected to date. These viruses fall into several major categories, depending on what they do and how they do it. Table 20.1 details the most common types of viruses.

Table 20.1   Common Types of Viruses

Category	Description
Worm	This type of virus spreads copies of itself without any user interaction. Viruses that take control of your computer and email themselves to other users are worms—and can spread like rabbits in heat.
Macro virus	This type of virus infects data files, such as Word or Excel files. These viruses rely on the pseudo-programming code in application documents to perform specific operations in the background when you load a document into your application program.
Trojan Horse	A Trojan Horse is a program that pretends to be another benign type of program but is actually a virus in disguise. This type of program enters your system under the guise of peace, but then goes to war when you're least expecting it—similar to the Trojan Horse of legend.
Script virus	These viruses are written in one of the script languages (Java, ActiveX, or VBScript) used to create certain Web pages and email messages, and are activated when the script is run. Virus-infected VBScript files attached to email messages are probably the most common means of virus distribution today.

Protecting Your System from Infection

The only sure-fire way to avoid the threat of computer viruses is to never use the Internet, never share disks, and never install a new piece of software on your PC. You can, however, be proactive in reducing the chance of downloading a virus from the Internet by following these words of advice:

- **Don't open email attachments from people you don't know.** If you get an unsolicited email message from someone you've never heard of before, and that message includes an attachment (a Word document, or an executable program), *don't open the attachment!* The attached Word file could contain a macro virus, and the attached program could wipe out your entire hard disk!

- **Don't run any executable programs attached to email messages.** This is an extension of the previous item. It's good practice to *never* run any email attachments that have the following file extensions: .EXE, .COM, .BAT, .VBS, or .PIF.

- **Don't execute programs you find in Usenet newsgroups.** Newsgroup postings often contain attachments of various types; executing a program "blind" from an anonymous newsgroup poster is just asking for trouble.

- **Don't accept files from people in chat rooms.** Chat rooms are another big source of virus infection; some users like to send pictures and other files back and forth, and it's relatively easy to sneak a virus file into the flow.

- **Download programs only from reliable sources.** If you're connecting to a non-commercial Web site run out of some guy's basement, avoid the temptation to download any files from that site. If you must download files from the Internet, use only those established and reliable Web sites that actually check their files for viruses before they post them for downloading. These sites include Download.com (www.download.com), Tucows (www.tucows.com), or the ZDNet Software Library (www.zdnet.com).

tip

Virus files can only infect your computer when they're run, typically when you click or double-click them from within the email message to which they're attached. They do no harm until they're run, which means receiving a virus-carrying email message in your inbox is completely safe—unless and until you open the attachment.

caution

Some email programs can be configured to not show file extensions. Virus creators take advantage of this by including .TXT or .DOC within the name of the virus file. If the actual .VBS or .EXE file extension is hidden by your email program, you can be tricked into thinking that you're opening a text or Word file, when you're actually running an executable program or script.

■ **Use antivirus software.** Antivirus programs protect you against all types of viruses—including both executable and macro viruses. Purchase, install, and run a program such as Norton AntiVirus or McAfee VirusScan—and let the antivirus program check all new files downloaded to or copied to your system.

Is it possible to completely protect your system against computer viruses? Unfortunately, the answer is no—unless you never add another piece of software (even *new* software) to your system, never accept disks from strangers, and never access the Internet, not even for email. That doesn't mean you have to live the rest of your computing life in fear, but it does mean you should take whatever precautions are prudent to reduce your risk factors.

> **caution**
>
> Here's a non-Internet piece of antivirus advice: If you must share disks and CD-ROMs with other users, do so only with those users that you know and trust. If you don't know where a disk comes from, don't stick it in your disk drive.

Using an Antivirus Program

Antivirus software programs are capable of detecting known viruses and protecting your system against new, unknown viruses. These programs check your system for viruses each time your system is booted—and can be configured to check any programs you download from the Internet, as well.

The most popular antivirus programs are

■ Command AntiVirus (www.commandsoftware.com)

■ Kaspersky Anti-Virus Personal (www.kaspersky.com)

■ McAfee VirusScan (www.mcafee.com)

■ Norton AntiVirus (www.symantec.com)

■ PC-cillin (www.trendmicro.com)

Whichever antivirus program you choose, you'll need to go online periodically to update the virus definition database that the program uses to look for known virus files. As new viruses are created every week, this file of known viruses must be updated accordingly.

Recovering from a Virus Infection

What should you do if your computer has been infected by a virus? A lot depends on the type of virus you've been blessed with, and the damage that it has done.

If your system is still working and you have full access to your hard disk, you can use one of the antivirus programs to clean infected files on your system. You can also go online and access either the Symantec or McAfee Web sites. From there you should be able to search (by symptom) for the particular virus infecting your system, and in many cases download a "fix" specific to that virus. These fix files will remove the specific virus from your system, and (if possible) repair damaged files.

If you can't start your system or access your hard disk, you'll need to restart your computer using your Windows installation CD and then repair/rebuild/restore your hard disk. After your system is up and running again, run an antivirus program to perform additional cleaning.

Know, however, that one of the dangers of catching a virus is that you might lose key data files. If your system has been hit hard, you might have to essentially start from scratch with a fresh system—losing any data that wasn't previously backed up.

Dealing with Internet Attacks

Connecting to the Internet is a two-way street—your computer is connected to the global network, and the global network is connected to your computer. That means that not only can your PC access other computers on the Web, but other computers can also access your PC.

If other users can access your computer, they can also take that opportunity to read your private data, damage your system hardware and software, and even use your system (via remote control) to cause damage to other computers. This risk is even more pronounced if you have an always-on connection, like that offered with DSL, cable modems, and other broadband providers.

This is not an idle risk. Hackers can and do access household-based personal computers—and are a real threat to the security of your system.

Potential Threats

Just what kind of damage can be done by someone who hacks into your system? It's a long and scary list, including the following:

- Steal your account information
- Read, copy, damage, or delete your personal data or data files
- Infect your system with computer viruses
- Hijack your computer and use it to carry out other attacks

Is your computer at risk for these types of attacks? If you have a persistent broadband connection, the answer is yes. Without proper security, the typical PC connected via DSL or cable modem will be probed several times a day by potential hackers. It's hard to believe, but it's true; the odds are that your system *will* be hacked, unless you take the proper precautions.

Protecting Your System with a Firewall

How do you protect your computer from unwanted intrusions?

You *could* disconnect your computer from the Internet, but that wouldn't be very practical. A better solution is to install a software utility, called a *firewall*, that can ward off these uninvited attacks.

A firewall is a software utility that forms a virtual barrier between your computer and the Internet. The firewall selectively filters the data that is passed between both ends of the connection, and protects your system against outside attack.

Firewalls designed for home and small business PCs (so-called *personal firewalls*) work by trying to make your computer invisible to other computers on the Internet; if hackers looking for IP addresses don't see your PC's address, the odds of attack are decreased, thus decreasing your chances for attack.

The firewall software does this by creating a type of *proxy server*. As shown in Figure 20.1, the firewall software acts as a type of virtual server that is inserted between your gateway PC and the Internet. The PCs in your home network interact with the proxy server, not directly with the Internet; the firewall acts as a gatekeeper, blocking access to your system by those computers that shouldn't have access.

FIGURE 20.1
A firewall acts as
a barrier
between your
home computer
and the Internet.

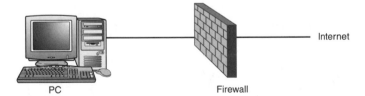

PC   Firewall   Internet

Popular Firewall Software

PC-based firewall software is low cost, easy to install, and operates in the background whenever you start your computer and connect to the Internet. The best of these programs not only block unauthorized access, but also create a log of all computers that try to hack into your system—and alert you of any successful attempts.

Among the most popular firewall programs for the home are

- BlackICE PC Protection (www.iss.net/solutions/home_office/)
- Kerio Personal Firewall (www.kerio.com)
- McAfee Personal Firewall (www.mcafee.com)
- Norton Personal Firewall (www.symantec.com)
- Sygate Personal Firewall (www.sygate.com)
- ZoneAlarm (www.symantec.com)

tip

After you have your firewall software installed and up and running, you can test its effectiveness at any of the following security Web sites: HackerWhacker (www.hackerwhacker.com), Secure-Me (www.broadbandreports.com/r3/dsl/secureme/), Shields UP! (www.grc.com), and Symantec Security Check (security.norton.com).

Using the Windows XP Internet Connection Firewall

If you're running Windows XP, you already have a firewall program installed on your system. You can make sure that Windows's Internet Connection Firewall is activated by following these steps:

1. Open the Windows Control panel and select Network and Internet Connections, and then Network Connections, to open the Network Connections folder.

2. Right-click the connection you use for your ISP and select Properties from the pop-up menu; this displays the Properties dialog box.

3. Select the Advanced tab.

4. Make sure that the Internet Connection Firewall option is checked.

THE ABSOLUTE MINIMUM

Here are the key points to remember from this chapter:

- Computer viruses are rogue programs that can damage or delete files on your computer—including key operating system files.

- Avoid computer viruses by not opening any unsolicited email attachments you receive, and by not unnecessarily sharing disks and CD-ROMs with other users.

- Any computer with a broadband Internet connection is at risk of malicious hacker attacks.

- Protect your computer from Internet-based attack by using a firewall software program—such as the Windows XP Internet Connection Firewall.

PART VI

TROUBLESHOOTING COMMON PROBLEMS

21

How to Deal with a Finicky PC

It doesn't matter how expensive your computer is, or how diligent you are. Computer problems happen.

Some of these problems are nothing more than minor annoyances. (You lose a few hour's worth of work on a Word document.) Some are major catastrophes. (You lose your entire hard disk.) All of them have to be dealt with, one way or another.

Dealing with a computer problem is a matter of understanding what could have gone wrong, and then working logically through a step-by-step process to pinpoint the most probable cause. After you know what caused your problem, it's easy enough (in most instances) to fix what is wrong.

Consider this chapter a primer on basic troubleshooting techniques. Follow these general instructions, and you'll be back up and running in no time!

Common Causes for Common Problems

Most computer problems are easy to solve because they're really not major problems. Oh, they might *appear* to be major—any problem that happens to *you* is major!—but in reality, most problems result from causes that are easily fixed. So, take a look here at some of the most common sources of computer problems and how you can avoid them.

User Error

Here's the thing about computers. They're logic machines, and they seldom, if ever, make mistakes of their own volition. So you can't always blame your problems on the computer, no matter how tempting that might be. The truth of the matter is that the most common cause of computer problems is *you*!

You see, most problems result when the user—that's you—does something wrong. You might hit the wrong key, type the wrong command, or enter the wrong input. Or maybe you click the wrong mouse button, highlight the wrong item, or double-click when you mean to single-click.

You're probably not even aware of your blunder until something goes terribly and unmistakably wrong with your work. The key to correcting the problem, then, is to remain calm and retrace your steps to figure out exactly what you did wrong.

The bottom line? If your computer doesn't seem to do what you tell it, make sure that you're telling it to do the right thing. When you input an error, you get an error in return.

Bad Connections

After you eliminate people problems, the next most common cause of computer malfunctions is the bad connection. Hooking up a handful of cables might sound simple, but it's easy to do wrong. If you plug a cable into the wrong connector, whatever is connected to that cable—on either end!—won't work. If the connection isn't solid—if the plug is loose—operation can be intermittent. If the cable is old, frayed, or sharply bent, the wires inside the cable might not transmit data effectively, again causing intermittent operation. And, of course, if you forget to turn the power on, well, nothing happens at all!

If an external device isn't working, the problem most likely lies in the connection. Make sure that all cables are solidly connected and, if necessary, securely screwed into their ports. Make certain that the printer cable actually is connected to the printer port, the keyboard cable to the keyboard port, and so on; it's easy to plug the right cable into the wrong connector. Finally, check that *both ends* of the cable are connected; a cable can work its way loose from the back of the monitor just as easily as it can from the back of the system unit.

When you're connecting multiple USB devices to your computer, you might have to resort to using a USB hub that lets you plug four or more USB devices into a single USB port. Problems sometimes result in your computer not always recognizing a device plugged into the hub; if you have a USB that isn't working, try plugging it directly into a port on your PC, rather than through the hub.

If it's an internal card that isn't working, a bad connection can also be to blame. Open up the system unit again and make sure the card is prop-

erly fitted into its slot. You might even need to remove the card and clean the edges, to ensure a proper connection. It's also possible that the card slot itself could be bad; try plugging the card into a different slot and see what happens.

If your entire system refuses to start, a faulty connection could be to blame here, too. In this case, however, you need to examine the *power cable*. Make sure that the power cable is securely connected to your system unit and firmly plugged into a power outlet. Then make certain that the power outlet actually is *turned on*. You can't imagine how many "major problems" can be caused by a wall switch in the "off" position. And while you're at it, make sure that all your peripherals are also turned on; it doesn't do you any good to have a functioning system unit with a monitor that's switched off.

And don't assume that because you connected everything just fine originally that you don't have a connection problem now. That's because *cables come loose*. Check those connections one more time, just to be sure.

Configuration Errors

Okay, so your entire system is hooked up and turned on—and you *still* have hardware problems. Then again, maybe not. In some cases, your "hardware problems" actually turn out to be *software problems*.

Any time you add a new peripheral to your system, Windows must be configured to recognize and properly work with the new device. Theoretically, Windows Plug and Play technology should automatically recognize most new components when they're first installed, but Plug and Play isn't perfect. Simply put, Windows doesn't recognize

100% of the devices you can potentially add to your system. Even worse, sometimes Windows thinks it recognizes one device but configures itself for *another* device instead. This means you might need to manually configure any new devices you add.

In addition, just adding a device to your system doesn't mean that that device will automatically be *used* by Windows or by any specific software program. For example, if you add a new printer, you'll probably have to manually instruct Windows to select the new printer as your *default* printer—and you might have to configure your software programs individually, as well.

Bugs

After you check for human error, make certain that everything is hooked up and turned on, and ensure that Windows is configured correctly for your hardware, what do you do if you still have problems? Well, the possibility exists—however slight— that your system actually is infested with software or hardware bugs.

How can you tell if you have a true hardware or software problem? The first thing to do is read the README file that comes with most new software programs and with hardware installation utilities. This file (variously labeled README, README.DOC, README.TXT, or READ.ME) contains last-minute instructions, changes, and additions that were developed too late to include in the standard documentation. If certain features of a program or device malfunction, the README file probably discusses those problems.

Next, go to the manufacturer's Web site. (The address is typically listed in the manual or on the box.) Click around the site looking for pages related to your specific program; look for technical notes or information, *FAQs* (lists of Frequently Asked Questions), or message boards you can search. If there are any last-minute changes to your software or hardware, they should be noted somewhere on the Web site— and you might even find software "patches" that you should download and install to bring your "new" program or peripheral even more up-to-date.

Two other potential sources of information include your dealer and other users. The latter group especially might be aware of bugs that could be causing your problem. (You can often find comments from other users in Web-based message boards or Usenet newsgroups devoted to your specific piece of hardware or software.)

As a last resort, you can always contact the manufacturer directly. Most manufacturers have contact information in their manuals and on their Web sites; you typically have the option of either email or telephone-based technical support.

Viruses

There is one final cause of computer problems to discuss—the *computer virus*. A virus is a computer program or file designed to deliberately cause other programs and data to malfunction. These malicious programs can infiltrate your system and inflict extensive damage to the data and programs on your hard disk.

How do you catch a computer virus? Like other computer data, viruses are transmitted primarily via email, and sometimes through the exchange of infected CDs and disks. Whenever you allow new programs from an outside source into your system, the chance exists—however slight—that within that data might lurk a hidden computer virus.

How do you avoid viruses? The only foolproof way is to sever your connection to the Internet and never use any media given to you by other users. However, such extreme measures are often impractical. Fortunately, you can take any of several more practical precautions, including the installation of special antivirus software. See Chapter 20 for more information on how to practice safe, virus-free computing.

note

Learn more about computer viruses in Chapter 20, "Protecting Your Computer from Viruses and Internet Attacks."

Dealing with Upgrade Problems

Because this book is about upgrading and fixing your PC, let's examine the intersection of these two topics—problems that occur after you upgrade something on your computer system.

There are a number of things that can go wrong during an upgrade, such as the following:

- You forgot to plug your computer back in, or to plug everything back into your system unit.
- You didn't connect something properly.
- Some part of your system isn't compatible with your new component.
- You broke something while you were inside your system unit.
- You left something loose inside your system unit, like a wire or a screw.
- You need to change your system configuration to recognize your new upgrade.

- The device driver for your new component conflicts with an existing device driver in Windows.

- The new peripheral you're installing isn't compatible with your operating system, or with your other PC hardware.

Whew—that's a lot that can go wrong!

Sometimes the best way to troubleshoot an upgrade problem is to uninstall the device that you just upgraded, and then reinstall it. Sometimes it takes Windows two (or more!) tries to get the configuration right. Sometimes you might need to consult with a technical professional to hunt down a pesky device conflict—or throw in the towel and not add the particular device that is giving your problems. The important thing to remember is to retrace your steps *backwards* through the upgrade process, and try to determine if everything was done correctly.

It's also possible that your system doesn't recognize your new component. Depending on what you installed, you might have to load new drivers (using the Add New Hardware Wizard); change your system's BIOS settings (using the initial CMOS setup utility); or physically reconfigure specific switches or jumpers on an expansion card or your system's motherboard.

In some cases old software simply won't work with new hardware. If you suspect this is the case, put in a call to the software manufacturer and see if they have a quick solution; if not, you might have to upgrade to a newer version of your software.

And, if all else fails, you can always call the technical support line for your new component, or consult with a technical professional.

note

Device drivers are discussed in the section "Fixing Driver Problems with the Device Manager," later in this chapter; learn more about changing BIOS settings in Chapter 2, "Preparing Your System for an Upgrade."

Basic Troubleshooting Tips

No matter what kind of computer-related problem you're experiencing, there are six basic steps you should take to track down the cause of the problem. Here they are:

1. Check for user errors—something *you've* done wrong. Maybe you've clicked the wrong button, or pressed the wrong key, or plugged something into the wrong jack or port. Retrace your steps and try to duplicate your problem. Chances are the problem won't recur if you don't make the same mistake twice.

2. Check that everything is plugged in to the proper place, and that the PC itself is getting power. Take special care to ensure that all your cables are *securely* connected—loose connections can cause all sorts of strange results!

3. Be sure that you have the latest versions installed for all the software on your system. While you're at it, be sure you have the latest versions of device drivers installed for all the peripherals on your system.

4. Run the appropriate Windows diagnostic tools. If you have them, use third-party tools as well.

5. Try to isolate the problem by *when* and *how* it occurs. Walk through each step of the startup process to see if you can identify which driver or service might be causing the problem.

6. When all else fails, call in professional help. That means contacting a technical support line, or taking your machine into the shop. Don't be embarrassed; if you need professional help, go and get it!

I should probably add a seventh step, before step number one:

Don't panic!

Just because there's something wrong with your PC is no reason to fly off the handle. Keep your wits about you and proceed logically, and you can probably find what's causing your problem and get it fixed. React irrationally, and you'll never figure out what's wrong—and you'll get a few gray hairs, in the bargain!

Using Windows Troubleshooting Utilities

Windows includes a raft of built-in utilities you can use to track down and fix many common problems. If you ever experience a problem with your computer system, it pays to know what tools you already have on hand.

Fixing Easy Problems with Windows Troubleshooters

Windows includes several built-in utilities, called *troubleshooters*, that can walk through various problems with your system. These troubleshooters are like wizards, in that you're led step-by-step through a series of questions. All you have to do is answer the interactive questions in the troubleshooter, and you'll be led to the probable solution to your problem.

In most cases, Windows troubleshooters can help you diagnose and fix common system problems. It's a good idea to try the troubleshooters before you pick up the phone and dial Microsoft's Technical Support line or start trying to track down problems manually.

To run a troubleshooter from Windows XP, open the Help and Support Center and click the Fixing a Problem link. When the next page appears, click the link for the type of problem you're having, and then click the link to start a specific troubleshooter.

To run a troubleshooter in earlier versions of Windows, click the Start button and select Help. When the Windows Help window appears, select the Contents tab and select Troubleshooting, and then select Windows Troubleshooters. Select the troubleshooter for your specific problem in the left pane; the troubleshooter itself will be displayed in the right pane.

Figure 21.1 shows a typical troubleshooter. All you have to do now is follow the interactive directions to troubleshoot your particular hardware problems.

note

Windows 98 was the first version of Windows to include troubleshooters.

FIGURE 21.1

Use Windows troubleshooters to help you track down system problems.

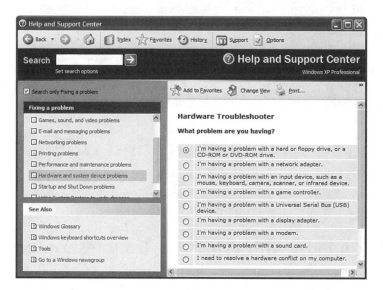

Fixing Driver Problems with the Device Manager

For any piece of hardware to work with Windows, Windows has to install and configure a device driver file. Windows includes drivers for most popular hardware devices. If you have a newer or less widely used peripheral, however, the manufacturer might have to provide its own drivers for Windows to use.

In most cases, Windows automatically recognizes your new device and installs the proper drivers. Even when that doesn't work, the Add Hardware Wizard can be used to install the proper drivers for new devices. Still, these methods can't add new and improved drivers if those drivers aren't available.

Windows Device Manager, shown in Figure 21.2, is where you can review your various hardware settings. (To open the Device Manager in Windows XP, select the Hardware tab in the System Properties utility and click the Device Manager button.) You also can use the Device Manager to determine which devices might have conflicts or other problems.

FIGURE 21.2

Use the Device Manager to find and fix driver problems.

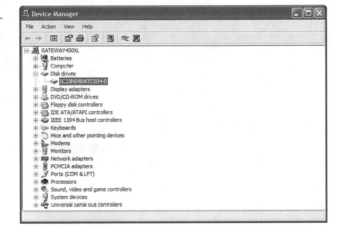

Identifying Problem Devices

When you open the Device Manager, any resource conflict on your system will be highlighted within the problematic Class group. Click the + next to the hardware device type to view all corresponding devices. If there is a problem with a specific device, it will be identified with one of the following symbols:

- A black exclamation point (!) on a yellow field indicates that the device is in what Windows calls a "problem state." Note that a device in a problem state can still be functioning, even though it has some sort of problem. The problem will be explained by the accompanying problem code.

- A red "X" indicates that the device is currently disabled. This usually means that the device is physically present in your system, but doesn't have a driver loaded—although it could also mean that a driver is loaded but not functioning properly.

■ A blue i on a white field indicates that the device is not using the automatic settings, but has a manual configuration instead. (This icon isn't necessarily bad, because it doesn't indicate a problem, only a different type of configuration.)

Solving Conflicts

If you have a device conflict, right-click that device and select Properties from the pop-up menu. This displays the Properties dialog box. When you select the General tab you'll see a message indicating the basic problem and the steps Windows recommends to solve the problem. The message might also display a problem code and number that can be useful when consulting with a technical support specialist—or prompt you to launch a troubleshooter for the device that is showing a problem.

Reconfiguring Devices

To reconfigure a device, select the Resources tab in the Properties dialog box. (If this device doesn't have a Resources tab, either you can't change its resources or it isn't using any resource settings.) Select the resource you want to change, uncheck the Use Automatic Settings option, and then click the Change Setting button. When the Edit Resource dialog box appears, edit the system resources as necessary. Click OK when done.

Note, however, that you probably won't need to bother with reconfiguring a device in this manner—it's pretty technical, all things said and done.

Updating Drivers

To update a device driver, select the Driver tab in the Properties dialog box, and then click the Update Driver button. When the Hardware Update Wizard appears, select where you want to search for an upgraded driver. If you have new driver software from your hardware's manufacturer, check the Install From a List or Specific Location option, and then insert the disk or CD-ROM and follow the onscreen instructions to install the specific driver.

If you'd rather have Windows search for a better driver, check the Install the Software Automatically option. Windows will now search for an updated device driver. If it finds one, follow the onscreen instructions to install it. If it doesn't find one,

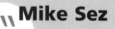

Mike Sez

You can always search for new and updated drivers at the device manufacturer's Web site. Also good are the big driver depositories at DriverGuide.com (www.driverguide.com) and WinDrivers.com (www.windrivers.com).

choose to keep your present driver. (And then go online yourself to try to find an updated version, if one exists.)

Fixing Big Problems with System Information

If your problem is so major that you can't fix it with the Troubleshooters or the Device Manager, you need to turn to a more powerful tool. That tool is called System Information; you launch it by clicking the Start button, and then selecting All Programs, Accessories, System Tools, System Information.

As you can see in Figure 21.3, the left pane of the System Information window displays information about the five key parts of your system: Hardware Resources, Components, Software Environment, Internet Settings, and Applications. Click the + next to one of the categories to display additional subcategories. When you highlight a specific subcategory, information about that topic appears in the right pane.

FIGURE 21.3

Use System Information to view more detailed information about your system and to access a variety of technical tools.

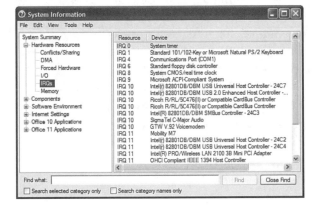

System Information is particularly useful for finding device conflicts. Open the Hardware Resources category and select Conflicts/Sharing. The right pane now displays a list of all shared IRQs—one of which is probably causing your current problem. Identify the problem IRQ, and then use the Device Manager to either reconfigure or reinstall the device to use a different IRQ.

Windows also uses System Information as a kind of gateway to a number of other system utilities. Many of the so-called "hidden" tools are accessible from the Tools menu in the System Information window. Some of these utilities are a bit technical in terms of what they monitor or do, but if you're having problems with some new piece of hardware you've installed, you'll probably find at least some of these utilities useful when you go to troubleshoot your problem.

Tracking Down Stubborn Problems with Dr. Watson

Dr. Watson, included with all versions of Windows, is a familiar tool to experienced Windows users. It takes a snapshot of your system whenever a system fault occurs, which aids in the diagnosis of tricky problems.

You start Dr. Watson from the System Information utility; just pull down the Tools menu and select Dr. Watson. On older versions of Windows you might have to launch Dr. Watson directly from the Run utility; click Start, Run and enter `drwatson` into the Run box. Click OK to run the utility.

Dr. Watson intercepts software faults and identifies the software that failed, offering a general description of the cause. In some cases, Dr. Watson will diagnosis the problem and offer a suggested course of action. You also can feed the information that Dr. Watson collects to tech support personnel; it will often provide the detailed technical information they need to find and fix tricky system problems.

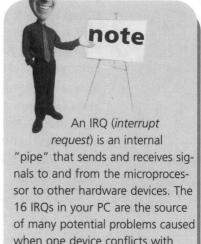

note

An IRQ (*interrupt request*) is an internal "pipe" that sends and receives signals to and from the microprocessor to other hardware devices. The 16 IRQs in your PC are the source of many potential problems caused when one device conflicts with another.

Older versions of Dr. Watson displayed a lot of information on a series of tabs. The new Windows XP version of Dr. Watson is more streamlined, saving all information it gathers into a separate log file (drwatson32.log); you can then access the log file to view the details of any program errors.

Turning Back Time with System Restore

Perhaps the best course of action when your system acts up—especially after you've performed an upgrade—is to use Microsoft's System Restore utility. This is a relatively new utility, first introduced in Windows Me, that can automatically restore your system to the state it was in before your problems cropped up.

Prior to Windows Me, it wasn't uncommon to run into problems that required you to reinstall your entire operating system. (That's a worst-case scenario of course; when nothing else works, you reinstall the whole shebang!) With System Restore, however, reinstallations are a thing of the past because it can automatically restore your system to a prior working state *without* reinstalling the entire operating system.

Think of System Restore as a safety net for your essential system files. It isn't a backup program per se, because it doesn't make copies of your personal files. It simply keeps track of all the system-level changes that are made to your computer, and (when activated) reverses those changes.

Setting System Restore Points

How does System Restore work?

It's quite simple, actually. System Restore actively monitors your system and notes any changes that are made when you install new applications. Each time it notes a change, it automatically creates what it calls a restore point. A *restore point* is a "snapshot" of the Windows Registry and selected system files just before the new application is installed.

Just to be safe, System Restore also creates a new restore point after every 10 hours of system use. You also can chose to manually create a new restore point at any point in time. This is a good idea whenever you make any major system change, such as installing a new peripheral or piece of hardware.

To set a manual restore point, click the Start menu and then select All Programs, Accessories, System Tools, System Restore. When the System Restore window opens (shown in Figure 21.4), select Create a Restore Point and click Next. You'll be prompted to enter a description for this new restore point. Do this and then click the Create button.

FIGURE 21.4

Use System Restore to create a new restore point before you install a new piece of hardware or software.

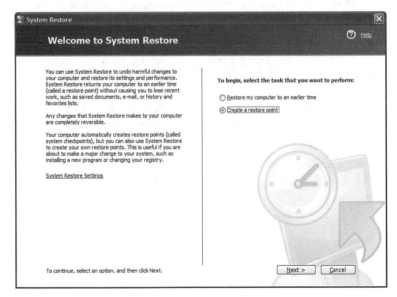

That's all you have to do. Windows notes the appropriate system settings, and stores them in its System Restore database.

Restoring Your System

If something in your system goes bad, you can run System Restore to set things right. Pick a restore point before the problem occurred (such as right before a new installation), and System Restore will then undo any changes made to monitored files since the restore point was created. It also replaces the current Registry with the one captured at the restore point. This will restore your system to its pre-installation working condition.

caution

Because System Restore only monitors system files and Registry settings, you cannot use it to restore changed or damaged data files. For complete protection, you'll still need to back up your important data files manually.

To restore your system from a restore point, all you have to do is follow these steps:

1. Click the Start button, and then select All Programs, Accessories, System Tools, System Restore.

2. When the System Restore window opens, check the Restore My Computer to an Earlier Time option, and then click Next.

3. When the Select a Restore Point screen appears (as shown in Figure 21.5), you'll see a calendar showing the current month. (You can move backward and forward through the months by clicking the left and right arrows.) Any date highlighted in bold contains a restore point. Select a restore point, and then click the Next button.

4. When the confirmation screen appears, click Next.

Windows now starts to restore your system. Be sure that all open programs are closed down because Windows will need to be restarted during this process.

When the process is complete, your system should be back in tip-top shape. Note, however, that it might take a half-hour or more to complete a system restore—so you'll have time to order a pizza and eat dinner before the operation is done!

FIGURE 21.5

Pick a restore point to restore your system to the way it used to be— before it started acting up.

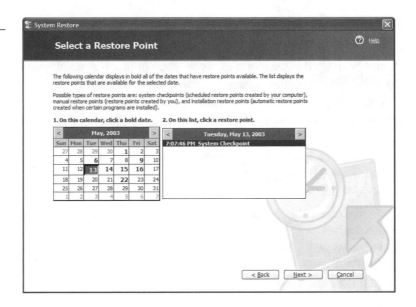

Managing the Windows Registry

There's one more Windows utility that can prove useful when you're trying to fix problems with your system—even though using it improperly can cause unpredictable behavior on the part of your PC. This utility is called the Registry Editor, and you use it to change key system settings in the Windows Registry.

The Windows Registry is a huge database that holds the majority of your system's configuration information. The Registry contains all the properties you set via the Control Panel, settings for each of the applications installed on your system, and configuration information for all your system's hardware and peripherals.

The Registry is updated automatically whenever you change a configuration through normal means. You also can make changes directly to the Registry, using the Registry Editor.

caution

Editing the Registry is a tricky proposition. If you do something wrong, you could make your system totally inoperable. For that reason, you should only edit the Registry if it's absolutely necessary to correct an otherwise hard-to-fix problem—and you should back it up before attempting any edits.

Backing Up and Restoring the Registry

Because editing the Registry is risky—even for experienced computer users—you should back up the Registry files before you commence making any changes. This will give you the option of restoring the pre-edited Registry, just in case anything goes wrong.

Fortunately, the System Restore utility automatically backs up your Registry whenever a restore point is created. If you're going to edit your Registry, be sure you create a new restore point immediately prior to making any changes. If anything goes wrong in the editing process, you can use System Restore to restore your system back to the previous restore point.

If you're using a version of Windows prior to Windows Me (which first introduced the System Restore feature), or if you just want to be extra safe, you can make a backup copy of your Registry and store it on some form of removable media, such as a Zip disk or CD-R/RW. The Registry is actually composed of two hidden files, SYSTEM.DAT and USER.DAT, located in the \windows folder. All you have to do is unhide these files and copy them to another location. That way you can copy them back later if you end up totally trashing your system with the Registry Editor.

Editing the Registry

Most of the time you won't need to bother with the Registry. However, there will come the occasion when you experience a particularly vexing system problem that can be fixed only by editing a particular value in the Registry. Typically, you'll be instructed to edit the Registry by a tech support person working for the company whose product is causing you problems. (Trust me, it happens.) If this happens to you, you'll need to know how to edit the Registry using the Register Editor utility.

You start Registry Editor by clicking the Start button and selecting Run to display the Run window. Enter `regedit` in the Open box and then click OK.

The Registry Editor window has two panes, as shown in Figure 21.6. The left pane displays the different parameters or settings, called keys. All keys have numerous subkeys. The right pane displays the values, or configuration information, for each key or subkey.

You display the different levels of subkeys by clicking on the + next to a specific item. You edit a particular value by highlighting the subkey in the left pane and then double-clicking the value in the right pane. This displays the Edit Value (or Edit String) window. Enter a new value in the Value Data box, and then click OK.

FIGURE 21.6

Use the Registry
Editor to edit the
(highly techni-
cal) values in
the Windows
Registry.

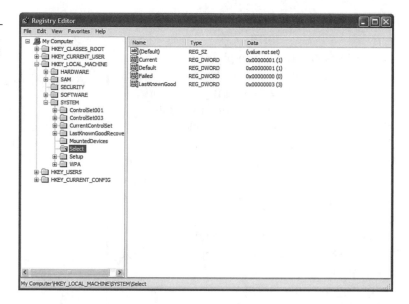

To add a new value to a subkey, right-click the subkey and select
one of the New, Value options from the pop-up menu. Type a name
for the new value, and then double-click the value
to display the Edit Value (or Edit String) window.
Enter the new value in the Value Data box, and
then click OK.

You also can add new subkeys to the Registry. Just
right-click the key where you want to add the
subkey, and then select New, Key from the pop-up
menu. A new subkey (with a temporary name)
appears. Type a name for the new subkey, and
then press Enter.

To delete a subkey or value, right-click the item
and select Delete. Remember, however, that all
changes are final. After a subkey is deleted, it's gone!

caution

Registry settings are
changed *as you make
the changes*. There is no
save command in the
Registry Editor. There is
also no undo command. So be very
careful about the changes you
make—they're final!

Upgrading for Bug Fixes

Many computer problems are caused by bugs in the operating system, typically
some sort of incompatibility between Windows and a particular piece of hardware or
software. That's why, if you have a problem you can't track down, it's always a good
idea to consult the Microsoft Knowledge Base, a huge database of official Microsoft

technical issues. You can search the Knowledge Base at the Microsoft Help and Support Web site (`support.microsoft.com`).

When Microsoft recognizes a problem involving Windows, the company more often than not tries to fix the problem. The fix might be in the form of a downloadable software patch (typically referred to in a Knowledge Base article) or it might come in a newer version of the operating system. This is one very good reason to upgrade your version of Windows.

Here's the thing. Windows 98 was more reliable than Windows 95. Windows 98 Second Edition was more reliable than the first edition of Windows 98. And Windows XP is much more reliable than any previous version of Windows. So if you're experiencing a lot of Windows-related problems, the easiest fix is to upgrade to Windows XP. No questions about it.

Not that Windows XP is perfect, of course. Microsoft continues to fix known bugs in XP, almost on a weekly basis. Use Windows Update (Start, All Programs, Windows Update) to go online and grab the latest bug fixes and patches. Even better, download Windows XP Service Pack 1 (and any subsequent service packs), which bundles all previous updates into a single big update. See Chapter 17, "Opening New Windows: Upgrading to Windows XP," for more information.

caution

If you're out on the Web you might find Registry hack utilities that will, when launched, automatically modify your Registry for you. (A lot of these hacks that change Registry settings purport to speed up your PC's performance.) Although most of these hacks are legitimate, as with any changes to the Registry, the changes they make are immediate—and can have all manner of unforeseen consequences.

Resorting to Repair

Sometimes, however, there's nothing you can do to fix whatever ails your PC. When your computer problems exceed your troubleshooting abilities, it's time to call in a professional. That's right—you sometimes have to take your PC into the shop for repairs.

Your first challenge in this situation is to find a competent and reliable service facility. One approach is to call your computer's manufacturer and have them recommend a repair center in your area. (They might also have quick factory service via Federal Express, UPS, or overnight mail.) You

"Mike Sez"

If you're a dedicated do-it-yourselfer, you can find lots of useful technical resources on the Internet. Check out Active-Hardware (`www.active-hardware.com`), CNET (`www.cnet.com`), Computing.Net (`www.computing.net`), Karbosguide (`www.karbosguide.com`), TechTV (`www.techtv.com`), and Tom's Hardware Guide (`www.tomshardware.com`).

should also ask your friends (or the tech support guy where you work) where they get their computers repaired. It's worth your peace of mind (and your PC's ongoing health) to do some homework before you entrust your computer to a stranger.

After you find a repair center, you need to do a little work *before* you hand over your PC to them. If your PC is still running, think about removing any sensitive files you have on your hard disk, such as online banking data, confidential documents, and dirty pictures you downloaded from the Internet. And if you think your hard disk might need replacing, back it up *before* you ship it off (if you can); most repair centers won't bother to transfer data from one hard disk to another unless it's a specific request.

The Absolute Minimum

The remaining chapters in this book detail the probable causes and solutions behind specific types of PC problems. Use the specific instructions in this and previous chapters to help you follow the troubleshooting advice in the future chapters.

With that in mind, here are the most important points you need to remember:

- Most computer problems are caused by user error, bad information, broken or poorly connected cables, incorrect system configurations, or computer viruses.

- It's also possible that your software or hardware actually is bug-infested; check with the manufacturer to see what problems they already know about.

- If your system doesn't work after an upgrade, it's probably the fault of the new component or the upgrade process in general. You can generally get your system working again by uninstalling the new component.

- Windows includes several built-in utilities you can use to track down and fix common problems; these utilities include Troubleshooters, the Device Manager, and System Information.

- If you think a problem was caused by something that you recently installed, you can use the System Restore utility to restore your system to the state it was in before the installation; it's a good idea to use System Restore to set a manual restore point any time you install a new piece of hardware or software.

- If you need to make key changes to your system's underlying configuration, use the Registry Editor to edit values in the Windows Registry.

- An almost-universal fix for Windows-related problems is to upgrade to Windows XP—and make sure you have the latest service pack installed.

- If you can't fix it yourself, don't hesitate to call in professional help and have your system prepared by a competent and reliable service facility.

22

WHAT TO DO WHEN YOUR COMPUTER DOESN'T START OR FREEZES UP

It happens.

You go to turn on or reboot your computer, and something bad happens. Either your system doesn't start at all, or it hangs in mid-startup, or it issues forth with some incomprehensible error message. It's then that you know that you have a bit of detective work ahead of you to track down and fix the problem.

If you're waiting in vain for your system to start, this chapter is for you. The good news is that there are some specific procedures you can follow to get your system up and running again after a crash, and I'll tell you about them. (I'll also remind you, right now, how important it is to back up your important files and settings—just in case this sort of disaster happens to you!)

Dealing with System Startup Problems

There's nothing scarier than turning on your computer and finding it doesn't start. What you do next depends on exactly what it is your computer is or is not doing. Let's work through some specific startup problems, and how to proceed in each instance.

Problem: Your Computer Doesn't Start—You Hear No Noises and See No Lights

First things first—*don't panic!*

Now, very calmly, look at the back of your system unit. Is the power cable plugged in to the right connector? Now follow the power cord to the other end. Is it firmly connected to a power outlet? Now check the wall switch. Is it turned on? Now walk to your fuse or circuit-breaker box. Is the fuse good or the circuit breaker set? Now go back to your computer. If it still isn't working, unplug the computer from the power outlet and plug in something that you know works—a lamp or a radio, perhaps. If the appliance doesn't work, you have a bad power outlet. If the appliance *does* work, you really do have computer problems.

If you're positive that your computer is getting power and that you're turning it on correctly, you probably have a hardware problem. The most likely suspect is the power supply in the system unit. To determine the culprit and fix the problem, however, you'll need to call in professional help at this point. Take your system to a certified repair center and let its technicians get to work.

Problem: Your Computer Doesn't Start, but It Makes the Normal Startup Noises

If your system is making noise, at least you know that it's getting power. Because you can rule out a bad power cord, the most common things to look for are poorly connected cables or a nonfunctioning monitor.

Begin by checking your monitor. Is it turned on? Is it plugged into a power outlet? Is the power outlet turned on? Is the monitor connected to the correct port on your system unit? Is the connection solid? Is the connection solid in the back of the monitor? Are the brightness and contrast controls turned up so that you can actually see a picture? If you have a newer monitor, try disconnecting the monitor from the computer (with the monitor turned on); if the monitor is working correctly, you should get a No Signal or Lost Signal message on the screen.

If everything is connected and adjusted properly, you might have a monitor that needs repair. Is the monitor's power light on? If not, your monitor might have power supply problems that need attention from a professional. If your monitor's little green light is on but nothing shows onscreen, the video card in your system unit might be loose or set up incorrectly. Try swapping monitors with another system; if the new monitor works on your system, your monitor is the problem. If you determine that your monitor is working fine, you should check your video card to make sure it's installed, seated, and connected properly. If that doesn't fix your problem, try plugging your video card into a different slot.

It's also possible that your keyboard isn't plugged in properly, or that you have some other internal problem that causes your system to halt during start-up. Check all your connections before you try rebooting.

Problem: Your Computer Starts, but the Monitor Displays an Error Message (Before Loading Windows)

Your system uses error messages to communicate with you when it encounters certain problems. Table 22.1 details some of the most common error messages you might encounter on startup (*before* Windows loads), their causes, and how to fix the problem.

Table 22.1   Startup Error Messages

Error Message	Causes/Solutions
Non-system disk or disk error	You see this message when you have a non-bootable disk in drive A:. Check the floppy disk drive and remove the disk, and then press any key to restart your computer using your hard disk drive. (You can boot from drive A:, of course, but you must have a bootable disk in that drive.)
Keyboard error, press F2 to continue	It sounds kind of silly to ask you to use your keyboard to confirm that your keyboard isn't working, doesn't it? This message is generated when the rest of your system works but the PC can't find the keyboard. If you receive this message, your keyboard probably is disconnected, has a loose connection, or has a stuck key. Check the connecting cable (at both ends) and reboot. If you still receive this message, you have a keyboard problem. Verify this fact by plugging in a keyboard from a friend's machine. If you do have a keyboard problem, it's probably cheaper to buy a new keyboard than to get your old one fixed. (See Chapter 24, "What to Do When Your Mouse or Keyboard Won't Work," for more information.)

Table 22.1 (continued)

Error Message	Causes/Solutions
File allocation table bad, drive X:	This message is not good. Something has messed up your FAT (File Allocation Table), the part of your hard disk that holds vital information necessary for your system to operate. One of the most common causes of this problem is a computer virus. Another cause is some sort of physical damage to your hard disk caused by contaminants or plain old wear and tear. If you have actual physical damage to your disk, you might need to use a third-party utility program to repair the damage— or you might want to drop back 10 and punt by letting a technical professional handle the situation from here. (See Chapter 23, "What to Do When You Can't Access Your Disks," for more information.)
General failure writing drive X: *or* General failure reading drive X:	If you get one of these messages when using a removable disk, check to see if you actually have a disk in the drive; you might also have a bad floppy disk. If these messages occur when you're accessing your hard disk, it's something much more serious—there's something wrong with your computer, but your PC doesn't really know what the trouble is. Try shutting down your system for a few minutes and then rebooting; sometimes this message is generated when your system gets a little cranky. More likely, however, you have something seriously wrong with your hard disk, which means it's time to hop in the car and drop off your PC at your local computer repair center. The pros there have diagnostic software and equipment that can pinpoint problems much easier than you or I can. (See Chapter 23 for more information.)
Invalid drive specification *or* Drive not ready	Either of these error messages indicates that you're having problems with the drive from which you're trying to boot. If you're booting from a floppy disk drive, your bootable floppy might be bad. Try using another bootable disk. If the problem persists, or if you're booting from a hard disk drive, the problem might reside in the drive mechanism itself. Sometimes an older drive can operate too slowly to always boot properly; try rebooting your system. If the problem persists, have a professional check out your system. The drive in question might need to be replaced. (See Chapter 23 for more info.)

Table 22.1   (continued)

Error Message	Causes/Solutions
CMOS RAM error	This message appears when something is bad in the setup held in memory by your system's CMOS RAM chip. (This chip holds important system information in permanent, battery-powered memory.) When you see this or any similar message, you are given the opportunity to press the F1 key to continue. Do this, and adjust your CMOS setup accordingly. (See your system's documentation for information on how to do the latter.) If this message persists, you might have a dead CMOS battery; see your repair center to replace the battery. (See Chapter 2 for more info.)
Memory size error *or* Memory size mismatch *or* Not enough memory *or* Insufficient memory *or* Parity check *xxx or* Parity error *x*	Any of these messages indicate that something is wrong with your computer's memory. Your CMOS setup might be incorrect, or you could have some bad or improperly seated memory chips. It's also possible that you recently added extra memory to your system and it isn't configured correctly—or you added more memory than your (typically older) PC can handle. If this is the case, enter your CMOS setup menu and reconfigure your system for the new memory. If you can't fix this problem via the setup routine, you should probably consult a computer professional for further assistance. (See Chapters 2 and 6, "You Must Remember This: Upgrading System Memory," for more information.)

Troubleshooting Windows Startup Problems

The previous problems are all caused by something wrong on your computer system, not your operating system. Of course, it's also possible that your computer is working fine and Windows is having problems.

If this is the case, the big challenge is getting into Windows to fix what's wrong when you can't even start your computer. The solution is deceptively simple; you have to hijack your computer before Windows gets hold of it, and force it to start without whatever is causing the problem.

Windows Startup Options

You hijack your computer by watching the screen as your computer boots up, and pressing the F8 key just before Windows starts to load. (You'll probably see some onscreen message about Windows starting, or pressing F8 for startup options, or selecting the operating system to start.)

When you press F8 your computer will display the Windows startup menu. This menu lists a number of different ways that you can start Windows:

- ■ **Normal**. This starts Windows in its normal mode as if you hadn't pressed F8 to begin with.
- ■ **Safe Mode**. Starts Windows with a minimal number of device drivers loaded. (You use this mode for most troubleshooting procedures.)
- ■ **Safe Mode with Networking**. A version of Safe mode that also loads key network drivers; you can still connect the ailing computer to your network.
- ■ **Safe Mode with Command Prompt**. Boots to the old DOS command prompt instead of to the Windows interface.
- ■ **Enable Boot Logging**. This logs all remaining startup operations to the NTBTLOG.TXT file (on Windows XP systems) or BOOTLOG.TXT file (on older systems), both located in your system's root folder.
- ■ **Enable VGA Mode**. Loads Windows as normal, but with a generic VGA video driver. (This is a good mode if you think you're having trouble with your video driver.)
- ■ **Last Known Good Configuration**. Uses the Windows Registry information and drivers that were saved the last time you shut down your system—presumably before your system got screwed up.

Starting in Safe Mode

When you see the Windows startup menu, the option you want to select is Safe mode. Safe mode is a special mode of operation that loads Windows in a minimal configuration, without a bunch of pesky device drivers. This means the screen will be low-resolution VGA, and you won't be able to use a lot of your peripherals (such as your modem or your printer). But Windows will load, which it might not have, otherwise.

note

Depending on your system configuration, you might have more, fewer, or just different options available on the Windows startup menu. The basic Safe mode option is available on all systems, however.

Any time you can't load Windows normally, you should first try the Last Known Good Configuration option. If this doesn't put things right, you should reboot again and revert to Safe mode. In fact, Windows will automatically start in Safe mode if it encounters major problems while loading. Safe mode is a great mode for troubleshooting because Windows still works and you can make whatever changes you need to make to get it up-and-running again in normal mode.

Once in Safe mode, you can look for device conflicts, restore incorrect or corrupted device drivers, troubleshoot your startup with the System Configuration Utility (discussed later in this chapter), or restore your system to a prior working configuration (using the System Restore utility, also discussed later).

Tracking Down Problems with the System Configuration Utility

After you have Windows started in Safe mode, you need to track down whatever is causing your startup problem. One way to do this is with the System Configuration Utility, a tool you turn to when you know you have a startup problem but you don't know what's causing it.

The System Configuration Utility troubleshoots your system by duplicating the procedures used by Microsoft's tech support staff when they try to diagnose system configuration problems. This utility leads you through a series of steps that, one-by-one, disable various components of your system on startup, until you're able to isolate the item that is causing your specific problem.

In Windows XP, you find the System Configuration Utility in the Tools section of the Help and Support Center. In previous versions of Windows, you start this utility by clicking the Start button and then selecting Programs, Accessories, System Tools, System Information; when the Microsoft System Information utility launches, pull down the Tools menu and select System Configuration Utility.

> **tip**
>
> You can also start the System Configuration Utility by entering `msconfig.exe` in the Windows Run box.

The easiest way to check your system is to use the System Configuration Utility to perform a *diagnostic startup*. This routine enables you to interactively load specific device drivers and software when you start your system.

You perform a diagnostic startup by selecting the General tab (shown in Figure 22.1) and selecting the Diagnostic Startup option. When you click OK, your computer will restart, but with only the most basic devices and services loaded. If you find that your problem is no longer present, you know that the problem was caused by one of the drivers or services that you *didn't* load.

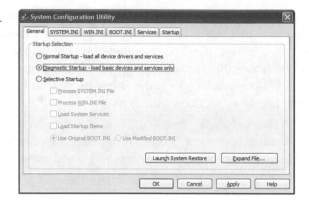

From here you need to return to the General tab and check the Selective Startup
option. Then, starting with the first available option, enable each option (one at a
time) and restart your system. By going through this admittedly time-consuming
process, you should be able to determine which file or service is causing your
problem.

Your job isn't done yet, however. You now have to find the item within that file—the
specific driver, in most cases—that is causing your problem. Click the tab that corre-
sponds to the problematic file or service, and work through one item at a time,
rebooting your computer after enabling each item.

Again, working through one item at a time is very time-consuming, but this is the
exact same procedure that the tech professionals use. Working methodically, you
can isolate the precise item that is causing your problem.

If, after working through these steps, your computer still acts up, select the Startup
tab. Here you see a list of all the programs that get launched every time you start
Windows. Work through this list line-by-line (rebooting your computer after each
change, of course) to determine if one of these programs is causing your system
problem.

Even though this process is time-consuming, more often than not it will help you
isolate your problem. Of course, after the problem is isolated, you still have to fix
it—normally by reinstalling a missing or corrupted driver file.

Using the Recovery Console

What do you do if you can't even get into Windows Safe mode? If you're using
Windows XP, you have access to a new startup utility that has all the functionality
of an old operating system. The Windows XP Recovery Console looks and acts just
like the old MS-DOS command prompt. If you can't boot into Windows at all, use

the Recovery Console to perform whatever simple command-line operations are necessary to get you up and running.

You start the Recovery Console by rebooting from the Windows XP installation CD; when you see the Welcome to Setup screen, press the R key on your keyboard. You're now presented with the Recovery Console's command prompt.

The Recovery Console provides you with a variety of different commands, all of which should be familiar to old-timers who still remember the MS-DOS operating system. Use of the Recovery Console is recommended for advanced users only, but it can be a real lifesaver in extreme situations. For a more complete description of how to use the Recovery Console commands, see the Recovery Console entry in the Windows XP Help system.

Dealing with Windows-Related Startup Problems

Now that you know how to get into Safe mode and troubleshoot the Windows startup process, let's look at some specific Windows-related startup problems.

Problem: Your Computer Starts, but Windows Doesn't—And You Receive an Error Message

If Windows doesn't load—if your system, after the standard boot procedure, just "hangs" in place—then there is probably something wrong with the way Windows is installed or configured. This typically happens after you add something new (hardware or software) to your system. The new thing changes the settings that used to work okay to a configuration that doesn't work okay anymore.

It's also possible for Windows to have trouble loading even when you've done nothing new or different to your system. Even the 32-bit Windows XP can be finicky at times, and can surprise you with what it does or doesn't do.

If you receive an error message while Windows is loading, it's likely that Windows is trying to load a bad or incorrect device driver of some sort. In fact, the error message will more often than not tell you exactly which driver it's having trouble with. After you know which driver is causing problems, you can either reinstall that driver or eliminate that driver from the loading process by using the options in the System Configuration Utility.

If the error message doesn't tell you which driver is causing the problem, you can determine that yourself by using the System Configuration Utility to perform a selective startup. Restart Windows in Safe mode, and then run the System Configuration Utility, as discussed previously.

If you'd rather not go through the entire selective startup business, just launch the System Restore utility, as discussed in Chapter 21, "How to Deal with a Finicky PC." Choose to restore your system to some prior restore point, and get on with your business. (Of course, you might not figure out what was actually causing the problem—but at least you'll be up and running!)

Problem: Your Computer Starts, but Windows Doesn't—And You *Don't* Receive an Error Message

What if you can't load Windows and *don't* receive an error message? In this instance you want to start Windows in Safe mode, and then disable any other programs that might be loading when Windows starts up. Click the Start button and select All Programs, Startup. Use your mouse to move all items in the Startup menu to another menu (any menu will do, as long as you remember which one it is). Now restart Windows and see what happens.

If Windows now starts properly, one of the programs that *used* to start up when Windows started is causing you problems. One at a time, drag those programs back to the Startup menu (using the same procedure as before), and then restart Windows. Each time Windows starts properly, you know that particular program is okay. When Windows doesn't start properly, you know that particular program is a problem—so leave it out of your Startup folder.

If, on the other hand, removing the programs from your Startup folder *didn't* fix your problem, you have a problem with a specific device driver. If you're technically minded (and very patient), you can use the System Configuration Utility's startup diagnostics to try and isolate the problem driver.

A better bet is to run the System Restore utility and restore your system back to an earlier state—presumably before you installed or updated the driver that is causing your problems.

If even this doesn't work, it's time to reinstall Windows. Use your Windows installation CD to initiate a complete installation and setup—and if *this* doesn't fix your problem, it's time to contact a technical professional.

Problem: Your Computer Starts, but Windows Doesn't—And You Can't Enter Safe Mode

Sometimes Safe mode isn't safe enough. Any number of conditions can cause Windows not to start in Safe mode:

- **Your system is infected with a computer virus.** You might need to reinstall Windows to eliminate the effect of the virus, and then use an antivirus program to initiate a more complete cleansing of your system.

■ **Your computer's CMOS BIOS settings are incorrect.** During boot-up, check your CMOS settings and make corrections as necessary. If your CMOS battery is weak and not holding its settings, replace the battery.

■ **You have a hardware conflict.** Some device in your system is conflicting with some other device; the most common conflicts are IRQ conflicts. Ask a technical professional (or just an old geek who knows how to use DOS) to hunt down the errant device with the Safe Mode with Command Prompt option.

If you have persistent problems starting in Safe mode, try choosing the Last Known Good Configuration startup option. If even this doesn't work, you might need to reinstall Windows from scratch.

Problem: Your Computer Starts and Windows Enters Safe Mode Automatically

Windows starts up in Safe mode automatically when it senses a major driver problem or conflict. Follow the steps in the "Your Computer Starts, But Windows Doesn't—and You Receive an Error Message" section to track down the source of the problem. (Or just launch System Restore and restore your system to some prior condition.)

Dealing with System Freezes

When your computer freezes, more often than not, you must reboot to get things working again. Rebooting loses whatever you typed since you last saved the file you were in when the machine froze, but the process really doesn't hurt either your computer or your software programs. (Of course, this is another reason why you should *save* and save *often* when you're working on important documents!)

Try first to reboot from the keyboard by pressing the Ctrl+Alt+Del key combination. This *should* bring up the Close Windows Task Manager. If you're lucky (!), your entire system really isn't frozen and you only have a problem with a single program not responding. If you have a frozen program, it will be listed on the Applications tab as "not responding." Select that program from the list and click the End Task button. After a few seconds (well, up to 10 seconds or so) a Wait/Shutdown dialog box appears; confirm that you want to shut down the selected application. This should close the offending program and return your system to normal.

If you can't close a non-responding program, or if there is no frozen application, or if your system is still frozen, click the Shut Down option on the Windows Task

Manager menu bar. If *this* doesn't have any effect, you need to reset your entire system and start over again. Press Ctrl+Alt+Del once, and then a second time to reboot your system.

If you can't reboot your system via the "three-fingered salute," use the Reset button or the main power switch on your system unit.

Naturally, your computer's system can stall for any number of reasons. Some of the most common causes of this annoyance, along with their solutions, are described next.

Problem: Windows Freezes—And Displays an Error Message

When Windows freezes up, it sometimes displays some sort of error message. A message of this sort is just a polite way of telling you that something (who knows what) has bombed.

> **caution**
>
> Before you reboot, make sure that your system is really and truly locked up. Don't mistake a long wait time during a complex operation for a complete system freeze. Look for signs that your computer is still working, such as noises from your disk drive or blinking lights on your system unit. The last thing you want to do is reboot and lose your current data when you don't have to.

More often than not, it's just your current program that has frozen, and not all of Windows. In this case you get a Program Not Responding error message. Try pressing Ctrl+Alt+Del to bring up the Windows Task Manager, and then manually shut down any unresponsive program.

If the error message you get is displayed on a blue screen (known in the industry as the "blue screen of death"), follow the onscreen instructions to get rid of the blue screen. You might have to press Enter to close the program causing the error, or press Ctrl+Alt+Del to reboot your computer. After you encounter the blue screen, your system typically gets unstable, so I recommend rebooting your entire system, even if you're able to close that particular program manually.

Blue screen messages are often caused when you start running out of space on your hard disk. This might sound odd, but Windows uses a disk cache to supplement conventional memory. (This is called *virtual memory*, if you're interested.) If you don't have enough free hard disk space, Windows thinks that it's low on memory and starts acting flaky.

The blue screen error messages also can be caused by errors on your hard disk. If you get a lot of these error messages, it wouldn't hurt to check for disk errors before proceeding.

Problem: Windows Freezes—And No Error Message Appears

Sometimes Windows freezes without displaying an error message. This typically means that one of two things has happened: Windows itself has locked up, or Your current Windows application has locked up.

In either case, the solution is the same: Press Ctrl+Alt+Del.

If Windows itself has frozen, either nothing will happen or you'll start hearing a beep every time you press a key on your keyboard. In this case you'll need to press Ctrl+Alt+Del again to fully reboot, or you might have to turn off your PC at the On/Off button (or at the power source).

If, on the other hand, it's an errant program that freezes up, you should see the Windows Task Manager when you first press Ctrl+Alt+Del. Select the "not responding" program and click End Task. If and when the Wait/Shutdown dialog box appears, go ahead and shut down the offending program.

> **note**
>
> For more information on error messages, see Chapter 30, "What to Do When You Receive a Windows Error Message."

If the Task Manager doesn't appear, or if you try to shut down a program but your system is still locked up, it's time to fully reboot by pressing Ctrl+Alt+Del twice in a row.

What causes Windows to freeze? There can be many different causes of a Windows freeze, including the following:

- You might be running an application that isn't compatible with your version of Windows. If so, upgrade the program.

- You might not have enough memory to run Windows effectively. Upgrade the amount of RAM in your PC.

- A memory conflict might exist between applications or between an application and Windows itself. Try running fewer programs at once, or running problematic programs one at a time to avoid potential memory conflicts.

- You might not have enough free hard disk space for Windows to use for temporary files. Use the Disk Cleanup Utility to automatically free up some space on your hard drive, or manually delete any unnecessary files.

- Your hard disk might be developing errors or bad sectors. Check your hard disk for errors.

If your system crashes or freezes frequently, call in a pro. These kinds of problems can be tough to track down by yourself when you're dealing with Windows.

Problem: Windows Freezes—Your System Unit Has Power, But Your Keyboard or Mouse Isn't Working

If your system appears to be working but you can't type a thing, you probably face a simple problem: Your keyboard is unplugged.

The solution is equally simple: Plug it back in.

Same thing if your mouse quits working. Check to see if it's firmly connected, and then try rolling it again.

In fact, you might have both your mouse and keyboard plugged in to the wrong jacks. It's all too easy to plug your mouse into the keyboard jack, and vice versa. (That's why most PC manufacturers now color-code their mouse and keyboard connectors and jacks.) Even if it looks like both your mouse and keyboard and plugged in, trace the cables to makes sure they're not mixed up.

Of course, the solution might not be quite that simple. If replugging your keyboard or mouse doesn't work, you might have to reboot your computer to recognize the replug. (You'll probably have to turn off your system with the main power switch or button—if you can't click or type, you can't exit Windows normally!)

If you still experience difficulties after rebooting, you actually might be the not-so-proud possessor of a bad keyboard or mouse. Try plugging in another keyboard or mouse to your PC, or your keyboard or mouse into another PC, to determine whether device failure is at the root of your problem.

Problem: Windows Won't Let You Exit

The most common cause for this situation is that you have a misbehaving program. Try closing all your open programs one at a time. If any individual program is frozen, use Ctrl+Alt+Del to close that "not responding" program.

Beyond a single misbehaving problem, a number of things can cause Windows to not shut down. Believe it or not, one of these things can be a bad sound file! It's that sound you hear every time you go to shut down Windows. If that file is corrupted, the shutdown sequence stops there, leaving Windows running. To fix this problem open the Control Panel and launch the Sounds and Audio Devices utility. When the Sounds and Audio Devices Properties dialog box appears, select the Sounds tab, and then pull down the Sounds list and select No Sounds. Now click OK and try shutting down your system again. (If you do have a corrupted sound file, you can reinstall this particular file from your Windows installation CD.)

It's also possible that Windows Power Management technology is keeping you from closing Windows. Disable Power Management by opening the Control Panel, selecting Performance and Maintenance, and launching the Power Options utility. When the Power Options Properties dialog box appears, select the Power Schemes tab, pull down the Power Schemes list, and select Always On. You can even go the extra step and configure each setting to always stay on.

If you still can't shut down Windows after trying all these actions, there is probably a fragment of a program still running somewhere in your system's memory. It's near impossible to track down that fragment. Instead, you need to reboot via the double Ctrl+Alt+Del procedure.

Problem: Windows Won't Wake Up from Standby Mode

What do you do when Windows doesn't wake up from standby mode? Normally you "wake up" your computer by moving your mouse, or pressing any key on your keyboard. Some keyboards have special "wake up" keys that need to be pressed to exit sleep mode. In any event, if you move and click your mouse a bit and then type furiously on your keyboard and Windows stays fast asleep, you have problems. (Make sure, however, that your monitor is actually plugged in and turned on. A switched-off monitor looks suspiciously like standby mode!)

The solution here is to reboot your computer—*somehow*. Try the Ctrl+Alt+Del method first. However, if your system is in a really deep sleep, it might not recognize any keyboard input. So you'll probably have to turn off your system at the main power switch button, wait a few seconds, and then turn it back on again.

If you're using a notebook computer and this happens, you might have to remove *all* your power sources. This means unplugging the computer from the wall *and* removing the battery. Wait a few seconds, and then plug your notebook back in. That should do the trick!

Finally, it's possible that your system woke up but your *monitor* stayed asleep. Yes, some monitors have their own sleep modes, and if they get stuck in that mode, you won't know whether or not your system is awake. It doesn't hurt to turn your monitor off and then back on (which definitely wakes it up!) just in case the sleep problem is the fault of your monitor, not your PC. (If this problem persists, of course, you might need to repair or replace your monitor.)

Problem: Your System Crashes—Nothing Remains Onscreen, and All Power Goes Off

This is a scary one, of which there are several possible causes.

First, you (or someone for whom you will soon have an intense dislike) accidentally cut the power to your system by turning off the system unit, turning off the wall switch, tripping over the power cord and yanking it from the socket, or tapping the off switch on your surge suppresser. Check all the power connections and switches and then turn your system back on.

Another possible cause is that your system is running too hot. This can happen if you have a lot of peripherals plugged into your machine and your power supply is a tad underpowered. (The power supply is a heavy-duty device inside your computer that "transforms" AC electrical current to a different type of current used by your system's electrical components.) Try turning off your PC and letting it cool off for five minutes or so; it might work fine when you turn it back on. If the problem persists, try moving your PC to a better-ventilated location; aiming a fan at the back of your system unit; purchasing a new fan for your system unit; or upgrading your power supply to a unit with a higher power output.

Finally, if your system is getting power and is turned on, there's a very good chance that a major calamity has just struck your system's power supply. If this is the case, it's time to take your PC into the shop.

THE ABSOLUTE MINIMUM

- There are easily explained (and corrected) causes to most startup problems. Before you panic, make sure that everything is plugged in and turned on—including your monitor and all external devices.

- While you're at it, make sure you don't have a disk in your floppy disk drive.

- If your startup problem is Windows-related, you can sometimes troubleshoot the problem by starting up in Safe mode—which you select by pressing the F8 key while Windows is loading.

- If you can't even get into Safe mode, use Windows XP's DOS-like Recovery Console to use basic commands such as format and copy.

- Most Windows startup problems are caused by bad or incorrect device drivers. You can use the System Configuration Utility to selectively load drivers, one at a time, to see which one is causing your current problem.

- If your system freezes while you're working, try pressing Ctrl+Alt+Del to close a stuck program or completely reboot your computer.

- When your computer completely crashes and goes dead, either someone turned off the power or your PC's power supply has gone bad.

23

WHAT TO DO WHEN YOU CAN'T ACCESS YOUR DISKS

Your disks—your hard disks, in particular—are where you store your valuable data. If, for some reason, you can't access your disk, you also can't get to your data. And if your disk is damaged beyond repair, your data is gone, as well.

Which is why you *really* don't want to run into hard disk problems!

Still, hard disk-related problems occur—as do problems with the other disk drives on your system, including your CD-ROM and DVD drives. Read on to learn more about what causes disk-related problems and how to deal with them.

Dealing with Hard Drive Problems

Yes, it happens. Hard disks endure a great deal of hard use and can—and do—go bad over time. This is especially so if your computer is in a space subjected to dirt and dust and cigarette smoke. The cleaner the room and the less abuse subjected, the longer your disks last.

But how do you know that your hard disk has died?

The first symptom is that when you try to turn on your computer, your hard disk spins and whirs and makes a lot of noise, but then nothing happens—your system appears to be stuck in the startup process.

The second symptom is that your system tries to start but then displays one of the following error messages (before launching Windows):

- ■ Bad or Missing Command Interpreter
- ■ Cannot load COMMAND, system halted
- ■ Cannot read file allocation table
- ■ Disk boot failure
- ■ Error loading operating system
- ■ File allocation table bad, drive C: Abort, Retry, Fail?
- ■ Invalid COMMAND.COM, system halted
- ■ Missing operating system
- ■ No system on default drive
- ■ Non-System disk or disk error: Replace and strike any key when ready

Whether your system won't start outright or you receive one of these error messages, there are a handful of steps you can take to try to get your PC up and running again, which we'll discuss next.

Problem: You Can't Access Your Hard Drive

Any number of problems can cause your hard drive to disappear. The key to diagnosing your specific problem is to follow a detailed troubleshooting procedure, outlined in the following steps.

In order, then, try the following:

1. Reboot your system. That's right. Turn your system off, wait about 30 seconds, and then turn it back on again. Don't ask why, but sometimes this fixes things.

2. If your hard disk still isn't accessible, try booting from the Windows installation CD or your Windows Emergency Startup Disk, as explained in Chapter 21, "How to Deal with a Finicky PC." If your system boots from this disk, enter MS-DOS mode and type the following command to copy a fresh version of the command interpreter to your hard disk:

COPY A:\COMMAND.COM C:\COMMAND.COM

Now remove the startup CD or disk and reboot your system by pressing Ctrl+Alt+Del.

3. If an error message tells you that you can't copy COMMAND.COM to your hard disk, or if step 2 doesn't get you up and running, you might have a completely trashed hard disk. Try booting from CD or disk again and using the DIR command to see what, if anything, is left on drive C. From MS-DOS mode, type the following command:

DIR C:

If you get an error message, you probably have a damaged or accidentally reformatted or repartitioned hard disk. If you don't get an error message, but no files are listed, something has erased the files from your hard disk; proceed to step 4 for more instructions.

4. If there are no files on your hard disk, something has wiped the disk clean. (This something could be a computer virus, a vengeful ex-employee, or some other fiend out to destroy your data.) You'll need to use your Windows installation CD to reinstall your operating system, and then proceed to reinstall all your software programs.

5. If your hard disk is totally inaccessible, you need to determine if the disk is salvageable or if it has some sort of irreparable physical damage. Get a copy of Norton Utilities or some other high-level disk-repair utility and examine your disk for physical errors. If possible, fix the errors and then proceed to step 6.

6. Assuming that your hard disk is in good physical condition, you'll need to repartition and reformat it, and then reinstall Windows. This procedure is described in Chapter 4, "Bigger Is Better: Upgrading System Storage."

7. If you can't reformat your disk, or if you continue to encounter problems after reformatting, you probably have more serious hard disk problems. You might need to consult a computer repair technician, or replace the hard disk.

tip

You can also perform the repartitioning and reformatting as part of a clean Windows install, as described in Chapter 17, "Opening New Windows: Upgrading to Windows XP."

If all else fails, don't be embarrassed about turning to a pro for help. A qualified computer technician often stands a better chance of fixing your system and restoring your data after a major disk disaster than you do. If you try and try and try again and still can't bring your hard disk back from the dead, then by all means call someone who gets paid to do the dirty work.

Note, however, that repairing a hard drive will probably cost more than just buying a new one—so the best course of action here is likely to be throwing the old one away and getting a new one.

Problem: You Just Installed a New Hard Disk and It Doesn't Work

Naturally, you might have just bought a lemon, but it's more likely that you did something wrong during the installation process. The two most likely culprits are (1) misconfigured jumpers and (2) incorrect connections. Let's tackle each one separately.

As you remember from Chapter 4, when you install a hard disk you have to configure its jumpers according to how the disk will be used. You typically have three choices: master, slave, and cable select. Chances are, you got the jumpers wrong. If the new drive is to be your main (C:) drive, you should choose the master position—*unless* your system is configured for cable select usage. If you had the jumpers one way, try them the other. And if this is to be a secondary (D: or later) drive, set the jumpers for the slave position or the cable select position, depending. Again, try it both ways.

While you're fiddling with the jumpers, check the installation manual and make sure you've properly configured the drive as either IDE 1 or IDE 2. You'll use the IDE 1 position if this drive is meant to be your main (C:) drive.

The second likely cause of your problem comes from incorrectly connecting the internal data cable. It's fairly easy (too easy) to connect the cable upside down. Try reversing the cable, taking care to line up the colored band on the side of the cable itself.

It's also possible that you can't run two drives off the same data cable. Although this configuration *should* work, sometimes it doesn't. That's why there are two IDE data cables inside your PC. (The second might be connected to your CD/DVD drive.) Both cables have two connectors, so you can try a variety of different connections to find one that works.

If the problem continues, you might need to update your PC's CMOS BIOS. (This likely involves downloading a BIOS patch from the manufacturer's Web site, or calling their tech support to obtain the update on disk.) When you update the BIOS, make any recommended changes to jumpers on your PC's motherboard; the updated BIOS should then recognize your new hard drive.

Problem: You Lost Valuable Data on a Bad Hard Disk

If you have irreplaceable data on a bad hard disk, all is not necessarily lost. There are companies that specialize in saving "lost" data from otherwise inaccessible disks. These data recovery services charge an arm an a leg—anywhere from $200 to $2,000—so you won't want to use them just to recover MP3 files and holiday recipes. But if you have truly valuable data on a disk that has gone bad, you should consider this option.

Some of the larger data recovery firms include the following:

- ActionFront Data Recovery Labs (www.datarec.com)
- Drive Service Company (www.driveservice.com)
- DriveSavers (www.drivesavers.com)
- Ontrack Data Recovery Solutions (www.ontrack.com)

Problem: Windows Doesn't Recognize Your Hard Disk's Full Size

In spite of what you might think, this isn't a Windows problem; it's a system setup problem. For some reason, when you installed the hard disk, your system BIOS didn't recognize the correct settings. You'll need to enter your CMOS BIOS setup utility and reconfigure the hard drive setting to "auto." When you reboot your system, your BIOS should recognize the hard drive during the startup process and register the proper size.

It's also possible that you're installing a really big hard disk on a much older PC. The BIOS on some older computers simply won't recognize hard disks over a certain size nor will some older versions of Windows. (For example, Windows 95 only recognizes hard disks up to 2GB.) If you're using an older BIOS, you can try updating the BIOS (check with your PC's manufacturer), but you're probably stuck using smaller-sized hard disks or using a utility like PowerQuest's Partition Magic (www.powerquest.com) to partition a single large drive into multiple smaller partitions.

Problem: Your Hard Disk Is Running Slower Than Normal

This problem is most often caused by a fragmented disk. You need to run the Windows Disk Defragmenter utility to clean up your disk and get it back up to speed. See Chapter 19, "Simple Steps to Keep Your System in Tip-Top Shape," for more details.

Dealing with CD-ROM or DVD Problems

Your hard disk isn't the only problematic drive on your system. Your CD-ROM or DVD drive can also be a source of problems mostly mechanical in nature.

Problem: Your CD/DVD Drive Doesn't Work—Nothing Happens

First, have you inserted a CD-ROM or DVD disc into your drive? Do you have the disc inserted *properly* (label side up)? If you're using an external drive, is it plugged in and powered on? Have you accessed the disc properly?

If you think you're doing everything right, you probably have some sort of power problem with your CD-ROM/DVD drive. (This is especially so if you can't open a motorized CD/DVD drive; if the drawer won't open, you're definitely not getting power.) If you're using an internal drive, you should check all the connections inside your system unit; not only should the drive be plugged into a drive controller, but it should also be plugged into your computer's power supply. If you're using an external drive, make sure all the connections are solid and that the drive actually has power (make sure the power light is on).

Problem: Your CD/DVD Drive Doesn't Work—The Drive Spins, But You Can't Access the Disc

Let's assume that you have power to your drive and have a CD-ROM or DVD inserted properly (right side up). Have you accidentally inserted a DVD disc into a CD-ROM drive? Most DVD drives will read CD-ROM discs, but not vice-versa.

If you still can't access the disc, you probably don't have the correct driver loaded into system memory. Open the Control Panel and launch the System utility; when the System Properties dialog box appears, select the Hardware tab and then click the Device Manager button. Select the entry for your CD-ROM or DVD drive, and then select Action, Update Driver. Follow the onscreen instructions to find and install the latest version of the driver software. (You can also download the latest driver from the manufacturer's Web site.)

Problem: Your CD/DVD Drive Doesn't Always Read Data Accurately

Inaccurate data can result from several problems, most likely a scratched or dirty disc. You can buy commercial CD/DVD cleaners that will remove surface dirt and debris; scratches are less easily fixed if at all.

It's also possible that the laser beam inside your CD-ROM/DVD drive is dirty or out of alignment. You can try to "blow" the dirt out of the drive with compressed air, or—in some cases—wipe the laser lens with a cotton swab. However, your best bet is to see a repair person ASAP to get this puppy fixed.

Problem: Your CD/DVD Drive Can't Read a Rewritable CD

First, are you trying to read a CD-RW disc in a CD-ROM drive? If so, you can't do it; CD-RW discs use a special data format that can only be read by CD-RW drives.

If you're having trouble reading a CD-R disc in a CD-ROM drive, you could have a simple incompatibility problem. Generally, this is more of a problem with playing CD-R discs on older, slower CD-ROM drives, or with discs recorded on older CD-R drives. If you encounter this kind of incompatibility, there's not much you can do about it, save for trying the disc in another machine or upgrading to a newer CD-ROM drive.

Problem: You Can't Play Music CDs on Your CD/DVD Drive

To get audio from your CD-ROM or DVD drive, an audio cable must be connected between your drive and your sound card. If you haven't connected this cable, you won't hear audio from *any* CD or DVD discs you play!

Also, and this might seem blatantly obvious, make sure that you actually have the volume turned up on your PC and the speakers plugged in and turned on. And make sure the volume isn't muted, either.

Problem: Your CD-R/RW Drive Won't Burn a CD

First, look to see that you have the right type of disc (recordable or rewriteable) in the drive, and that the disc is blank. Second, make sure you have a spare 1GB or so on your *hard disk*, as Windows writes the files to your hard disk before it burns them to CD; if you don't have enough free space, you can't copy files from one CD to another.

If you have trouble with skips and dropouts on CDs you burn (or if the burn fails altogether), there are two things to check. First, you might need to reduce the recording speed; recording faster than your drive can handle will result in write errors. Second, try burning the disc again, but this time close all your other applications including your Internet connection. If your computer has to multitask during the burning process, it can cause your drive to stutter, with resultant skips and gaps. (The technical name for this problem is a *buffer underrun*, and you might even see an error message referring to this; some newer drives include technologies that prevent this underrun problem.) A good rule is to not use your computer at all when you're burning a disc; let the burner have all the resources it needs to make a clean recording.

Problem: Your Newly Installed CD/DVD Drive Doesn't Work Right

Post-installation problems are typically caused by improper or missing device drivers.

The first thing to check is if your CD/DVD drive shows up in the Device Manager. Look for an entry for CD-ROM or DVD; if no such entry exists, your system doesn't know that it has a CD-ROM or DVD drive attached. Use the Add Hardware Wizard to properly install the drivers for your drive.

What if there *is* a CD-ROM or DVD entry in the Device Manager? Then you'll want to delete the entry and reinstall the drive from scratch. Highlight the drive entry and click the Uninstall button, and then return to the Control Panel to run the Add Hardware Wizard.

You should also check for conflicts between your new CD-ROM/DVD drive and some older peripheral. This is easy to do; just open the Windows Help utility and launch the Hardware Troubleshooter (called the Hardware Conflict Troubleshooter in older versions of Windows). All you have to do is follow the Troubleshooter's onscreen instructions to find and resolve any conflicts you're having. In the end, if you have a conflict, you'll need to change the DMA or port assignment for one of the conflicted devices.

If you still can't fix the problem, you'll probably need to call in a technician to help you track down the apparent DMA or port conflict.

THE ABSOLUTE MINIMUM

When you're experiencing drive-related problems, keep these key points in mind:

- Hard disks are like any other mechanical device—they go bad over time.
- If you can't access your system's hard disk, you'll need to boot from your Windows installation CD or Windows Emergency Startup Disk.
- Some physical problems can be found and fixed by using a third-party disk repair utility.
- If your data is scrambled or corrupted, you might need to repartition and reformat your hard disk if you want to use it again—although it's probably cheaper to buy a new drive than fix an old one.
- Data recovery services can often save lost data from a crashed drive—if you haven't reformatted or repartitioned the disk since the disaster occurred.
- CD-ROM and DVD problems are often driver-related; you might need to update the device driver, or uninstall and reinstall the device within Windows.
- Optical drives can sometimes conflict with other devices in your system; use the Hardware Troubleshooter to track down and fix potential conflicts.

24

WHAT TO DO WHEN YOUR MOUSE OR KEYBOARD WON'T WORK

Until we get computers with workable voice recognition, you have to rely on your mouse and keyboard to communicate with your PC. And if these input devices break down, there's no way to control your machine.

The good news is, even if you have really bad mouse or keyboard problems, the most likely fix is cheap and easy—just buy a new one. Mice and keyboards are inexpensive enough that you don't want to spend a lot of time troubleshooting problems. If it breaks, replace it.

And if it isn't broken, you probably have a connection problem—also easily correctable. So don't let yourself be plagued by an ongoing input crisis. Do some simple plugging and unplugging, and then buy a new device if you need it.

Dealing with Mouse Problems

Next to your keyboard (both metaphorically and physically), your mouse is the part of your system you use most often. Your mouse is constantly in your right hand (unless you're left-handed, of course), rolling along your mouse pad as you point your cursor at one or another part of Windows.

So what do you do if it quits working?

Fortunately, a mouse needs little maintenance, and few things can go wrong with it. But given the right circumstances, things can and will go wrong. Look at this list to determine what problems your mouse might be causing you.

Problem: Your Mouse Doesn't Work at All

First, make sure that your mouse is connected correctly to the back of your system unit. You might have the mouse connected to the wrong port on your machine—it's easy to confuse the mouse and keyboard connections as they're physically identical—or it might have come loose or become disconnected. Even if it looks like both your mouse and keyboard are plugged in, trace the cables to makes sure they're not mixed up.

If simply replugging your mouse doesn't work, you might have to reboot your computer to recognize the replug. You'll probably have to turn off your system with the main power switch or button; if you can't click or type, you can't exit Windows normally.

Next, check to see whether your PC has the right mouse driver loaded. Open the Device Manager and click the + next to Mouse. Confirm that the mouse driver listed is correct; if there is no driver listed or if the icon has a red X through it, you'll need to reinstall your mouse driver with the Add Hardware Wizard. If there is more than one mouse listed, highlight the one that you're *not* using and click the Remove button.

Finally, your mouse driver might conflict with some other device on your system, which is not an uncommon occurrence. Your mouse is probably using your system's COM1 port. This is fine and dandy, but if another device in the system (like a modem) is using the COM3 port, conflicts might develop between the two devices. (Don't ask me why, but it all gets pretty technical and has to do with IRQ lines and interrupts and other stuff regular people don't understand.)

You can reconfigure a device's COM port from the Windows Device Manager. For example, to reconfigure your modem's COM port (in Windows XP), go to the Control Panel and open the System Properties utility; then select the Hardware tab and click the Device Manager button. Right-click the modem listing and select Properties from the pop-up menu. When the Properties dialog box appears, select the Advanced tab and click the Advanced Port Settings button. When the Advanced Settings dialog box appears, pull down the COM Port Number list and select a different COM port. (It's sometimes easier to reconfigure your modem's COM port than the one for your mouse.)

If you can reconfigure your mouse to use port COM2, or your other device to use port COM4, you might solve the problem. Each type of device has its own methods for changing ports, so you'll need to check the instructions for your specific mouse and other devices. (More often than not, you'll have to *uninstall* the device you want to change, and then reinstall it to a different port.)

If this adjustment is beyond you, call in a technician.

Now, you're probably asking, how do you make all these configuration changes if you can't use your mouse? Simple—most mouse operations can actually be performed from the keyboard! See Table 24.1 for a list of these "hidden" keyboard shortcuts.

Table 24.1   Keyboard Shortcuts for Common Mouse Operations

Key(s)	Operation
Ctrl+Esc *or* Windows logo key	Opens the Start Menu; use arrow keys to navigate items on the menu
Shift+F10 *or* Application key	Opens a context menu for the selected item (same as right-clicking)
Alt+Tab	Switches between running applications
Alt+F	Switches between multiple windows in the same program
Alt+-(Hyphen)	Lets you restore, move, resize, minimize, or maximize a window
Alt+underlined letter in menu	Opens corresponding menu and runs commands in menu
Alt+F4	Closes the active window
Tab	Move to the next control in an open dialog box
Shift+Tab	Move to the previous control in an open dialog box
Spacebar	Clicks the active button or selects check boxes and option buttons in an open dialog box
Ctrl+Tab	Cycles through property tabs in an open dialog box
Enter	Same as clicking the selected button
F1	Launches Windows Help

Problem: Using Other Peripherals Causes Your Mouse to Act Up

If your mouse quits working after you initiate a print job or use your modem, chances are you have this peripheral on a conflicting interrupt with your mouse. (It's the old COM1/COM3 problem again.) You'll need to change the port assignment of either your mouse or your other peripheral (probably your modem) to resolve this conflict.

Problem: Your Mouse Moves Erratically

If you find your mouse jumping around of its own accord or not holding its position correctly while you're moving it around, chances are you have a bad or incorrect mouse driver installed. Check with your mouse manufacturer (via their Web site, typically) to get the latest version of the mouse driver.

This problem can also be caused by a dirty or broken mouse—especially if your mouse is of the old-fashioned rollerball type. Try taking the mouse apart and cleaning it.

In addition, this problem can be caused by the old interrupt conflict (COM1 versus COM3). Make sure that you have your mouse hooked up to a port that doesn't conflict with other accessories in your system.

It's possible, too, that you need to adjust the settings in the Mouse Properties dialog box; select the Mouse icon in the Control Panel and make any necessary changes.

Problem: Your Wireless Mouse Moves Erratically—If at All

This problem has a simple solution—replace your batteries! Low batteries in a wireless device will cause all sorts of problems. In a mouse, this typically means that the cursor slows down, jerks around, or seems to hit an invisible wall. Fresh batteries should fix things right up.

If new batteries don't fix the problem, you have some sort of wireless interference. Try moving the wireless receiver to a new position—preferably away from other wireless devices (wireless network adapters/base stations, cordless phones, baby monitors, and the like). If interference continues, see if you can change transmitting/receiving channels on one of the devices, or consider turning off the interfering device while you're computing.

Problem: You Receive an Error Message About Your Mouse

If you receive an error message saying that the mouse driver could not find the mouse, the mouse was not connected correctly when you booted your computer.

Reconnect your mouse and reboot. If you still receive this message, you could have a dead mouse. Buy a new one.

Problem: You Spilled Something on Your Mouse

Mice don't like water or other liquids. Don't spill stuff on your mouse!

If you have a wet mouse, all hope is not lost. First, if possible, take your mouse apart and remove the roller ball. Carefully wash the ball with soap and water (*don't* use rubbing alcohol or anything similar!), and use a soft cloth to soak up any excess liquid on the outside and inside of the mouse. Dry the mouse (and all mouse parts) overnight, and then reassemble your mouse. If you plug it in and all works fine, good job! If not… well, fortunately a new mouse isn't that expensive. Just remember to use the Device Manager to delete your old mouse driver (if you can) before you add the new mouse to your system.

tip

You might want to try swapping your (apparently) dead mouse with a friend's still living rodent. If your friend's mouse works and yours doesn't, that means you really do have a dead mouse. If your friend's mouse *doesn't* work, that means you have problems inside your system unit or with some system settings!

Dealing with Keyboard Problems

Keyboards aren't much more complex than mice. After all, a computer keyboard is nothing more than a bunch of switches, covered by plastic key caps. So there's not much to go wrong.

Right?

Here's a short list of keyboard-related problems you can run into:

It can get unplugged. The keys can start sticking. (This is exacerbated when you pour soda or coffee on the keyboard; try to avoid doing this.) The key mechanisms can simply go off and not transmit the proper electrical impulses. Some of the other electronic parts in the keyboard can go bad. You can type so fast that your system can't keep up with you. (Keyboard signals are stored in a kind of temporary memory called a *buffer* until your system can get around to processing them; you can actually fill up the buffer if you type quickly enough, causing a "buffer overflow" effect.) And, finally, you can set up parts of your system incorrectly so that your keyboard seems to be messed up.

If your keyboard does happen to go bad, you should just throw it away. You can buy new keyboards for less than $50, and you'd probably pay that much trying to get your old one fixed. It's cheaper to buy a new one.

Problem: Your Keyboard Won't Type—No Characters Appear Onscreen

First, check to make sure that the keyboard is firmly connected to the system unit. If need be, reboot so that your system realizes that the keyboard is actually there.

If that doesn't solve your problem, you probably have a bad keyboard. Try hooking another keyboard to your computer. If the new keyboard works and your own keyboard doesn't, you have a bad keyboard.

If another keyboard doesn't work on your system either, you might have some weird problem in your system unit—maybe a bad keyboard port. You can call the repair shop and take your PC in for repairs or just buy a USB keyboard, instead.

It's also possible that a frozen keyboard is caused by an incorrect keyboard driver within Windows. Open the Device Manager, scroll down to the Keyboard section, and highlight the keyboard driver. If the driver is nonfunctional, it will appear with a large red "X" over its icon. If this is the case, click the Remove button to delete the driver, then return to Control Panel and run the Add Hardware Wizard to reinstall your keyboard driver.

Problem: Your Keyboard Quits Working After You Install a New Peripheral

The most probable cause of a frozen keyboard after a major system change is a memory conflict. Your new device is now trying to share the same memory space needed by your keyboard.

The first thing to do is to remove the device that is causing the conflict. So whatever you just installed—uninstall it!

Now reinstall the new device again, and see if there are any settings you can affect manually during installation. (There probably aren't.) If you continue to have keyboard problems after reinstalling the new device, contact the device's manufacturer for assistance.

Problem: Your Keyboard Won't Type—Every Time You Press a Key, You Hear a Beep

Your keyboard is probably connected, but maybe not correctly. Make sure that the connectors are firmly plugged into one another. If that isn't the problem, something funny has happened while you were typing—maybe you typed too fast and filled the keyboard buffer. Try rebooting. (If your keyboard is really dead, you can't reboot by pressing Ctrl+Alt+Del, so you have to turn the system on and off from the reset button or the main power switch.)

If, after rebooting, you still have keyboard problems, try hooking up another keyboard to your PC. (Make sure you turn the PC off before you replace the keyboard, and then reboot with the new keyboard connected.) If the replacement keyboard works, you need to buy a new keyboard. Fortunately, keyboards aren't that expensive to replace.

Problem: You Spill Some Liquid on the Keyboard

When you spill the contents of your glass onto your keyboard, several things might happen:

- *Nothing.* You're lucky—though you should turn off your computer and let your keyboard dry out before using it again, just to make sure that none of the electronics are damaged.
- *It shorts out.* Liquids and electronics don't mix. Spilling water or any other liquid onto your keyboard could cause the circuitry to short-circuit. Whatever you do, don't use the keyboard again until it dries out—or you get it fixed or replaced.
- *It gets gummed up.* The sugar in most soft drinks can get down into the switches under the keys on your keyboard, which can cause them to malfunction or stick.

If you spill something on your keyboard, the first thing to do is turn off your computer and unplug your keyboard. Then use a soft cloth to wipe up the spill, as much as possible. You can then pull off individual keycaps, taking care not to damage the switches underneath, and clean up any excess liquid there.

It's a good idea to let the keyboard dry overnight, before testing it again. After drying, plug it back in and fire up your PC; if you're lucky, everything will work fine.

The worst that can happen is that you spill a liquid with a high sugar content (like a cola or other soft drink), and the residue gunks up your keyboard switches. If this happens, you can take the keyboard in for a professional cleaning, or just spring for a new keyboard.

Problem: You Type a Lowercase Letter, but an Uppercase Letter Appears Onscreen

You have the Caps Lock key on. Press the Caps Lock key again to turn it off. (The Caps Lock light should reflect the position of the key; if the light is on, the key is on.)

Sometimes your system can get confused and think that Caps Lock is on when it really isn't supposed to be. I don't know what causes this, but it happens to me sometimes when I type just a little too fast in some programs. If this happens to you, you might have to reboot to reset the system.

Problem: You Type a Number, but the Onscreen Cursor Moves Instead

You have the Num Lock key off. Press Num Lock again to turn it on. (The Num Lock light should reflect the position of the key; if the light is on, the key is on.)

As noted in the previous problem, sometimes your system can get confused and think that Num Lock is on when it really isn't supposed to be. If this happens, you might have to reboot to reset the system.

Problem: You Type One Key, and a Different Character Appears Onscreen

This is an interesting problem with four possible causes:

- You really didn't type what you thought you did. Look at your fingers. Now look at the screen. Now look at your fingers again. Is everything the way it should be? Good!

- If you have a programmable keyboard, you or someone else might have reprogrammed the keys so that they don't do what they normally do. Refer to the keyboard's manual for instructions about how to reprogram the keys.

- If you're in a specific software program, some programs let you reprogram the keyboard from within the program. When you exit the program, your keyboard should be back to normal.

- It's possible your keyboard is broken. Try hooking another keyboard up to your system and see how it works.

Problem: Your Keyboard Isn't Responding Properly

What do you do if you hold down a key and it repeats too fast or too slow? Windows lets you make adjustments to your keyboard via the Keyboard Properties dialog box.

Just open the Control Panel and select Keyboard, and then select the Speed tab. Adjust the Repeat Delay and Repeat Speed settings to your liking, and then test your settings by clicking in the blank box and holding down a key. After you have things adjusted to your liking, click OK.

Problem: Your Wireless Keyboard Isn't Responding Properly

This is the same issue as with a wireless mouse—your batteries are getting weak. Replace the batteries in your wireless keyboard to put things right.

It's also possible that you're experiencing interference with some other wireless device. Try moving your wireless receiver or the offending device, or turning off the other device while you're at the computer.

Problem: You Press the Page Up or Page Down Keys, but Your Window Doesn't Scroll

Check to see if the Scroll Lock on your keyboard is activated. Sometimes having Scroll Lock on will cause strange scrolling problems with some programs.

THE ABSOLUTE MINIMUM

- A mouse can get quite dirty over time, which can effect movement; remove and clean your mouse's roller mechanism periodically.

- One common cause of mouse-related problems is a COM port conflict.

- Most keyboard problems are caused by age and poor maintenance; remember to clean your keyboard regularly and avoid spilling anything on the keys.

- Typing too fast can cause commands to jam up the keyboard buffer and cause your keyboard to freeze.

- If you have a bad mouse or keyboard, just replace it; new models aren't that expensive.

IN THIS CHAPTER

- Your printer won't print
- Your printer's output is garbled
- You have a paper jam

25

WHAT TO DO WHEN YOUR PRINTER WON'T PRINT

If you have to have a computer-related problem, it might as well be a problem with your printer. That's because even if your printer quits working completely, it really doesn't throw all your plans into jeopardy.

You can, after all, copy the files you want to print to a CD and take that disc to another PC or a service bureau (such as Kinko's) to print. Or you can borrow a friend's printer, or—if you're connected to a network— use another printer on the LAN for your print job. You can even email your file to someone else to print.

That said, if you have a problem with your printer, you need to fix it. Read on to learn more about printer problems and how to deal with them.

Understanding Potential Problems

Printers are mechanical devices with lots of moving parts. And any time you have moving parts, you have something that can break or wear out over time.

So when you click the old print button and nothing happens, what are the likely causes?

First, you might have the wrong printer driver installed in Windows. You might have either simply selected the wrong driver for your printer, or Windows might have mistaken your printer for another model, or the driver selected might be out of date. While we're in this area, it's also possible that various aspects of your printer setup might be incorrect, which can cause some highly unusual problems. You should also check your font setup because fonts themselves can cause perplexing problems if they're not installed correctly.

In addition, any new input or output device you've installed since you installed your main printer could have changed your printer's settings. (It's kind of like the last device installed gets dibs on key system settings.) If you've recently added a scanner or a digital camera or fax software or anything like that and then experienced printer problems, try uninstalling your printer (and all printer drivers) and then reinstalling your printer so that your printer is now the last device installed—and thus controls key system settings.

It's also possible that if you're printing large or graphically complex documents, you might not have enough disk space or memory to print. Make sure that you have plenty of both, because Windows needs all the space it can get to complete the printing operation.

Finally, you could have real printer hardware problems. These problems range from the mundane (you're out of paper, you forgot to turn on the printer, a cable came loose) to the fairly serious (your printer is broken!). Check all your cables and connections and make sure that your printer is actually turned on.

The bottom line is there are a lot of things you need to check if you have printer problems, both hardware- and software-related. So if you have printing problems, hunker down and plow through the problems/solutions section, coming up next.

tip

One of the best ways to track down a printing-related problem is to use the Windows Print Troubleshooter, found in the Help utility.

Dealing with Printer Problems

The types of problems you might encounter with your printer fall into four basic categories: The printer has no power, the printer doesn't print, the printout is garbled, or pages of the printout are missing. Read on to find out more about each problem and ways to solve it.

Problem: Your Printer Has No Power

This is the perennial problem with computer hardware. By now you know the drill:

Make sure that the power cord is plugged into both the power outlet and the back of the printer. Make sure that the power outlet has power; check all fuses and circuit breakers, as well as surge suppressors. Make sure that the printer is online. (This is normally accomplished by a front-panel button of some sort.) And check the internal fuse in the printer itself.

If all the right parts in your system have power and your printer is online, your problem is more serious. The biggest potential source for this type of problem is the power supply in the printer. If this is causing your particular problem, it's time to call the repair center and ready your checkbook.

Problem: Your Printer Has Power but Doesn't Print

The first item to check is whether your printer is connected correctly to your computer. Check the connecting cable to make sure that the connections are tight. You also should unplug each end of the cable to ensure that none of the connecting wires are bent, making a bad connection. You might also want to change the printer cable. Cables can get old, and the wires inside can break; try a new cable and see whether this change fixes the problem.

Next, you should make sure that the printer is connected to the correct port on the back of your computer. Checking the port connection is not always as simple as it seems. Some computers come with more than one printer port, and your printer might be hooked up to the wrong one. If you have multiple printer ports, try plugging your printer into the other ports.

Next, check the paper feed of your printer. If you're out of paper, your printer can't print. You

caution

Anytime you change *any* connection between your system unit and any external device (such as your printer), you probably need to turn your computer off and then back on again for the connection change to register with your system. So if you're plugging in cables, reboot your system when you're done.

also should check the paper path inside the printer to make sure that no stray pieces of paper are lodged inside. Make certain, too, that your printer is online, or set in the *on* position.

You should also check to see if your printer is paused. Check your front panel buttons to make sure that your printer is online. You should also double-click the Printer icon in the Windows system tray to open the Print Manger and make sure the job isn't paused from within Windows.

Another potential cause of this problem is having the "manual feed" option selected in Windows or on your printer. If this option is selected and there is no paper in the manual feed tray, your printer just sits there waiting for someone (like, oh, *you!*) to insert some paper. The solution to this is to either add some paper to the manual feed tray or switch off the manual feed option.

It's also possible that you have the wrong driver installed or selected within Windows. Right-click on this printer's icon in the Printers window and select Properties. Check the Details tab to make sure you're printing to the correct port using the correct driver. If you need to change drivers, pick one from the pull-down list, or click the New Driver button to add a new printer driver.

It's possible that the correct driver is installed, but something has gone screwy with how Windows reads the driver information. Go to the Printers Window and *delete* the current printer, and then use the Add Printer Wizard to reinstall the printer driver. You might also want to check with your printer's manufacturer to see if there is an updated version of your driver available.

note

The tabs in the Printer Properties dialog box are specific to the brand and model of printer you have installed. If your Print Properties dialog box doesn't have a Details tab, look for a Ports or Advanced tab instead.

In addition, it's possible that a recently installed device has somehow mucked with your printer configuration in Windows. Try deleting your printer driver and then reinstalling it, as described in the previous paragraph. Because the last device installed on your system can overwrite previous configuration information, go ahead and make your printer the last installed device.

If none of these suggestions solves your problem, you're looking at a major computer or printer problem. Try hooking up another printer to your computer; if the new printer works, it's time to take your old printer into the shop. If the new printer doesn't work, you probably have a defective port in your computer.

Problem: Your Printer Prints, but Output Is Smudged or Garbled

If your printout is not as you expected, there might be several causes. The most likely cause, believe it or not, is our old friend the poorly connected cable. If all the instructions don't make it from the computer to the printer, your printout will be incomplete, if not totally out of whack. Check all cable connections to ensure a good throughput of data. If that doesn't fix the problem, just change the printer cable. An old or damaged cable could be causing your problems.

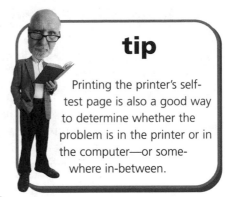

tip

Printing the printer's self-test page is also a good way to determine whether the problem is in the printer or in the computer—or some-where in-between.

Another cause of print garbage might be the printer itself. If you have a low or old toner cartridge in a laser printer or a near-empty ink cartridge in an inkjet printer, your printout will be lighter than normal, perhaps even unreadable. If necessary, change the cartridge and run the print job again.

If you're using a laser printer, you might get black streaks on your output. This problem is most often caused by an old toner cartridge, or by a dirty roller or printer cleaning bar. If you replace the toner cartridge and clean the suspect parts (using a cotton swab) and you *still* experience black streaks, your printer might need service.

If you're using an inkjet printer, it's possible that your print jets are clogged. You'll need to unclog the print jet by inserting a small pin into the jet.

It's also possible that a paper misfeed in your printer caused the printout to become smudged or out of line; if this is the case, straighten the paper feed and start the print job again.

An incorrect printer setup in Windows can also cause unusual printouts. Make sure that Windows is configured for the exact type of printer you're using. Also make sure that you have the correct landscape (horizontal) or portrait (vertical) printing option selected.

If none of this works, you probably have a problem somewhere in your printer. Although a bad printer port on your PC could be the culprit, more than likely some internal problem with your printer is causing the poor printout. (You can confirm this by printing a self-test page; if it looks bad, the problem is in your printer.) Consult your friendly repair center.

Problem: Your Printed Page Looks Half-Finished

If you're trying to print a document with a lot of graphics (especially on lower-priced laser printers), you might find that your printer doesn't have enough memory to print the entire document. What you'll get is about half the document—and not always a contiguous half! You can do one of several things to rectify the problem:

- *Add more memory to your printer.* If you do a lot of heavy graphics printing, you probably need at least 1MB of RAM installed in your printer. You might be able to add the memory yourself, or you might want to have a qualified laser printer technician do the job for you.

- *Instruct Windows to print this document at a lower resolution.* Go to the Printer Properties dialog box for your printer and select the Graphics tab (if your printer has this option). Select a lower resolution (which requires less memory and gives you less finely detailed output) and see if you can now print your document.

- *Simplify your document.* If you're using a lot of different fonts and graphics, take some out. It's not an ideal solution, but it might be the only way you'll get this particular document printed on time!

Problem: Your Printer Prints, but the Fonts Aren't Correct

If you create a document on a PC with one set of fonts installed, and try to print it on another PC with different fonts installed, you could be in for a real surprise! Windows will try to "match" missing fonts, but quite often the match leaves a lot to be desired—resulting in different line lengths and page breaks than what you had originally. Your options are to install the missing fonts on the PC you're printing from, or change the fonts in the document in question. (A word to the wise: stick to common fonts such as Arial and Times New Roman if you think you'll be sharing a document on multiple PCs.)

Problem: Your Color Printer Doesn't Print All Available Colors

This problem is most likely caused by an old ink cartridge. It's not unusual for some colors to get depleted before others, throwing off your color output. If you're seeing less blue (or red or yellow or black) than normal, chances are it's time to change your cartridge.

Problem: Paper Jams in Your Printer

It's possible that your printer's internal paper feed mechanisms are getting dirty. You can try taking the printer apart yourself to clean out any pieces of scrap paper or other debris, or you might want to take it into the shop to let a pro deal with it.

You might also be getting some paper sticking to other sheets of paper in your paper tray. (This happens more often with cheaper paper—spend a little more and get the good stuff!) Try thumbing through the stack of paper before inserting it into the tray; this should loosen up the paper and make it feed easier into your printer.

Finally, you might need to change the grade of paper you use with your laser or inkjet printer. Lightweight papers tend to jam up the works, so switch to something heavier if you experience a lot of problems.

THE ABSOLUTE MINIMUM

- Most printer problems are caused by a bad cable connection, a misconfiguration in Windows, or a bad or outdated print driver.

- All printers need periodic maintenance; make sure you regularly change toner or ink cartridges, clean the paper path and feed, and—if you have an inkjet printer—use the cleaning option to clean the ink jets and cartridge.

- If you're having trouble printing graphically intense documents on a laser printer, you might need to add memory to the printer or simplify the documents.

- Lightweight paper can cause unexpected paper jams; use a better grade of paper to keep things running smoothly.

IN THIS CHAPTER

- Your monitor goes blank
- Your monitor displays a screen full of garbage
- Your monitor displays at the wrong resolution
- Your monitor whines—or pops and crackles
- Your dual-monitor display doesn't work properly

26

WHAT TO DO WHEN YOUR DISPLAY LOOKS FUNNY

Displaying a picture on your computer screen is a complicated procedure. First, your operating system (Windows) has to generate the instructions to display a character or image. Next, a video card has to interpret this command and generate the electronic impulses that create the image. Finally, these impulses have to be transmitted (via a cable) to your display monitor, which fires up a series of phosphor dots in such a way that a picture is displayed.

So why do you care? Simple—any one of these things can go bad, causing you to have display problems.

What Can Give You Bad Video

All this video card and monitor business sounds fairly complicated although, if it's all running right, it's no big deal. Only when something goes wrong in the process do you need to get involved.

So what can go wrong? Here's a short list:

■ *Your cables might be disconnected.* If the cable from the video card to your monitor isn't firmly connected, all sorts of strange images can show up onscreen. Or, sometimes, absolutely nothing at all shows up. Cable problems are like that. So if you have a video problem, you should *always* check your connections, including the power cable. And while you're at it, make sure that you don't have any bent pins on your cable plugs.

■ *Your monitor might need adjusting.* Most monitors have the same type of picture controls as your TV set—contrast, brightness, and even vertical and horizontal hold on some models. Some monitors let you adjust the size and position of the display image itself. If your display doesn't look right, adjust it.

■ *You might have a bad monitor/card combination.* Believe it or not, some newer video cards don't work with some older monitors. In particular, you can't use a higher-resolution card with a lower-resolution monitor. Check with your dealer to make sure that you have the right monitor/card combination.

> **tip**
>
> To keep your monitor in tip-top shape, avoid dusty areas and strong magnetic fields. You should also use a soft, static-free cloth (or special "screen cleaner" wet pads) to clean your monitor screen at least once a week.

■ *Your video card might be inserted improperly.* The video card is just like any other expansion card in your computer. If the video card isn't seated in its slot properly, it won't work right.

■ *Your video card might be set up incorrectly.* Some video cards use either separate software programs or switches on the card itself to adapt to a particular monitor and system. If the card's switches are set wrong, the display might not work at all. Check your card's switch settings against those recommended in the card's documentation.

■ *Your drivers might be set up incorrectly.* If you've loaded the wrong video driver for your video card, you could get gibberish on your screen. If Windows doesn't recognize your video card, it will run a generic video driver—which will display the lowest possible resolution. It's also possible that Windows will recognize the *wrong* video card, mistaking your card for another card and causing all sorts of havoc. As is the case when installing any new device, you should always double-check your driver setup.

■ *You might need a new video driver.* Check with the manufacturer of your video card to make sure that you have the latest version of their video driver. Older drivers might not work with newer versions of Windows.

■ *Your monitor might be on the fritz.* If your TV can go on the fritz, your PC monitor can go on the fritz, too. If you get lots of lines onscreen, or smoke out the back of the monitor, or if nothing at all happens, suspect the worst.

■ Your video card might be bad. Enough said.

Dealing with Video Problems

Let's get right to it and start troubleshooting a variety of video-related problems.

Problem: Your Monitor Is Dead—The Power Light Isn't On

Check the monitor's power cable. Is the power cable plugged into a power source? Is the power source turned on? Is the monitor turned on?

If the cables are okay and the monitor is turned on and has power, you have a problem with your monitor, probably a blown fuse or a bad power supply. See your local repair center—don't try to fix it yourself.

Problem: Your Monitor Doesn't Display— But the Power Light Is On

If the power light for the monitor is on, all the power cables are okay. The cable from the monitor to the system unit, however, might have a bad connection. You should also check your video card to make sure that it is installed and set up

caution

Never open up your monitor's case even if it's turned off and unplugged. You could get a nasty shock fiddling about inside what is essentially a miniature television set!

properly. In addition, check your monitor's contrast and brightness controls to make sure that they're turned up enough to display a picture.

If you still don't have a picture, try connecting another monitor to your system. If that monitor displays properly, you have some sort of hardware problem with *your* monitor. If the second monitor doesn't work either, the problem is probably with your video card. Try installing a new card or having your existing setup examined by a professional.

Problem: Your Monitor Doesn't Display—The System Unit Issues a Series of Beeps

Your PC uses beeps to communicate with you when something is wrong with the video setup. Check the settings on your video card to make sure that they're correct for your system. Also check any switches on the motherboard to make sure that they're set up correctly for your type of video card. (You should consult your system's instruction manual for details on this procedure.) Check to make sure that your video card is seated properly in its slot; you may even want to try inserting the card in another slot. If none of these suggestions works, try a new video card, or have your system examined by a professional.

In a pre-Windows 98, system, if you have two video cards installed at the same time, they can sometimes interfere with each other and cause neither to work properly. Try removing one of the cards; if this results in the remaining card working, you need to reconfigure one or both of the cards to better work together. (With Windows 98 and later you can install two video cards to run multiple monitors simultaneously.)

Problem: Your Monitor Works, but Displays an Error Message Before Windows Loads

If you see an error message, you at least know that video signals are getting to your monitor. Look for these common messages:

`Bad or missing FILENAME`

In this message, the `FILENAME` refers to your video card's device driver file. Make sure that the driver has been copied to your hard disk and selected properly within Windows.

`NUMBERxx`

This type of message (such as **24xx**) indicates that you have a defective video card or a problem on the motherboard, or that you are trying to display in a mode that your system can't display. Check all the switch settings on your card and mother-board, and if the problem persists, see a repair technician.

Problem: Your Monitor Works, but Displays a Screen Full of Garbage

If the display isn't displaying properly, you most likely have a loose connection or a bad cable between your video card and your monitor. Check all your connections and cables, as well as your video card installation. Make it a rule to be certain that all the parts of your system are hooked up and set up properly.

It's also possible that the configuration of the video card itself is wrong. Check the instructions for your video card to see if there are any switches that need to be set; when in doubt, configure your card for the lowest possible (default) resolution, which all monitors can display.

If your display looks fine on initial startup but goes to garbage when Windows launches, your monitor is working fine but you have a Windows-related problem, such as one of the following:

- You've selected a resolution that your monitor can't display.
- You're using the wrong video display driver.
- You're using an outdated video driver.

At this point, your challenge is to get into Windows and make the appropriate changes—which you can do from Windows Safe mode. When Windows loads in Safe mode, you can open the Display Properties dialog box (from the Control Panel) and update or change the resolution of the current video driver. You can also use the Device Manager to delete the current driver and the Add Hardware Wizard to install a new one.

Windows *should* recognize your monitor and automatically display only compatible resolutions—thus preventing you from setting an incorrect resolution. However, if Windows *doesn't* recognize your monitor (which sometimes happens), you're free to misconfigure your system's display resolution.

Problem: Windows Displays at a Lower Resolution Than Normal

Chances are that, for some reason, Windows started in Safe mode. (You can verify this by looking at the corners of your screen; the words "Safe Mode" should be displayed in all four corners.) Safe mode uses a minimal driver configuration—including a generic VGA driver for your video display, which explains the lower resolution.

Try rebooting your PC to see if it restarts in normal mode. If it still boots into Safe mode, you'll need to figure out what kind of problem is causing this behavior.

See Chapter 22, "What to Do When Your Computer Won't Start or Freezes Up," for more about Safe mode.

Problem: Your New Video Card Doesn't Display at Its Maximum Resolution or Color Depth

You installed a video card that is supposedly capable of 1920×1080 resolution with 32-bit color, but the only options in the Display Properties dialog box are for 640×480 and 800×600 at 256 colors. What gives?

The most likely cause of this problem is that you somehow installed the wrong video driver. Use the Device Manager to either update or uninstall the video driver, and then use the Add Hardware Wizard to reinstall the driver(taking care to select the right one this time). Alternately, reinstall the driver via your video card's installation utility.

Problem: Your Screen Display Flickers

Some high resolution displays use what is called *interlaced* display technology. An interlaced display lets you run higher resolutions on lower-cost hardware, but sometimes results in a very annoying screen flicker. Your options are to buy a video card/monitor combination that can run in *noninterlaced* mode, or to select a lower video resolution.

Problem: Your CRT Monitor Doesn't Display—It Makes a High-Pitched Whine

This whine indicates that your CRT-type monitor, for some reason, is operating at the wrong frequency. Turn it off *immediately*—this problem could seriously damage your monitor! Now check the settings on your video card. Chances are that it's set to a higher resolution than your monitor is capable of displaying. If this isn't the problem, your video card itself could be defective. If your video card is okay, your monitor might be defective.

Problem: Your CRT Monitor Pops and Crackles and Starts to Smell

Like the rest of a computer system, monitors can get dusty. When dust builds up inside the monitor, it can generate static charges.

It's also possible that the power supply inside the monitor has become defective. If the monitor demonstrates these symptoms, turn it off immediately and take it to a repair center. The technicians can either clean your monitor or replace the power supply if necessary.

Problem: Your Dual-Monitor Display Doesn't Work Properly

Configuring your system to run two monitors, as explained in Chapter 9, "The Big Picture: Upgrading Video Cards and Monitors," can expose you to a variety of potential problems. Naturally, any type of problem you can experience with one monitor can also be experienced on your second monitor. In addition, you can run into the following problems:

- You have trouble moving windows from one monitor to another. Chances are you have the primary and secondary monitors switched; you'll need to open the Display Properties dialog box and reconfigure the order of the monitors.

- You have trouble getting your second monitor to work. Make sure you've enabled the second monitor in the Display Properties dialog box. (Select the Settings tab, select the secondary monitor icon, and then select Extend My Windows Desktop Onto This Computer.)

- If your second monitor still doesn't work, you might have the display adapters connected to the wrong slots inside your system unit. Your primary adapter has to be a PCI adapter, installed in your computer's first PCI slot. You can't install an AGP adapter as your primary adapter; the AGP adapter has to function as the secondary adapter.

- Another cause of a blank second monitor is if you have Adobe Type Manager installed on your system. This program is incompatible with dual monitor support, and will cause your second monitor not to work. Uninstall the program and see if that fixes things.

- An MS-DOS program won't run full-screen on your second monitor. You can't do this; you have to run full-screen MS-DOS programs on your primary monitor only.

THE ABSOLUTE MINIMUM

Remember these points when you have a video-related problem:

- Most display problems are caused by video card/monitor mismatches, bad or outdated display drivers, or improperly connected cables.

- One good way to determine whether a video problem is card-related or monitor related is to connect a different monitor to your system. If the new monitor works fine, the problem is in your old monitor; if it doesn't, the problem is with your video card.

- Most video card–related problems will manifest themselves before Windows launches.

- Most driver-related problems will manifest themselves after Windows launches.

27

WHAT TO DO WHEN YOUR SOUND SYSTEM DOESN'T SOUND RIGHT

Seems like every time you click something in Windows, it makes a sound. Your computer talks to you when something good happens ("you've got mail!") and buzzes at you when something bad happens (that awful noise associated with error messages). You listen to music on your system via audio CDs, and depend on background sounds to entertain and direct you on a variety of Web pages.

So what do you do when you can't hear the sounds anymore—or when the songs you hear are the wrong ones? If your system develops audio problems of any sort, it's time to quit listening and start reading!

What Can Cause Bad Sound

The most common problems with your system's sound are often similar to the problems you find with CD-ROM or DVD drives. (You can refresh your memory by rereading the last half of Chapter 23, "What to Do When You Can't Access Your Disks.")

■ *Things might not be hooked up right.* Remember to seat all the cards and connect all the cables, including the power cables for your powered speakers.

■ *Things might not be configured properly.* Don't forget to configure Windows for your specific sound card and make sure you have the latest sound driver loaded.

■ *Things might be in conflict—in particular, ports (also called input/output addresses), interrupts, and DMA channels.* It's important to make sure that your sound card is set up so that it doesn't use ports, channels, or interrupts assigned to other devices on your system. If you have conflicts, you might find that *several* devices don't work right.

■ *Things might not be properly associated.* If you find events that used to make noise have suddenly become silent, chances are the .WAV file has been deleted or moved or associated with an inactive media player. Check the Sounds and Audio Devices Properties dialog box to make sure that real sounds are associated with all key events and actions.

> **note**
>
> Your sound card, like most peripherals, uses a direct memory access (DMA) channel to pipe information directly to your system's memory, bypassing the microprocessor. Most systems have eight DMA channels available.

As you can see, your problems can come with the sound card itself, with your speakers (and their connections), or with Windows sounds properties configuration. You especially need to familiarize yourself with the configuration settings, which you access (from the Control Panel) in the Sounds and Audio Properties dialog box. This dialog box lets you change the playback volume, display a volume control icon in the Taskbar tray, change the preferred playback and recording devices, select what type of speakers are hooked up to your system, and associate specific sounds with various system operations.

Dealing with Audio Problems

Now that you understand the general causes of audio problems, let's look at some specific problems—and what you can do about them.

Problem: Your New Sound Card Doesn't Work—You Don't Get Any Sound

Let's look at the simple stuff first. Is the card installed properly in your system unit? Have you connected the audio cable from your sound card to your CD-ROM/DVD drive? Are speakers (or headphones) hooked up to the card? Are the speakers plugged in and turned on? (And are they plugged into the correct jack? You don't want to plug your speakers into your microphone jack!) Are you performing a task on your PC that actually produces sound? Is the volume turned up loud enough (both on your speakers and in Windows)?

Okay, now that the easy stuff is out of the way, let's turn to something more difficult. The most likely cause of no sound is some sort of conflict. One by one, change your card's DMA, IRQ, and port settings. (This might entail resetting some jumpers on the card itself, as well as making some software-based changes.)

This problem can also occur if you add a new sound card to a system that has sound capabilities built into the motherboard. You'll need to disable the onboard sound before the new sound card can work.

Problem: Your New Sound Card Crashes Your System

If you've just installed your sound card, you might not have the card properly installed. Check your installation (is the card properly seated and connected?) and then reboot your system.

If this doesn't fix it, you have something wrong in your setup. Check your software setup to make sure you have the same DMA, IRQ, and port assignments as selected on your sound card itself (usually via DIP switches or jumpers). If the settings are correct, you probably have a conflict of some kind. You should methodically change the DMA, IRQ, and port assignments in Windows so that they don't conflict with the assignments for other devices on your system.

Problem: Windows Generates an Error Message About Your Sound Card

There are a number of error messages you can receive about your sound card when you launch Windows. Perhaps the most common is one that looks something like this:

`SOUNDCARD ERROR: DRIVER.XXX not installed`

This error message occurs when the driver file for your sound card either isn't found or is incorrect. The obvious fix is to open the Device Manager and make sure the driver is being loaded properly.

This message can also be generated when you have an interrupt conflict between your sound card and another device. If this is your problem, change the IRQ setting for one of the two devices.

Problem: Audio from Your Sound Card Skips—Or Plays Continually

This problem generally results from an IRQ conflict. Change the interrupt setting for your sound card to one not used by another system device and then reboot your system. You might want to change the sound card's interrupt to one between 3 and 8; in some systems using a higher interrupt (between 9 and 15) might cause playback problems.

Problem: You Only Get Sound from One Channel of a Stereo Setup

The most likely cause of this problem is using the wrong kind of plug for your powered speakers. It's possible that you're using a mono plug; you need a stereo plug to connect to your sound card's stereo jack.

Let's not overlook the obvious, either—make sure you actually have both speakers connected. (Most speaker setups are terribly confusing; even *I* have occasionally plugged the wrong plug into the wrong jack—or left one of the speakers accidentally unplugged!) And don't forget to check the balance slider in the master volume control, shown in Figure 27.1. This control is accessible from the Sounds and Audio Devices Properties dialog box; select the Volume tab and then click the Advanced button. Make sure that the balance isn't set all the way to the left or the right.

This problem also can occur if you don't have the proper driver for your sound card loaded into memory. Check your Windows configuration to make sure you have the proper driver installed and selected.

FIGURE 27.1
Adjusting your system's master volume control.

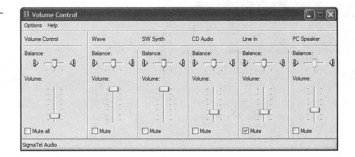

Problem: Your System's Audio Level Is Too Low or Too High

This is normally a simple problem with a simple solution. First, try adjusting the volume on your powered speakers. If this isn't the problem, you need to adjust the volume within Windows; use the master volume control, accessible from the Sounds and Audio Devices Properties dialog box.

Next, check your setup to make sure you have the right sound driver loaded. Next, try moving your speakers farther away from your video monitor; electrical "noise" from your monitor might be affecting the speakers' sound. Finally, try moving your sound card to another slot inside your system unit. Sometimes proximity to another card can cause your sound card to generate poor-quality sound.

Of course, poor quality sound could simply be the result of using poor quality speakers with your system. You might want to invest in some better speakers if you're really picky about this sort of thing.

> **tip**
>
> Make the Windows volume control permanently visible by opening the Sounds and Audio Devices Properties dialog box, selecting the Volume tab, and checking the Place Volume Icon in the Taskbar option.

Problem: Program- or Event-Specific Sounds Don't Play

If you can't play sound files from a specific program (for example, if you don't hear "you've got mail" when you log onto America Online), check the association in the Sounds and Audio Devices Properties dialog box—select the Sounds tab and evaluate each item in the Program Events list, as shown in Figure 27.2. It's possible that the sound file has been moved (this might happen when you upgrade to a newer version of a program, and the upgrade is made to a different directory or folder) or even deleted.

FIGURE 27.2

Checking sound associations in the Program Events list.

If the sound file exists and is associated properly, make sure you can actually play the sound; click the Preview arrow below the Program Events list on the Sounds tab. If you can hear the sound in the dialog box but *not* in the associated program, you have a program-specific problem; check with the technical support department of your software's manufacturer for help.

If you can't preview a specific sound but other sound files play properly, you have a corrupted file. The only way to fix a corrupted file is to reinstall it, either from your Windows installation CD or from a specific program's installation media.

It's also possible that two applications on your system are trying to generate sounds at the same time—and they're essentially canceling each other out. Stop or close all open applications (particularly games and the Windows Media Player) and then see if you can hear your normal system sounds.

If you can't hear *any* system sounds—or if all sounds play back incorrectly—you have a bigger problem. Your sound card might not be capable of playing .WAV files, or might not be configured properly for .WAV playback. There could also be some sort of resource conflict between your sound card and another device installed in your computer that only affects .WAV playback. (Don't laugh, I've seen it happen.) Check all your sound configuration settings and make any necessary changes.

THE ABSOLUTE MINIMUM

When you experience some sort of sound problem, remember these key points:

- PC sound is generated from a sound card and typically fed to an external speaker system; these speaker hookups are often confusing and can cause many problems.

- Sound cards can be one of the most temperamental devices in your system; I/O address, DMA, and IRQ conflicts are common.

- Most Windows audio settings are configured from the Sounds and Audio Devices Properties dialog box.

28

WHAT TO DO WHEN YOUR FILES ARE LOST OR CORRUPTED

All of your data is stored in files. All the good things you do with your computer involve files, and some of the bad things do, too. This means you must be careful when working with your files because any mistake you make can cause your files—and your valuable data—to disappear.

Most file problems are caused by something you do. You press the wrong key, click the wrong button, or select the wrong item, and—shazam!—you have a problem. Fortunately, these problems are easy to prevent and, in most cases, easy to recover from.

Why Files Go Bad

What file problems might you encounter? Let's see…You can accidentally delete a file you really didn't want deleted, or you can inadvertently copy one file over another existing file, which erases the latter. (There's not much you can do about this one, I'm afraid.) In fact, if you try hard enough, you can even sabotage your entire hard disk by using Windows file commands incorrectly. (Scary thought, isn't it?)

Before you get too paranoid about all this, know that Windows normally gives you ample warning (in the form of an onscreen message) before it carries out a potentially dangerous command. If you heed the onscreen warning, you can halt any such operation before it destroys your files.

Know also that hard disk problems can inflict severe damage on your files. Bad sectors on a hard disk, for example, can scramble the data in affected files, making them unreadable. And, of course, computer viruses can cause the same type of damage to your files—and in many cases, even worse. Because all your efforts at your computer depend on the integrity of your files, it's imperative that you understand how fragile their existence can be.

Dealing with File Problems

Because most file problems are caused by user error, the most important information you need to know is how to recover from your own mistakes. Let's look at the most common file-related problems and how to fix them.

Problem: You Accidentally Delete an Important File

Deleting an important file can be one of the most disconcerting—and most common—errors you will make in the course of using your computer. Fortunately, Windows makes it relatively easy to recover from this self-inflicted problem.

That's because Windows doesn't actually get rid of the files you delete—instead, it temporarily stores all deleted files in a file called the Recycle Bin. As long as the file hasn't been dumped from the Recycle Bin, it can still be recovered.

To undelete a file in the Recycle Bin, follow these steps:

1. Double-click the Recycle Bin icon on your desktop.
2. When the Recycle Bin window opens, select the item you want to undelete.
3. Select Restore This Item from the Recycle Bin Tasks panel.

If you open the Recycle Bin and the file you want isn't there, that means it has been dumped. Windows only allocates a certain amount of storage space for the Recycle Bin folder, so it's "first in, first out" for your deleted files; as the Recycle Bin fills up, the oldest files are excised as necessary.

If a file has been "permanently" deleted from the Recycle Bin, there still might be a way to bring the missing file back from the dead. You see, just because a file isn't accessible doesn't mean that it's been physically deleted from your hard disk. In fact, all deleted files continue to reside on your hard disk, although all reference to the data in the file allocation table (FAT) has been removed—at least until the reference data has been overwritten by newer data.

There are several third-party programs that include special "undelete" utilities. These utilities will recover any existing data from the FAT that hasn't been overwritten and thus "restore" the deleted file to your hard disk. The most popular of these utilities include:

- Active@ UNDELETE
  (www.active-undelete.com)
- Norton Utilities (www.symantec.com)
- R-Undelete (www.r-tt.com)
- Undelete (www.executive.com/undelete/)

caution

The fact that "deleted" data isn't really gone can lead to a variety of security issues; any dedicated individual with minimal technical knowledge can recover and read confidential or damaging files you thought you deleted. (Which is a good reason not to write nasty things about your boss and then think you're safe just because you pressed the delete key!)

Problem: You Can't Delete a File

This is the opposite of the previous problem. You try to delete a file, but it won't delete. This problem can occur for one of three reasons:

- *The file is currently in use by another program.* Try closing that program and then deleting the file.

- *You're trying to delete a file from a floppy disk that is write-protected.* If you're trying to delete a file on a floppy disk, slide the tab in the lower-left corner so that the hole is closed, and then try the procedure again.

- *The attributes of the file have been set so that you can't delete it.* Every file has multiple attributes. One such attribute makes a file read-only, meaning that you can't delete it or write to it. To change a file's attributes, right-click the file's icon and select Properties from the pop-up menu. When the Properties dialog box appears, uncheck the Read-Only attribute, and then click OK.

Problem: You Can't Find a File

Is it possible to actually lose a file on your hard disk? Of course it is. When you have thousands of different files in dozens of different folders, you can easily forget where you stashed a certain file.

Windows makes it easy to find specific files, however. Just follow these steps:

1. Click the Start button and select Search to open the Search window.
2. Select what type of you want to search for.
3. Enter all or part of the filename, or a word or phrase in the file.
4. Select where on your system or hard drive you want to search.
5. Click the Search button.

Windows will now return a list of files that match your search parameters.

If this doesn't find the file you're looking for, the file might actually be on another disk (maybe on a disk instead of your hard disk), or you might have accidentally deleted the file. To look for a possibly deleted file, just open the Recycle Bin; any files you find here can be undeleted, following the steps outlined previously.

> **tip**
>
> If you're not sure of the exact filename, you can use wildcard characters to broaden your search. For example, the asterisk (*) character stands in for all subsequent characters; when you search for **bob*** you'll find files named **bobby**, **bobbie**, **bobcat**, and **boboboreebob**.

Problem: You Attempt a File Operation and Get a Windows Error Message

Windows error messages often appear to let you know that you incorrectly clicked or typed something. So if you get such a message, the first action is always to try the operation again, more carefully this time. However, even when you do whatever it is you're doing more carefully, you can still get error messages.

Table 28.1 presents those you're most likely to encounter when working with files.

Table 28.1 Windows File-Related Error Messages

Error Message	Probable Cause and Solution
Cannot find file	The most common cause behind this message is that the file in question is either missing or corrupted. Use the Search utility to search for the file. Reinstall the file in question if necessary.

Table 28.1   (continued)

Error Message	Probable Cause and Solution
Cannot read from drive *X*	Windows is looking for a file on drive *X*: (probably drive A:) and there isn't a disk in the drive. Insert any disk to end the Windows look loop. If a disk *is* in drive *X*: and you get this error message, you either have a bad (or unformatted) disk, or something is wrong with your disk drive.
Folder *xxx* does not exist	You have specified a folder that does not exist. Check the spelling of the folder and pathname. You might also try selecting View, Refresh to refresh the file/folder display.
File already exists. Overwrite?	You're trying to create or save a file with a name that already exists. Windows is asking if you wish to overwrite the existing file. If so, answer yes. If no, answer no, and assign a new name to your file.
File is missing	When Windows loads, it tries to load any programs that are included in the Startup folder. This message is generated when one of these files no longer exists or has been entered incorrectly. Use My Computer to open the Startup folder and check all programs and associations, removing or editing those that are not correct.
Not a valid filename	You typed an invalid filename. Try again.
The specified path is invalid	You typed an incorrect path for a file operation. Check the path and retype the command.
Write protected disk	You're trying to perform a file operation on a disk that is write protected. Change disks, or slide the write-protect tab into the down position.

Problem: You Open a File and Its Data Is Scrambled or Incomplete

Scrambled data can be caused by a number of factors. The most likely reason is that you accidentally rebooted or turned off your system while that file was being accessed, causing the file to become corrupted. Another cause for scrambled data is a bug in a software program or a computer virus. Whatever the cause, you can't do much about it—after data is scrambled, it's scrambled.

Of course, if you have a backup copy of the data on another disk (or on a backup disk) you can always use that copy to replace your scrambled copy. Experiencing scrambled data is strong motivation for backing up your data files on a regular basis.

It's possible that your data isn't *really* scrambled, however. If you try using an old version of a software program to open a document saved with a *newer* version of that program, it might appear (from within the old version of the program) that the file is scrambled. In reality, the file is fine, it's just saved in a format that your version of the program can't read. Make sure you're using the newest version of a program, or that someone saves the file in question "down" to an older version, for compatibility.

note

See Chapter 19, "Simple Steps to Keep Your System in Tip-Top Shape," for more information on using the Microsoft Backup utility.

Problem: You Can't Open a Document File

When you go to open a document file, Windows automatically launches the associated application. If you can't open a document file—that is, if the associated application doesn't open—then you likely have an association problem.

This type of problem is most often caused when the document's file type is not associated with a program type—or with the correct program type. When you select a document file, it should launch the associated program, with the selected document preloaded. If, instead of launching the program, Windows displays the Open With dialog box, you need to select an application to associate with the file.

When you install a new application, it usually registers its file types automatically. You might also need to reassociate a file type, however, if you install a new program that hijacks the original file associations for itself—and you'd rather go back to the default associations.

To associate a file type with a particular application, follow these steps:

1. From the Control Panel, select Appearance and Themes, then launch the Folder Options utility.

2. When the Folder Options dialog box appears, select the File Types tab, select the file type you want to change, and then click the Change button.

caution

This is one very good reason to pay attention to every screen when you're installing a new program. You'll typically be prompted if the new program wants to change your file associations; don't automatically click OK on every screen!

3. When the Open With dialog box appears, as shown in Figure 28.1, select the application you want to associate with the file type. (If the program you want isn't listed, click Browse to search for and select another program.)

4. Click OK.

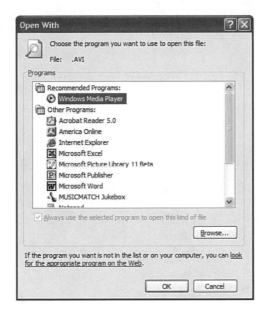

FIGURE 28.1

Associating file types.

THE ABSOLUTE MiNiMUM

File problems are either easily recovered from or not recoverable from at all; there's not a lot of inbetween. Just remember these key points:

- Most file-related problems are caused by user error—which argues for being more careful before you click that OK or Delete button.

- Fortunately, all files you delete are sent to the Recycle Bin folder. Until the Recycle Bin is filled up, you can restore any file you've recently deleted.

- File types must be associated with applications in order to launch an application by selecting a specific file.

IN THIS CHAPTER

- You can't find another computer on your network—or your PC doesn't recognize your network

- Your modem doesn't work, or doesn't dial

- You can't connect to the Internet

- Your online session disconnects unexpectedly

- You can't retrieve your email

- You can't connect to a Web site

29

WHAT TO DO WHEN YOUR NETWORK OR INTERNET CONNECTION STARTS ACTING UP

Think about all the problems you can encounter on your personal computer. Now imagine connecting two computers together—the number of potential problems increase geometrically!

That's not entirely true, of course. But there are a lot of problems that can occur when you connect your computer to a network or to the Internet. This chapter examines both types of problems and how to troubleshoot them.

Dealing with Network Problems

Just a few short years ago, setting up a network was an extremely complicated procedure that required a technical degree and years of experience. Today, however, small networks have become relatively simple to connect and configure, thanks to Plug and Play hardware and easier-to-use networking software. The process isn't totally painless, but there's a lot less to go wrong than there used to be.

That said, even small networks can sometimes pose large problems. Read on to learn about the most common problems and how to fix them.

Problem: You Can't Find Another Computer on Your Network

You open up My Network Places looking for another computer on your network, but it isn't there. Where did it go?

First, try looking a little harder. Click the View Workgroup Computers link in the Network Tasks panel. This *should* display all connected computers.

If the missing computer isn't there, click the Search button in the My Network Places toolbar. When the Search Companion appears, enter the name of the computer, and then click Search. If you don't know the name of the computer, enter an asterisk (*). This should search for (and then display) all the computers on the network.

If you still can't see the missing computer, it's time to check the obvious. Is the other computer turned on? (Sleeping computers don't show up on the network.) Is it connected to the network? (Double-check both ends of the cable.) If you're on an Ethernet network, are both your computers connected to the hub, and does the hub have power? You should also check the ends of the network cables; if the connection is working, there should be a blinking light where the cable connects to the PC.

Here's another simple thing to try—reboot your computer. For whatever reason, "lost" computers on a network will often get found when you reboot the computer that can't see them. (I have to reboot my main computer a few times a week for this very problem.)

It doesn't hurt to check the cable itself at this point—especially if it's run over a long distance. Ethernet cables can become cracked or bent or otherwise damaged. Check any cables that run under a carpet; getting walked on isn't good for long cable life.

More basics: If you're running Windows XP, have you run the Network Setup Wizard on the second computer? If not, run it now, from the Windows installation CD. (And don't assume that because your network worked pre-XP everything will show up after you install XP on your main PC. You'll probably have to run the XP Network

Setup Wizard on all your networked PCs.) Try running the wizard again. (Sometimes it takes two tries to get everything recognized.) Now reboot both your PCs and see if they recognize each other.

Now for some serious troubleshooting. Open the Help and Support Center, click the Fixing Problem link, click Networking Problems, and then run the Home and Small Office Networking Troubleshooter. Chances are this will fix most simple networking problems.

You might have a bad network connection on either one of the two computers. To repair a host of connection problems, open the Network Connections utility from the Control Panel. Right-click the problem connection, and then select Repair from the pop-up menu.

If worse comes to worst, delete the problematic connection from the second PC, and then rerun the Network Setup Wizard to reinstall the network. You also might have to rerun the wizard on your host PC (to recognize the new PC) .

Problem: Your PC Doesn't Recognize Your Network

Let's assume you've run the setup software and your PC still doesn't think your network exists. If you're running a wired network, make sure you have all the cables connected to your computer's Ethernet port, *not* to the modem port. Try rebooting the problem computer. If that doesn't work, try rebooting the network's gateway computer, and then rebooting the problem computer again.

At this point, you should run the Windows Home and Small Office Networking Troubleshooter. You can also try repairing the connection via the Network Connections utility. Then, if you have to, rerun the Network Setup Wizard.

Problem: Your PC Can't Connect to Your Wireless Network

The most common cause for this problem is a weak wireless signal. Check the signal strength on the problem PC—if it's poor, that's your problem. You might need to reposition the wireless network adapter or your wireless base station to improve the signal strength.

You might also be experiencing interference with another wireless device, such as a wireless mouse or keyboard, or a cordless phone—or even a microwave oven! (Yep, microwaves operate in the same RF band as WiFi networks.) Again, moving either the wireless adapter or base station might solve the problem; moving or disconnecting the interfering device might also be in order.

Dealing with Internet-Related Problems

Connecting to the Internet can be problematic. You can experience connection problems, of course, as well as all sorts of problems doing what you want to do online.

What kind of connection problems might you experience? First, you can hook up your modem incorrectly. Maybe you fail to seat an internal modem securely into its slot on the motherboard, or perhaps you plug an external modem into the wrong port on your system unit. It's also common to connect your telephone line to the *Ethernet* port instead of the modem port; the plugs are close enough in size for this to happen.

Next, you can sabotage your setup, partially or entirely, by configuring the modem's switches or Windows modem settings—or both—incorrectly. It's possible, too, to create a COM port conflict by designating your modem and your mouse for either the same COM port or a conflicting COM port.

If you're relying on a dial-up connection, you can also be cursed with a noisy telephone line. You'd be surprised at the amount of trouble this seemingly minor annoyance can cause—everything from slowing down your connection speed to thwarting your connection altogether. Even if you get everything else right, Ma Bell can send you back to square one with just a little line noise.

Finally, your *Internet Service Provider* (*ISP*) might not be operating up to par. Now that the Internet is experiencing astronomic growth, it's not uncommon to run into "traffic jams" at popular sites, and access in general often slows down during the heaviest-trafficked times of the day.

Of course, your problems don't stop once you get connected. Read on to learn how to deal with the most common Internet problems, connection-related and otherwise.

Problem: Your Modem Doesn't Work—Nothing Happens

If you attempt to use your modem but it does nothing at all, start by checking all your connections—especially the connection to the phone line. A malfunctioning modem usually results from a bad connection. If you use an external modem, make sure that it's hooked to the correct port in the back of your PC. Make certain, too, that the modem is plugged into a power source (if necessary) and connected to a phone line. If you use an internal modem, check to ensure that the card is firmly seated in its slot. You should also try hooking a normal phone to the line hooked to your computer, just to be sure that you have a dial tone. After you've taken care of a poor or overlooked connection, you might need to reboot your system to recover from the problem.

Next, you should check to see if your modem is communicating with your computer. In Windows XP you can do this by going to the modem's Properties dialog box, selecting the General tab, and then clicking the Troubleshoot button. This initiates a troubleshooting sequence that, more often than not, will identify your problem.

Problem: Your Modem Is Working, but It Doesn't Dial

After you've confirmed that your modem is working and communicating with your computer—but you still can't dial a number—you should confirm that you're not trying to make one Internet connection while a previous connection is still open. (You can't dial two places at the same time!) Then be sure that the phone line your modem is connected to is working by disconnecting your modem and hooking a working telephone to the same phone line. If the phone doesn't pick up a dial tone, neither will your modem. Try another phone line, or call the phone company for repairs.

If you have voice mail on your phone line, some voice mail systems change the dial tone to indicate when you have messages waiting. This modified dial tone might not be recognized as a real dial tone by some modems. Answer your voice mail to change the tone back to normal, and then try dialing again.

It's also possible that you have your phone line plugged into the wrong jack at your modem. Most modems have two jacks—one labeled "line" and the other labeled "phone." Be sure that the phone line is plugged into the one labeled "line."

If your problem persists and it clearly isn't caused by a bad connection, an inoperable phone line, or a defective modem, the most likely source of your woes is an incorrect configuration within Windows. Make certain that you've selected the correct COM port and check the modem initialization string. (Your modem's documentation should list the correct commands to use for your device.) Also check the Maximum Port Speed setting in the Modem tab of the modem's Properties dialog box. You might try *reducing* this setting if your modem is having difficulty communicating with your computer. And check for any COM port conflicts between your modem and another device, such as a mouse.

You should always check the port settings from within Windows to be sure that they're configured correctly. You can do this from Device Manager, where it pays to examine the Properties for ports COM1 through COM4.

If Windows appears to be configured correctly (or it wasn't and you've fixed it) but your modem still doesn't dial, check your hardware. Many modems have physical switches that must be set in certain positions for the device to operate. Refer to your modem's documentation for the correct switch settings for your system.

Problem: Your Modem Dials, but It Doesn't Connect

Many common causes for this problem are the same as for the previous problem—either your hardware or software is set up incorrectly. If you think this is the case, see the previous problem for troubleshooting instructions.

It's also possible that your modem is dialing an incorrect phone number, or that something is screwy at your ISP. Be sure that your modem's speaker is enabled, and then listen to the connection in process. If you hear your modem dialing, dialing, dialing—and it receives no answer from your ISP—check the phone number you entered for your ISP. If the phone number is correct, it's possible that your ISP is having problems and temporarily can't accept incoming calls. (Dial your ISP's voice support line to confirm or report this problem.) If you hear a busy signal after dialing, that means that too many people are trying to dial in at one time, and your ISP can't accept any more incoming calls right now. Wait a few minutes and try dialing in again.

Problem: Your Broadband Modem Doesn't Connect

If your cable or DSL modem appears to be working (the lights light up, although they might be blinking) but you can't actually access the Internet, it's a sign that your modem has lost connection with your ISP's network. The solution might be as simple as unplugging your modem for about 60 seconds and then turning it back on and letting it resync to the network. If this doesn't work, either your ISP's network is down, or there is a real problem with your broadband connection. If it's the former, all you can do is wait for your ISP to fix their problems. If it's the latter, it's time to call your ISP and have it send a repairman out to fix the connection.

Problem: You Connect to Your ISP, but at a Slower Speed Than Desired

There are many factors that determine at what speed you actually connect over a dial-up line. The most common cause of slower-than-expected connections is line noise. I run into this problem a lot when traveling. Many older hotels have very noisy phone systems, which cause my modem to connect at speeds as slow as 14.4Kbps. (Man—that's slow!)

In addition, the busier your ISP is, the more likely that you'll connect at a slower speed even with a broadband connection. If you try to connect during "prime time" (from just after dinner to bedtime in your specific time zone) chances are you'll get a slower connection than if you try to connect after midnight.

Problem: Your Online Session Disconnects Unexpectedly

You can get disconnected in the middle of a session if you have more than one phone in your house hooked to the same phone line. If someone picks up an extension while your modem is online, the resulting interruption can scramble the connection. Sometimes the problem can be rectified simply by hanging up the extension; other times, you must cancel the current modem session and start over again.

Call Waiting also can be the cause of disconnect problems. When the Call Waiting signal comes down the line it stands a good chance of either scrambling your modem session or disconnecting your modem completely. Although you can simply abstain from ordering the Call Waiting service, you also can turn it off while you're online by editing the settings on the Dialing Rules tab in the Phone and Modem Options utility.

Some ISPs and commercial online services (AOL is notorious for this) will disconnect you if you've been idle for too long. (They don't like users staying connected without actually doing anything.) If you want to stay connected, do *something* every few minutes, even if it's just checking your email inbox or clicking to a different Web site.

Sometimes a Windows-related problem can cause your modem session to shut down. If Windows is low on memory, it might not have enough resources to let your modem do its thing. If you think this is the problem, try closing a few Windows applications and then restarting your modem. If you have continual modem problems under Windows, you might need to add more memory to your system.

Another increasingly common cause of this problem is a noisy phone line. If you have frequent trouble connecting or staying connected, it might not hurt to have your local phone company check your line for excess noise.

Problem: Using Your Modem Causes Your Mouse to Act Funny—Or Vice Versa

This is actually a common problem. It results from weird hardware bugs that force two different COM ports to use some of the same system resources. Fortunately, however, resolving the conflict is relatively simple.

First, check the port settings for your mouse and your modem. (You do this from the Windows Device Manager; right-click on a device listing and select Properties, and then navigate within the Properties dialog box to the port setting.) If they're both configured for the same COM port, change one of the devices' settings so that it can use a different port.

Now, check that they're not both set for COM ports with even numbers (COM2 and COM4). If so, reconfigure one of the devices to use an odd-numbered port.

At the same time, check that the two devices aren't both configured for COM ports with odd numbers (COM1 and COM3). If so, reset one of the devices to use an even number.

If you're running your modem on COM2 and there is no COM1 on your system you might not be able to get your modem to work at all. This is because Windows looks for COM ports in order, and if COM1 doesn't exist, well, you've got problems. Reassign your modem or some other accessory to COM1, and you'll fix your problem.

Problem: You Can't Connect to Your Email Server

This problem is most often caused by an incorrect configuration in your email program. Make sure you have the right incoming and outgoing mail server names for your ISP, as well as the correct username (typically your email address) and password, if required. (And remember that some ISPs use case-sensitive usernames and passwords.)

If you have everything configured properly, it's possible that there is some sort of problem with your ISP's mail server. Wait a few minutes and try connecting again. If you continue to have problems connecting, call your ISP's voice support line and report the problem.

Another cause of this problem is if your email program crashes while it's in the middle of retrieving your email. This causes all sorts of problems on the server end of things; you'll need to wait a few minutes (for the email server to reset) before you restart your program and go back online.

Problem: Your Email Program Connects to Your ISP, but You Have Trouble Sending or Receiving Email Messages

Just because you connect to your ISP doesn't mean you can actually send or retrieve messages. Again, check your email program's configuration; be especially sure that you have the right protocols (POP3, IMAP, and so on) selected.

If you receive a timeout message after connecting, there might be problems with the ISP's mail server. Things can really slow down during busy times of the day; if it takes too long to complete an action (such as downloading a list of messages), your program times out and reports an error. Try clicking the Send/Receive button again to initiate a new upload/download of messages. (If you receive a lot of timeout messages, reconfigure your email program to allow more time before timing out.)

Sometimes a really large message (or a message with a large attachment) can take so long to retrieve that it times out your email program. (Any message more than 1MB in size could cause this sort of problem on a normal 56Kbps connection.) The bad thing is, if you can't download this message, it clogs up your message retrieval so you can't grab any other message after this one, either. If you run into this sort of problem, you might have to call your ISP's voice support line and ask them to remove the extra-large message from the queue so you can retrieve the rest of your message. (And email the person who sent the large message and ask him or her to either compress it using a Zip utility or break it up into several smaller messages.)

Problem: An Email Message You Sent Is Returned as "Undeliverable"

This might be the most common Internet-related problem, period—and the one with the simplest solution.

If you get an email message bounced back to you, there is a very good possibility that the recipient's email address was incorrect. (This is just like when you get a letter returned from the postal service as "addressee unknown.") Double-check the email address (perhaps by calling the recipient and inquiring by voice), correct it, and resend the message.

It's also possible that the address was correct but there was a problem with the recipient's mail server. If you're positive you have the right address, go ahead and resend the message and hope the server problem has been corrected.

You can sometimes track down the cause of the error by carefully deciphering the error message that accompanies many returned messages. You'll often find specific reasons that the message was returned, which can help you formulate your reaction.

Finally, know that Internet users often move from one email account to another as they play a game of musical chairs with multiple ISPs. It's possible that you sent your message to what was formerly a viable address, but one that has since been abandoned by the user. Again, checking with the recipient personally (*not* via email!) might be the only way to get their current email address.

Problem: You Don't Receive a Message Someone Sent to You

Just as you sometimes get email bounced back to you as undeliverable, people sending *you* email sometimes receive an "undeliverable" message in return. The causes are the same, of course—the sender could have an incorrect email address for you, or there might have been temporary problems with your ISP's mail server that bounced the message back to the sender.

It's also possible that the message is still in transit. We kind of expect email delivery to be instantaneous, but sometimes ISPs get a bit of a backlog going, which can hold up email delivery anywhere from a few minutes to a few days. The solution, of course, is to be patient and to ask the sender to resend the message anyway, just in case.

In addition, don't forget that extra-large messages (over 1MB, in many cases) can screw up your mail delivery. One large message can clog your entire retrieval, blocking dozens of other messages from being downloaded to your inbox. If you think you have a message that you haven't actually received, it doesn't hurt to call your ISP's voice support and have them check on it.

Finally, some spam-blocker utilities will block email messages from entire domains. (The utilities use lists of servers frequented by spammers, and paint all messages coming from those servers with the same brush.) If your ISP is using this type of utility and if the sender just happens to be using a suspect server, the message will be automatically blocked and you'll never know it. The sender, however, should receive some sort of message indicating that the message was returned, and (sometimes) why. The only solution is for the sender to change email services, or for the blocked server list to be somehow modified. (Or, if this is antispam software you're running on your own machine, you might be able to modify the blocked-sender list—or just turn off the software in order to receive the message.)

Problem: You Have Trouble Sending an Attachment to an Email Message

Most email programs let you "attach" files to your email messages. You can use this feature to send pictures, word processing documents, and even complete executable programs along with your email messages.

Note, however, that some email programs might set a limit on the size of your email attachments, and that some ISPs might not let their users receive attachments. (For example, AOL lets users select whether they want to receive attachments or not; some parents turn off the attachment-receiving option for their children's email accounts.) Also note that overly large (more than 1MB) attachments might cause retrieval problems for your intended recipient(s). It might not be a bad idea to contact your recipients ahead of time to warn them that a really large email is on its way; they can then prepare themselves for what will be an annoyingly long download.

Problem: Your Computer Acts Oddly Soon After You Download a File or Open an Email Attachment

What now? You've just pulled several files—including a great new game—from this new Internet site you found, and now your computer acts as though it needs to be decked out in an electronic straitjacket. It doesn't seem to have any problems with loose connections, incorrect settings, or excess line noise. In fact, your online session went without a hitch. So what's wrong?

Well, along with your nice new files, you have probably downloaded a not-so-nice computer virus! Any time you download a file, run the file, and then find your computer starting to do strange things (running more slowly, mysteriously losing files, displaying unusual messages onscreen), you might have accidentally infected it with a virus.

Even more common is the case of the unexpected email attachment. Most computer viruses today are sent (unwittingly, in most instances) as attachments to email messages. If you open a file attached to an email message, you're running a really big risk—even if the message is from someone you know. (A lot of viruses hijack a user's system and send out infected email messages automatically without the user knowing.)

If you think you've been infected by an Internet-borne virus, turn to the advice I gave in Chapter 20, "Protecting Your Computer from Viruses and Internet Attacks." And get yourself an antivirus software program!

Problem: Your Web Browser Won't Connect to Any Web Site

If you try connecting to one site, and then another, and then another—all unsuccessfully—you know you don't have a problem with a single URL or Web server. When you can't connect to *anything*, there's either a problem between you and your ISP, or between your ISP and the Internet.

Try doing something non–Web-related on the Internet; check your email, or try to access a chat room. If you can do other Internet-related tasks, your ISP has a problem with its gateway to the Web. You might have to wait a few minutes (or hours!) for the gateway to unclog; if the problem persists, call your ISP's voice support line and report the problem.

If you can't perform other Internet-related tasks (if you get errors when trying to check your email, for example), your problem lies in your connection to your ISP. End your current connection, and then reconnect. Oftentimes establishing a new connection solves this type of problem. If you continue to lack Internet access on subsequent connections, check your configuration information, as detailed previously. If the situation persists, call your ISP's voice support line and report the problem.

Problem: Your Web Browser Won't Connect to a Specific Web Site

The first thing to check if you can't connect to a specific site is the URL. If you entered the URL manually, it's possible you mistyped it; try re-entering the address more carefully this time. It's also possible that the address doesn't actually exist; either the URL is wrong or the page *used to* exist but has been taken offline for some reason or another. (Dead pages are an increasing problem on the Web.) Next, the link to the page might be incorrect (someone had to manually enter the code for the link when the page was being created; human beings sometimes make mistakes!). And, finally, the page might be *temporarily* unavailable (sometimes Web servers *go down*—break—and leave all the pages they host unavailable until repairs are made); trying again later is the best suggestion in this situation.

tip

One trick to try if you can't access a specific page on a Web site is to try to access other pages on the site. You can do this by *truncating* the URL. For example, if you couldn't access `www.mysite.com/mydirectory/mypage.html`, then truncate the last part of the URL and try accessing `www.mysite.com/mydirectory/`. If that doesn't work, keep truncating until you get to the main site URL (in this case, `www.mysite.com`).

Problem: Your Web Browser Gives You an Error Message When You Try to Load a Specific Page

Quite often, your browser will display an error message when it can't access a specific Web page. Learning how to decipher these messages will help you determine *why* the page in question is inaccessible.

Table 29.1 details the most common Web error messages, what they mean, and what to do about them.

Table 29.1 Web Error Messages

Error Message	Cause	Recommended Action
`400 - Bad request`	Page can't be found; URL is incorrect.	Reenter URL; check uppercase and lowercase.
`401 - Unauthorized`	Page is protected and you're not on the guest list —or you entered an incorrect password.	If you're not on the guest list, you can't get in; if you *are* on the guest list, recheck and reenter your password.
`403 - Forbidden`	Page is protected and you're not on the guest list—or you entered an incorrect password.	If you're not on the guest list, you can't get in; if you *are* on the guest list, recheck and reenter your password.
`404 - Access denied`	Page is protected and you're not on the guest list—or you entered an incorrect password.	If you're not on the guest list, you can't get in; if you *are* on the guest list, recheck and reenter your password.
`404 - Not found`	Page can't be found; URL is incorrect.	Reenter the URL or try going one level up in the site directory.
`503 - Service unavailable`	Something between you and the page is down, probably the site's server or your ISP's Internet gateway.	Wait a few minutes and try connecting to the page again.
`Bad file request`	Your browser isn't compatible with a form on the page.	Upgrade your browser to the latest version.
`Cannot open... You do not have permission to open this item`	Page is protected and you're not on the guest list—or you entered an incorrect password.	If you're not on the guest list, you can't get in; if you *are* on the guest list, recheck and reenter your password.
`Connection refused by host`	Page is protected and you're not on the guest list; you typed an incorrect password; or this page is blocked to your ISP.	If you're not on the guest list, you can't get in; if you *are* on the guest list, recheck and reenter your password; if this site is blocked to your ISP, complain to your ISP.
`Connection reset by peer`	The Web site reset your connection for some reason.	Reload or refresh the Web page.
`Connection timed out`	Either the site or your Internet connection stopped responding.	Wait a few minutes and try reloading the page; if you get this message at multiple sites, close your current connection, wait a few minutes, and then reconnect to your ISP.

Table 29.1 (continued)

Error Message	Cause	Recommended Action
Failed DNS lookup	Page can't be found; URL is bad or there are temporary connection problems.	Recheck the URL and try again; if the URL is correct, try again a few minutes later.
File contains no data	You have the right site, but there's nothing there.	It's possible the site might be updating its pages; if so try again in an hour or so. It's also possible the site has been closed down, even though the domain name is still active.
Helper application not found	Your browser isn't capable of reading a particular file.	Update your browser to the latest version, or add the "plug-in" to read this particular file type.
Host unavailable	The site you're trying to access is down.	Try accessing the site in a few minutes or hours; if you continue to get this message, the site might have been closed.
Host unknown	The site you're trying to access is down or you have an incorrect URL.	Recheck and reenter your URL, then try accessing the site in a few minutes or hours; if you continue to get this message, the site might have been closed.
Network connection was refused by the server	The site's server is too busy to handle any more users.	Wait a few minutes, and then try again.
Socket is not connected	There's a bad connection somewhere between your PC and the site.	Try reconnecting to site; if you get the same error message, wait a few minutes, and then try again.
Too many connections - try again later	The site's server is too busy to handle any more users.	Wait a few minutes, and then try again.
Too many users	The site's server is too busy to handle any more users.	Wait a few minutes, then try again.
Unable to locate host	The site you're trying to access is down.	Try accessing the site in a few minutes or hours; if you continue to get this message, the site might have been closed.

Table 29.1 (continued)

Error Message	Cause	Recommended Action
Unable to locate the server	Page can't be found; URL is bad or there are temporary connection problems.	Recheck the URL and try again; if the URL is correct, try again a few minutes later.
Unable to open http://www.site. com/page ... The site reports that the item you requested could not be found.	The overall site exists, but the individual page you want doesn't.	Make sure you have the correct page URL; try truncating the URL to access a higher-level directory.
Viewer not found	Your browser isn't capable of reading a particular file.	Update your browser to the latest version, or add the "plug-in" to read this particular file type.

Problem: You Connect to a Web Page, But It Only Partially Loads

There can be a number of causes if a page "hangs" while loading—or if parts of a page don't display properly. First, the page might actually still be loading, but it's a really big page. Click the Stop button on your browser and then try reloading the page. If the page still takes too long to load, try turning off graphics in your browser, so that you only load text. (In Internet Explorer, select Tools, Internet Options to display the Internet Options dialog box; select the Advanced tab and then uncheck the Show Pictures option.)

Also note that pages that load background sounds and music can *appear* to be hung, but are actually just waiting for the music file to download. If this is the case, just be patient; the page will load, eventually.

Second, the connection to this site might have gone bad in mid-load. Try reloading the page; if you still have trouble loading this and other pages, disconnect from your ISP, wait a few minutes, and then reconnect.

Third, the problem might be with your Web browser. Try "flushing" your browser's cache and history files to clear disk space and memory. In Internet Explorer, select Tools, Internet Options to display the Internet Options dialog box; select the General tab and then click (sequentially) the Delete Files and Clear History buttons.

Fourth, some Web pages incorporate advanced technologies such as Java and Macromedia Shockwave that might not be compatible with older Web browsers. If you get a blank space on your page, try reloading—but then check to make sure your browser is capable of displaying these elements. (That might mean adding a plug-in to your browser, or upgrading to a more recent version.)

Finally, it's possible that parts of the page referenced in its HTML code actually aren't there. This is somewhat common when dealing with graphics files; site designers will reference .JPG and .GIF files elsewhere on the site (or on another site) that subsequently disappear. Try right-clicking on the empty space and selecting Load Picture from the pop-up menu; if the picture still doesn't load, it's a problem with the page, not with your browser.

The Absolute Minimum

Whew—that's a lot of problems! When you're experiencing problems with your network or Internet connection, keep these key points in mind:

- Most network problems can be resolved by rerunning the network setup utility.

- Wireless network problems are typically caused by poor reception; try repositioning either the wireless adapter or the wireless base station.

- If you're having trouble connecting to the Internet, look for configuration mistakes, incorrect settings, and noisy phone lines—and try to connect when your ISP isn't so busy!

- Undeliverable email typically results from problems at your recipient's ISP mail server or an incorrect email address.

- If you can't access a particular Web site, double-check the URL and try accessing it again at a later time—but if you can't access *any* Web page, your ISP is having trouble with its gateway to the Internet.

30

WHAT TO DO WHEN YOU RECEIVE A WINDOWS ERROR MESSAGE

Windows uses error messages to try and tell you why something bad has happened. Sometimes the messages are easy to decipher. Sometimes they're not.

Because Windows can display literally thousands of error messages—some of them fairly obscure—I've tried to narrow it down to the most common messages you're likely to encounter, sorted in alphabetical order. I've listed error messages common in Windows 95, 98, Me, and XP, although not all versions of Windows generate the same error messages. (In fact, the newer your version of Windows, the fewer error message you'll encounter—although when you *do* see them, they're likely to be slightly more understandable.)

If your message isn't in this list, don't despair—it just means you have something *really weird* happening with your system. Write down the message and call a competent computer technician. They'll be glad to help you out.

Understanding Common Error Messages

To help you figure out what Windows is trying to tell you, here's a list of the most common Windows-specific messages you're likely to encounter. The messages are listed in alphabetical order, along with the most probable cause(s) of the message.

A fatal exception <XY> has occurred at xxxx:xxxxxxxx

Windows does not cause these fatal exception errors; these messages are just Windows' way of reporting a problem encountered by your system's microprocessor, often caused by faulty or mishandled RAM. In many cases, a fatal exception error will freeze or crash your entire system, and you'll have to reboot to continue.

This error is typically caused by a software bug that causes two drivers (or applications) to try to use the same area of memory. After you get past the error message (and close one of the applications in question), you probably won't see the error again; it's an intermittent thing.

If the error message repeats, you'll need to try to track down which applications or drivers are causing the problem, and then contact the appropriate manufacturers for more detailed technical support.

tip

The best place to look up Windows-related error messages is in the Microsoft Knowledge Base. You can access the Knowledge Base from Microsoft's main support page (support. microsoft.com).

Abnormal termination

This message occurs when a Windows application crashes unexpectedly, most often due to memory problems. Sometimes this kind of program crash will also crash Windows itself.

Another application is using communication port

You are running two programs that are both trying to access a single communication port, such as two communications programs. Close one of the two programs to avoid the current conflict.

Application execution error: Cannot find file. Check to ensure path and filename are correct

This message results when Windows tries to load a program that either doesn't exist or isn't located where Windows thinks it is. If this message appears when you start Windows, it means you have an incorrect file inserted in your Startup folder. Check all the programs in this folder to make sure the filename and path are correct.

Application execution error: No association exists for this file

You receive this message if no program file is associated with a data file you're trying to launch. To associate a program file with a file type, open the Control Panel and launch the Folder Options utility. When the Folder Options dialog box appears, select the File Types tab. Add a new file type by clicking the New Type button and filling in the blanks in the Add New File Type dialog box.

Application is still active

You're trying to exit Windows while an application is still running. Close the program and then exit Windows.

Call to undefined dynalink

This message results when a Windows program tries to use an incompatible DLL file. You'll probably need to wipe the program from your hard disk and reinstall it from scratch. It's also possible that an old printer driver can cause this problem. The solution is similar; erase the old driver and install an updated version.

Cannot communicate with modem

For some reason, Windows cannot access your modem. Check all connections and setup configurations to make sure that your modem is working and properly set up.

Cannot copy file

For some reason (generally something wrong with either the original or the destination disk) the current file cannot be copied. If you encounter this message when installing Windows, try to continue without copying the file. If the problem is that you don't have enough free space on the destination disk, you'll need to rethink the copy operation or free up some space before you retry the copy.

Cannot find a device file that may be needed

This message is typically followed by a filename (often with the .VXD extension), and indicates that a virtual device driver (VXD) file is missing or corrupted. If you've recently installed a new device or program, uninstall it and then reinstall it; if the problem persists, you might need to obtain a new or updated version of the driver file.

Cannot find the file "*XXX*" or one of its components

The most common cause for this message is that the file in question is either missing or corrupted. Click the Start button and select Find to search for the file. Reinstall the program in question if necessary.

Cannot format disk

Windows generates this message when you try to format a disk that is write-protected. Change disks or slide the write-protect tab into the down position.

This message can also appear when you're trying to use a damaged disk, or if the disk contains a virus. If either of these are the case, you probably want to throw away this particular disk and start again with a new one.

Cannot print. SoftRIP error.

Some printers print an entire page as a graphic image, forming that image in memory before printing. If your system doesn't have enough memory, this message is generated. Close any other open applications to free up additional memory.

Cannot read from drive *x*

Windows is looking for a file on drive *x*:. If no disk is in drive x:, insert any disk to end the Windows look loop. If a disk is already in drive *x*:, you either have a bad (or unformatted) disk, or a bad disk drive. If the message refers to drive C: (your hard disk), your hard disk is going bad.

Cannot replace xxxx: Access Denied.

A common cause of this message is if you tried to copy a file to a write-protected disk or to a drive that doesn't have a disk inserted. Make sure the disk is inserted correctly before you resume the operation or change the disk's write-protect status.

Another cause of this problem is when the file you're trying to copy (or save) is marked as read-only. Reconfigure the file's status before retrying the operation.

In addition, this message can be generated if you try to access a file that is in use by another application or, on a network, by another user.

Cannot run program—No application is associated with this file

If no program file is associated with a document you're trying to launch, you receive this message. To associate a program file with a file type, open the Control Panel and launch the Folder Options utility. When the Folder Options dialog box appears, select the File Types tab. Add a new file type by clicking the New Type button and filling in the blanks in the Add New File Type dialog box.

Cannot run program—Out of system resources

Resources include system memory as well as space taken by everything you see on your screen—icons, fonts, dialog boxes, and so on. When too much is going on at one time, Windows runs out of resources. Try closing any open programs or simplifying your screen in any way—minimizing windows, closing dialog boxes, and so on.

Cannot start application

Windows cannot start the desired application. Check to make sure the correct directory path and filename was specified. It's also possible that sufficient memory was not available to run this application.

Cannot start more than one copy of *xxx*

Some programs cannot be loaded twice in Windows. If a program is already running, avoid starting a second instance of the program.

Could not print page x

Windows could not print a particular page in your printout. This is often due to low memory or insufficient disk space to print a page with lots of graphics. Try printing this page at a lower resolution.

Dangerously low on system resources

Windows is running low on system memory—which you've probably already noticed by the increasingly sluggish performance of your system. With Windows 9X/Me, this is sometimes caused by the operating system not releasing the entire amount of memory used when you close a program. (It's called a memory leak, if you're interested.) The more programs you open and closed, the more unreleased memory you have—and the more likely it is you'll see this error message.

The only way to release unreleased memory is to reboot your computer. Fortunately, this problem is minimized (if not completely eliminated) with Windows XP.

Deleting this file will make it impossible to run this program

This message appears when you try to delete a program file. Make sure you *really* want to delete this program before you proceed.

Destination disk drive is full

You receive this message when you're trying to copy data to a disk that has run out of free space. Either delete files from the disk or use another disk that has more free space.

Disk error

If Windows generates a disk error message, it's normally because you're trying to use a bad or unformatted disk. If you receive a disk error message while reading or writing from a disk, try another disk. If you receive this error message regarding your hard disk, it's possible that it is starting to fail. Run ScanDisk to find any hard disk errors, and consider replacing your hard disk (after you've backed up your critical data, of course).

Divide by zero

This message generally results from software bugs. When it occurs, close Windows, reboot your computer, and then restart Windows and the problem application. If this message occurs with frequency, consult the publisher of the software.

Drive x: is inaccessible

This message is displayed when a specified drive can't be accessed. Make sure you actually have a disk correctly inserted in the drive and that the disk is formatted. If the drive does exist, there might be a problem with your Windows setup.

Explorer caused a fatal exception xxxxxxx in module KER-NEL32.DLL at xxxx:xxxxxxxx

This message is displayed when either Windows Explorer or Internet Explorer (they both use the same base code) has misbehaved. If you receive this error frequently, try upgrading to a newer version of Internet Explorer (which upgrades all the underlying code).

Another cause of this message is a damaged Control Panel file (.CPL extension). You may need to repair or reinstall Windows to get the error message to go away.

Extremely low on memory, close applications and try again

This message results when your system doesn't have enough memory to run the application or perform the operation you specified. Just like the message suggests, close some applications and try the operation again. You might also need to exit Windows (to free up some unreleased memory), restart Windows, and then run the application or perform the operation.

This message can also be caused when you have too little free space left on your hard disk. (Windows uses your hard disk for virtual memory; too little hard disk space equals too little virtual memory.) Try deleting unnecessary files to free up hard disk space.

File already exists. Overwrite?

You're trying to create or save a file with a name that already exists. Windows is asking if you want to overwrite the existing file. If so, answer yes. If no, answer no and assign a new name to your file.

File not found

If you get this message when Windows is loading, the likely culprit is a corrupt or missing driver or program file. The problem can be fixed if you know *which* file is missing; sometimes the message tells you what is missing, sometimes it doesn't. If you can track down the missing or corrupt file, you can either reinstall it or delete its reference from the Windows startup routine.

There are several places where Windows specifies which drivers to load:

- Startup folder, accessible by clicking Start, All Programs, Startup
- WIN.INI file, used by many older programs (but few newer ones)
- Windows Registry, under the following key: **HKEY_LOCAL_MACHINE\ SOFTWARE\Microsoft\Windows\CurrentVersion\Run**

Oftentimes this error message occurs when you've deleted a program from your system but not the reference to load the program. If you can find the reference in one of these places, you can delete it.

General protection fault

The general protection fault (GPF) is a very common type of error message under Windows 9X/Me. It indicates that there is a problem with a specific software program, or that you need to update a device driver. If you can't figure out the cause of the GPF, run Dr. Watson to track it down for you.

note

The predecessor to the GPF in earlier versions of Windows was the UAE (unrecoverable application error).

Illegal operation

This message is similar to the fatal exception error, the result of two drivers (or applications) trying to use the same area of memory. After you get past the error message (and close one of the applications in question), you probably won't see the error again; it's an intermittent thing. If the error message repeats, you'll need to try to track down which applications or drivers are causing the problem, and then contact the appropriate manufacturers for more detailed technical support.

Insufficient disk space

Your system is short on hard disk space. Try deleting some unneeded files and then restarting the operation at hand.

Insufficient memory to run this application

You're trying to launch a program but don't have enough free system memory to do so. Try closing down any open applications before relaunching the new application; if this message occurs again, reboot your system to clear up memory clogs.

Invalid destination specified

Windows displays this message when you try to copy a file to a folder or drive that doesn't exist. Check your commands and try this operation again.

Invalid page fault

This message is similar to the fatal exception error, typically the result of two drivers (or applications) trying to use the same area of memory. After you get past the error message (and close one of the applications in question), you probably won't see the error again; it's an intermittent thing.

This message is also generated when you run low on RAM, or when your system's virtual memory becomes unstable due to a shortage of free disk space. If the message persists, reboot your PC to release any memory leaks and, if necessary, delete unnecessary files from your hard disk to free up some disk space.

Invalid VxD Dynamic Link Call

This message is generated when a device driver is either missing, corrupted, or incompatible with your version of Windows. If you recently installed a new device or program, try uninstalling and reinstalling it to fix the driver file. If the problem continues, contact the manufacturer of the problem device for an updated driver file.

The problem that causes this message can sometimes stop Windows from loading. If so, you'll need to restart in Safe mode to remove the device.

Invalid system disk, replace the disk, and then press any key

This message appears when you've tried to start your system with a non-bootable disk in your A: drive. Remove the disk and press any key to continue.

Keyboard error. Press F1 to continue

This error is generated when your computer can't find a keyboard attached to your system during startup—or if one of your keys is stuck. Make sure your keyboard is connected (and the keys unstuck) and then reboot with the power button/switch on your system unit. (Because your keyboard is recognized, you actually can't press F1 to continue!)

No association exists for this file

If no program file is associated with a data file you're trying to launch, you'll receive this message. To associate a program file with a file type, open the Control Panel and launch the Folder Options utility. When the Folder Options dialog box appears, select the File Types tab. Add a new file type by clicking the New Type button and filling in the blanks in the Add New File Type dialog box.

No COM ports available

You're trying to add a new device to your Windows and all of your COM ports are filled. You'll need to uninstall one of your current devices before you can add the new device.

Not a valid filename

You typed an invalid filename for a file operation. Remove any illegal characters from the filename. See "This filename is not valid" later in this chapter for a list of characters you can't use in filenames.

Not enough disk space

There isn't enough free space on the current disk to continue with the operation. Delete some files and try again.

Not enough memory

This error occurs when you try to launch an application but your system is low on available memory. Here are some solutions to try:

- Close any open applications—including background utilities—and then restart the latest program. The more applications you have open, the less system memory you have available for additional applications.

- Close all applications, exit Windows, and restart your computer. Sometimes Windows applications don't free up all their memory when they close. This memory "leakage" can build up over time and drain your system resources. Exiting and relaunching Windows frees up this stolen memory.

- Free up extra disk space on your system. You can do this by emptying the Recycle Bin or deleting unused files or applications. Because Windows uses extra disk space as virtual memory, having too little disk space free can result in insufficient memory problems.

Open With

Windows displays this message when you try to open a document and there is no file type associated. Choose a program to open the file with from the list in the dialog box, or click the Browse button to choose from other programs on your system.

Out of memory

Windows has trouble running under low memory conditions. When this message is generated, try closing some open applications to free up memory space. If Windows continues to generate this message, exit Windows and reboot your system to free up any unreleased memory.

Parity error

This message most often results when something is wrong with your system memory. It's also possible that a power supply problem can cause this message. Whatever the cause, rebooting your system and restarting Windows generally clears things up.

If this message appears with some degree of regularity, you might have a defective memory chip or some sort of mismatch between old memory and newly installed memory. In any case, you may need to replace your system memory.

Print queue is still active

You're trying to exit Windows while a print job is still in progress. Either finish or cancel the print job before you try exiting again.

Rundll32.exe has performed an illegal operation

The error message is caused by a problem with your modem driver. You might need to uninstall and then reinstall your modem to continue.

Sector not found reading drive X

Windows encountered a problem reading one of your drives, most probably due to a bad sector on the disk. If the drive is your hard drive, you might be developing a serious hard drive failure. Call a computer technician for advice.

Setup detects that an earlier version of SetupX.dll or NetDi.dll is in use

While installing a new version of Windows, you have one or more applications open. Close the open applications and then continue with your installation.

Setup cannot create files on your startup drive and cannot set up Windows. There may be too many files in the root directory of your startup drive, or your startup drive letter may have been remapped (SU0018)

This is an odd problem you might encounter while installing Windows. The root folder of a drive holds a maximum of 512 files and/or folders, and your root folder apparently contains more files/folders than this. Move or delete some files to continue the installation.

Setup could not back up your system files

You're trying to install a new version of Windows, but your hard drive does not have enough free space to back up the previous system files. Because you need up to 75MB or more free space to continue, try deleting as many files as you can.

System Error

When some piece of hardware in your system stops working, this message is generated. You'll see it often when something is wrong with your disk drives—like you're using an unformatted disk or you forgot to close the disk drive door. Cancel out and fix your problem before retrying the operation.

The file or folder that this shortcut refers to cannot be found

When you see this message, it means that the file associated with this shortcut has been moved or deleted. If the file's location has changed, right-click the shortcut icon, select Properties from the pop-up menu, select the Shortcut tab when the Properties dialog box appears, and enter a new location in the Target box. If the file has been deleted, delete the shortcut by dragging the shortcut icon into the Recycle Bin.

The network could not validate your user name

This message is generated when you are starting up Windows on a network, or when you are logging on to the network after another user has logged off, and tells you that either the username or password you entered was incorrect. Check both and try logging in again. If you're sure you entered the correct information, contact your network's administrator for assistance.

You should also check the Ethernet cable running from your PC to your network hub. Make sure it's still connected and that the link light is working.

The printer on LPT1 is offline or not selected

This message appears when your printer is not ready to print. It might be offline or out of paper. Check your printer and click the Retry button to resume the print job.

There was an error writing to LPT1:

This message appears when something is wrong with your printer or your printer setup. Here are some possible solutions to the problem:

- Make sure your printer is actually turned on and is online.
- Make sure you have paper in your printer. If not, refill your paper tray.
- Check your printer for paper jams.
- Double-check all cable connections; make sure both ends of the printer cable are securely fastened.

If these simple solutions don't fix your problem, check your printer configuration.

This filename is not valid

This message appears when you type an illegal name for a filename. An illegal name would include characters that you can't use for filenames. Remove any illegal characters from the filename and save the file again.

caution

The following characters (called "illegal" characters) cannot be used to name a file in Windows: **/ \ * | < > ? " :**

This program has performed an illegal operation and will be shut down.

This message appears when a program has ceased proper operation, for whatever reason (typically untraceable). Click the Close button to close the offending program.

The system has recovered from a serious error

This is a new error message in Windows XP that is displayed after you've had a program crash. (In Windows XP—in most cases—a program crash doesn't crash the entire operating system.) The message goes on to tell you that a log of this error has been created, and then prompts you to "please tell Microsoft about this problem." If you click the Send Error Report button, your computer will connect to the Internet and send the aforementioned error report to Microsoft. You also have the option to not send the report.

What happens when you click the Send Error Report button? Well, you can see for yourself by clicking the "To see what data this error report contains, click here" link. Windows will now display a totally incomprehensible collection of technical information that doesn't tell you diddly squat.

The big concern, of course, is how much of this information is technical and how much is personal; most users don't want to send Microsoft any more personal data than they absolutely have to. Microsoft *says* that they don't intentionally collect your name, address, email address, or any other personal information—however, the error report itself might include data files that contain this type of information.

So, should you send the error report? I'd recommend not, as you don't directly benefit from it; Microsoft uses this information for future bug fixes, not to help you with your specific problem. Just click the Don't Send button and continue with whatever you were doing before the message appeared.

By the way, if you get this message every time you turn on your PC, you need to update your version of Windows XP with Service Pack 1. This is a bug in the original Windows XP code that affects a small number of systems, and was fixed by Microsoft in SP1.

Unmountable boot volume

This message is generated when certain Windows XP files become garbled, making your hard disk inaccessible. The solution is to use XP's new Recovery Console utility to repair the installation. Follow these steps:

1. Reboot your computer using the Windows installation CD.
2. When you see the Welcome to Setup screen, press the R key on your keyboard to start the Recovery Console.
3. You're now presented with a command prompt. Enter `chkdsk` and press Enter.
4. Enter `exit` and press Enter to quit the Recovery Console and restart your computer.

If this doesn't fix the problem, restart the Recovery Console and run the **chkdsk /r** command.

Windows protection error

This error typically occurs when your computer attempts to load or unload a problematic virtual device driver (VXD). In most cases, the problematic driver is mentioned in the error message; in other cases, however, you'll have no clue as to what is causing the problem.

If you can track down the driver causing the problem, you can usually fix things by reinstalling or updating the driver, repairing any damaged Registry entries, or eliminating any driver conflicts.

Windows Setup was unable to update your system files

You might see this message if you're trying to install (or reinstall) Windows and you're running antivirus software. This can also be caused if you have "Boot Sector Protect" enabled in your systems CMOS BIOS settings; check your BIOS on system startup to disable this setting.

Windows was not properly shut down

On a pre-Windows XP system, this message is displayed the next time you restart your computer after you've improperly exited Windows. (Windows then proceeds to run ScanDisk to search for any disk errors resulting from the improper shutdown.) Remember to shut down Windows properly next time by clicking the Start button, selecting Shut Down, and—when the Shut Down Windows dialog box appears—selecting the Shut Down the Computer? option.

Write protected disk

You're trying to perform a file operation on a disk that is write protected. Change disks, or slide the write-protect tab into the down position.

X:/ is not accessible. The device is not ready

This message appears when a disk drive is not yet ready; the *X* represents the drive with the problem. If the problem is with a disk, CD-ROM, or DVD drive, insert the proper diskette or disc in the drive. If the problem is with a hard disk drive, you might have some major problems with your system; consult a technician for more information.

You'll also see this message if you insert a CD into your PC and then try to explore it via My Computer before Windows has had a chance to recognize the disc. Just hold your horses until all the lights quit blinking, and *then* go ahead and access the disc.

You cannot format the current drive

You're trying to format a disk that is write-protected. Change disks or slide the write-protect tab into the down position.

THE ABSOLUTE MINIMUM

Well, that's all there is. I hope you've enjoyed this book, and picked up some useful information and advice about upgrading and fixing your PC. As to the information in this chapter, keep these points in mind:

- Windows generates error messages when it encounters most common (and uncommon!) problems.

- When you receive an error message, read it carefully and *write it down*—then proceed as instructed.

- Unfortunately, you might never find out the exact cause of any error message you might receive; sometimes the best way to deal with an error message is to figure out the best workaround.

Index

How can we make this index more useful? Email us at indexes@quepublishing.com

How can we make this index more useful? Email us at indexes@quepublishing.com

X-Z

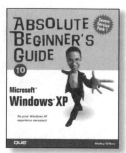

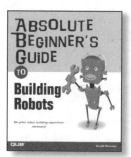